CISTERCIAN STUDIES SERIES: NUMBER ONE HUNDRED EIGHTY-NINE

A Life Pleasing to God

CISTERCIAN STUDIES SERIES: NUMBER ONE HUNDRED EIGHTY-NINE

A Life Pleasing to God

THE SPIRITUALITY OF THE RULES OF ST BASIL

Augustine Holmes OSB

CISTERCIAN PUBLICATIONS

Kalamazoo, Michigan — Spencer, Massachusetts

The work of Cistercian Publications is made possible in part by support from Western Michigan University to The Institute of Cistercian Studies.

First published in 2000 by
Darton, Longman and Todd Ltd
1 Spencer Court
140–142 Wandsworth High Street
London sw18 4jj

and by

Cistercian Publications
WMU Station
Kalamazoo, Michigan 49008

© 2000 Augustine Holmes osb

isbn 0 87907 689 5

Cum permissu superiorum.

Designed by Sandie Boccacci
Phototypeset in 10½/13½pt Minion by Intype London Ltd
Printed and bound in Great Britain by
Redwood Books, Trowbridge, Wiltshire

Contents

St Basil: Select Chronology

c.300	Birth of Eustathius
>325	Eustathius enters the clergy
325	Council of Nicaea
c.330	Birth of Basil at Caesarea
c.340 (or >360s)	Council of Gangra
346–348	Basil a student at Caesarea, meets Gregory
349–355	Basil a student at Athens
c.350	Basil's mother and sister take up the ascetic life at Annisa in Pontus
356	Basil follows Eustathius in visiting ascetic centres of the western Mediterranean
>357	Eustathius elected bishop of Sebaste
357 or 358	Basil baptised, begins ascetic life at Annisa
358	Gregory of Nazianzus joins him
359–360	Basil at Synod of Constantinople
362	Basil ordained presbyter, returns to Caesarea
363	Basil returns to Annisa
365	Basil recalled to Caesarea and takes up public ecclesiastical career
370	Basil elected bishop of Caesarea
372 or 373	Meeting between Basil and the Emperor Valens
372	Gregory ordained bishop of Sasima
373–375	End of friendship between Basil and Eustathius
c.377	Death of Eustathius
379	Death of Basil
381	Council of Constantinople

(Dates taken from the work of Gribomont, Fedwick and Rousseau. Many of them are the subject of controversy amongst scholars.)

Acknowledgements

This work started life as a series of papers given to monks and nuns of various Christian traditions at the 'East–West Monastic Meeting' held at Minster Abbey, Kent in 1996. The Conference was a response to the Apostolic Letter of Pope John Paul II, *Orientale Lumen*, which invited Catholics and Orthodox to meet and study 'the many unifying aspects of the monastic experience' and called on Western Catholics to rediscover the riches of the Christian East. It was organised by Sr Benedict Gaughan OSB of Minster, and I would like to thank her and Dom Hugh Gilbert, Abbot of Pluscarden, for inviting me to speak on St Basil. They are thus the book's grandparents. Abbot Hugh has also given constant encouragement to this project and has read through the whole text, making a number of helpful suggestions.

Gratitude is also due to others who assisted the progress of the book. Sr Hilda Wood OSB of Stanbrook Abbey first suggested that the papers be developed into a more substantial work. Dom Bede Kierney OSB of St Mary's, Petersham did some very helpful computer wordsearches in the Greek text. I also received advice from Fr Anthony Meredith SJ, Fr Gregory Woolfenden, and my friends Dr Lewis Ayres and Mr Hidemi Takahashi. I must record a special debt to Professor Andrew Louth, who read all three parts, for his encouragement and for many helpful comments. I obviously take full responsibility for the final product.

This book was largely written in the interstices of the monastic horarium and I would like to thank my brethren at Pluscarden for their tolerance of a Basilologist in their midst. I am also grateful to Abbot Richard and the community of Downside Abbey and Dom Henry Wansbrough of St Benet's Hall, Oxford for their hospitality, and to Dom Daniel Rees of Downside, the staff of Aberdeen University Library and the Bodleian Library for help in tracking down obscure items of Basiliana. I should also mention Dr Paul Magdalino

of the University of St Andrews who taught me Byzantine History
and laid the foundations for my subsequent interest in the Greek
Fathers and early monasticism. Finally I must thank Katie Worrall
and all at DLT for efficiently guiding this project to completion.

On the closure of the monastery at Fort Augustus on Loch Ness,
our community inherited their extensive collection of sacred relics.
Among them are relics of St Basil and St Gregory Nazianzen and so
the last stages of this book were written in the presence of the bodily
remains of the great saints who inspired it. May they call down
special blessings on all who read it.

HOLY FATHER BASIL, PRAY FOR US TO GOD!

Dom Augustine Holmes OSB
Pluscarden Abbey, Moray
Solemnity of St Andrew, 1999

Abbreviations

ABR	*American Benedictine Review*
ACW	*Ancient Christian Writers,* The Works of the Fathers in Translation, J. Quasten et al. (Westminster, Md./New York 1946–)
CHA	*Basil of Caesarea: Christian, Humanist, Ascetic,* Fedwick (Pontifical Institute of Mediaeval Studies, Toronto, 1981)
CPG	*Clavis Patrum Graecorum,* vol. 2, ed. Moritz Geerard (Turnhout, Brepols, 1974)
CS	*Cistercian Studies Series* (Kalamazoo, Cistercian Publications 1969–)
CSEL	*Corpus Scriptorum Ecclesiasticorum Latinorum* (Vienna, 1886–)
DACL	*Dictionnaire d'archéologie chrétienne et de liturgie,* edd. Fernand Cabrol and Henri Leclercq (Paris, Letouzey et Ané, 1907–1953)
DIP	*Dizionario degli Istituti di Perfezione,* edd. Guerrino Pelliccia and Giancarlo Rocca (Rome, Ed. Paoline, 1973–)
DSp	*Dictionnaire de spiritualité,* edd. Marcel Viller et al. (Paris, Beauchesne, 1937–1995)
DTC	*Dictionnaire de théologie catholique,* edd. A. Vacant and E. Mangenot (Paris, Letouzey et Ané, 1908–1972)
É&É	*Saint Basile, Évangile et Église,* Gribomont (Bellefontaine, 1984)
ET	English translation
FC	*The Fathers of the Church: A New Translation* (Washington, CUA Press, 1947–)
HE	Historia Ecclesiastica

LR	Longer Rule
NPNF2	*Nicene and Post-Nicene Library of the Fathers,* Second Series (New York, 1890 ff)
PG	*Patrologiae cursus completus, series Graeca, accurante J. P. Migne* (Paris, 1857–1866)
R	Answer in the Small Asceticon tr. by Rufinus
SC	*Sources Chrétiennes* (Paris, Cerf, 1942–)
SO	*Collection 'Spiritualité Orientale': Monachisme primitif* (Abbaye de Bellefontaine)
SR	Shorter Rule

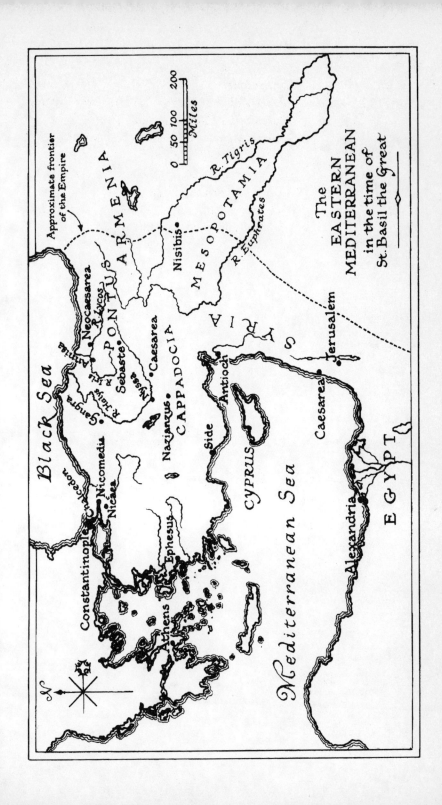

The
EASTERN
MEDITERRANEAN
in the time of
St. Basil the Great

Approximate frontier
of the Empire

Miles
0 50 100 200

R. Tigris

MESOPOTAMIA

ARMENIA

R. Euphrates

Nisibis

PONTUS

Neocaesarea

R. Lycos

Amnia

R. Iris

Sebaste

Nyssa

Caesarea

CAPPADOCIA

Nazianzus

Gangra

Nicomedia

Nicaea

Constantinople

Chalcedon

Black Sea

Athens

Ephesus

Side

CYPRUS

Antioch

SYRIA

Jerusalem

Caesarea

Mediterranean Sea

Alexandria

EGYPT

N

Introduction

St Basil the Great, bishop of Caesarea in Cappadocia from 370 to 379 is one of the most important figures in the history of the Christian Church. He stands in the midst of that creative period from Constantine to Chalcedon and has left his mark on many areas of Christian life. In theology, canon law, liturgy, social teaching, monasticism and spirituality his influence has remained strong down to our own day, not only in the Churches of the East but also in the Christian West. Living as he did before the divisions of the fifth, eleventh and sixteenth centuries, he is also a figure of ecumenical significance. This book is concerned with his spirituality as it is expressed in a work called the *Asceticon* or *Rules*, a collection of Basil's answers to questions from his disciples.

The study of St Basil

The last decades of the twentieth century have seen a decline in the number of people in Western Europe and North America entering consecrated life as monks or religious. Paradoxically, the same period has also witnessed a great increase of interest in the Christian ascetic tradition among the wider community and the publication of many books on this subject. This interest takes two main forms.

In the English-speaking academic world there has been a significant change in the way that early monasticism is viewed. There is a move away from a narrowly monastic perspective to a broader understanding of asceticism in the context of what has come to be known as Late Antiquity (roughly defined as the second to the sixth centuries in the area of the Roman Empire and its successors). Under the influence of modern intellectual movements, social, political, cultural, feminist and literary analyses of the evidence have come to predominate. Many of the results of this are positive, such as a better

understanding of the place of monks in society and the rediscovery
of the important part played by women in ascetic movements. But
there are problems. Columba Stewart, in a series of three very percep-
tive review articles,[1] has pointed out a serious deficiency in the
current academic landscape: an absence of the spiritual and theological element in the understanding of early Christian asceticism.
This is a fundamental flaw as the desire for God and hope for heaven
was the defining motivation of the ascetics themselves. For them,
asceticism was merely a means to this end.

The same desire and hope has produced the second type of interest
in early monasticism. This is among modern Christians, primarily
among the laity, and is focused on monastic spirituality. A plethora
of books have been produced, most notably perhaps those by Esther
de Waal, to enable non-monastics to appropriate the spiritual riches
of the Rule of St Benedict. A similar phenomenon attends the pithy
and down-to-earth sayings of the Egyptian Desert Fathers and also,
more ambiguously, the strongly monastic Celtic spirituality. This is
part of a general return to the sources in contemporary Christianity
and is a recognition both of the normative nature of sacred
tradition and of the essential unity of Christian spirituality. The
inadequacy of both modern liberal Christianity and the forms of
piety of recent centuries has caused many to seek authentic spiritual
teaching in the monastic tradition.

Basil has been badly served in both of these areas. In *Reading
Renunciation* (1999), Elizabeth Clark notes that scholars studying
asceticism now concentrate on geographically specific areas 'especially
in Egypt, Syria and Palestine'.[2] Despite its significance Asia Minor
is left out. Anthony Meredith, in his excellent introduction to the
Cappadocian Fathers, notes of his writings that 'little of Basil is easily
available'.[3] The only complete translation of the Rules in English, by
W. K. L. Clarke, was published in 1925 and is now out of print. A
subsequent version by Sr Monica Wagner, published in 1950, only
includes the Longer Rules. The same neglect is noticeable in studies
of his ascetic teaching. While Basil is frequently mentioned in
studies of early Christian asceticism, the only substantial investi-
gations of his ascetic teaching in English are *St Basil and his Rule* by

E. F. Morrison (1912), *St Basil the Great: A Study in Monasticism* by W. K. L. Clarke (1913) and *St Basil and Monasticism* by Sr Margaret Gertrude Murphy (1930). When one considers the many studies of early asceticism in Egypt which have appeared in the past couple of decades, and the texts and studies relating to Palestine, Syria and the early Latin West, this is not a satisfactory situation.

There are, however, two excellent recent studies which have influenced the present work. Philip Rousseau's *Basil of Caesarea* (1994) is an elegantly written book focused on Basil as bishop but doing justice to his ascetic life and teaching. Susanna Elm's *Virgins of God: The Making of Asceticism in Late Antiquity* (1994) is one of the best products of the new approach to early monasticism. Dealing with female ascetics in Asia Minor and Egypt, it clarifies Basil's role against the background of contemporary ascetic developments. One does not have to subscribe to secular and feminist interpretations to appreciate the new vistas she has opened. Two post-war writers in French have also made major contributions to the study of Basilian asceticism. Dom David Amand's *L'ascèse monastique de saint Basile* (1949) is enlightening but unfortunately marred by his jaundiced attitude to the Christian monastic tradition, exacerbated by his own disillusionment with monastic life. Dom Jean Gribomont is the undoubted master of Basil's texts and doctrine but, while we have his articles collected in *Évangile et Église* and his thorough analysis of textual transmission in *Histoire du texte des Ascétiques de s. Basile*, it is a cause for great regret that he did not produce a definitive study of the subject. Finally one should also mention the continuing work on Basil of Paul Jonathan Fedwick who edited the two volumes of *Basil of Caesarea: Christian, Humanist, Ascetic* (1981).

Parallel to this academic work there is no popular interest in 'Basilian Spirituality'. This is both strange and regrettable as Basil's teaching is scriptural, practical and avoids the ascetic extremism of the Egyptians and Syrians. It also has a strong social and community dimension which should appeal to modern concerns. Part of the problem is the lack of an accessible translation into contemporary English.

The scope of this book

It is clear that there is need for a presentation of Basil's ascetic teaching that takes account of modern developments in Basilian studies. There is also an imperative for Basilian spirituality to be made known to a wider Christian audience. This book is perhaps not the ideal solution to either of these problems. It is neither a reworked doctoral thesis nor is it 'popular spirituality'. One hopes, though, that it will be of use in both areas: as an introduction to the ascetic teaching of St Basil for the student and as an initiation into Basilian spirituality for the thoughtful Christian.

The over-used and much abused word spirituality is, however, problematic. One modern writer notes that it is 'a word so widely used now as to mean, to quote Humpty Dumpty, "what I chose it to mean"'.[4] It is here understood as life according to the Spirit of God in its active and contemplative aspects.[5] One would not be true to Basil's teaching, though, if one left this at the personal and theoretical level, and so, as well as showing why he believed one should live in community, the actual practice and institutions of community life will also be studied.

This division gives the structure of the book which, like that of David Amand, is an extended commentary on selected Basilian texts. After setting the Asceticon in context and looking at the various influences on Basil's ascetic development in Part 1, Part 2 discusses the first Longer Rules. These, starting from the double commandment of love, lay the foundations for the whole spiritual life. One of their key conclusions is the desirability of living in a community of the devout. Part 3, therefore, considers selected texts dealing with the practicalities of community life. The commentaries on the Rules constitute the main body of the work.

The texts commented on are deliberately restricted to the Rules, in a translation based on that of Clarke but modernised and modified with reference to the Greek. Significant Greek words are indicated in the text, but they have usually been put into their basic form (nominative/ first person present) to help those with little or no Greek. Although Basil also gives ascetic teaching in Letters and Homilies, the Rules are chosen as they were collected by Basil himself as representing his spiritual doctrine. Limited space has precluded the incorporation of other important texts from the Asceticon, such as the Preface to the Longer Rules, Longer Rule 8 on renunciation and Longer Rule 16 on self-control. Those chosen, however, should be sufficient to achieve the aim of presenting a representative and balanced outline of Basilian spirituality, set in its historical context, using the results of recent scholarship. One hopes that the reader will then be able to go on to make a more fruitful reading of the rest of the Asceticon and other Basilian ascetic writings. As the last similar work in English was published 70 years ago, this seems a worthwhile and useful objective.

St Basil and monasticism

The subsequent influence of the Rules is a complicated subject which is worthy of further study. This book aims only to elucidate Basil's teaching, but it is worthwhile outlining this influence to give an idea of their importance.

The original scene of Basil's teaching was Pontus, Cappadocia and the surrounding areas. The Armenian Catholicos Nerses was influenced by Basil's ascetic mentor Eustathius and Basil was in close contact with the Armenian Church.[6] It is therefore not surprising that the Asceticon was soon translated into Armenian and the early monasticism of the area shows Basilian influence. Basil was also in regular contact with Syria and the Small Asceticon was translated into Syriac. His ascetic teaching was familiar to early sixth-century Syrian writers such as Severus of Antioch and John of Tella, and the Monophysite monasticism of the area has a strong Basilian colouring. Nestorian Syrian monasticism, however, shows no Basilian influence until the ninth century, with no reference to the Asceticon in ascetic authors such as Abraham of Kashkar and Isaac the Syrian.

To the south in Palestine, where Basil had been in contact with monks on Mount Olivet, we find that many of the great fifth-century monastic leaders such as Theodosius and Sabas were Cappadocian. There was Basilian influence, especially in the cenobia, and the sources record that Theodosius and Peter the Iberian (dd. 489) used the Asceticon, but local monasticism, especially in the Judaean desert, developed along different, more ascetic, lines.[7] Peter was from Georgia and it was a monk of Mar Saba in Palestine who first translated the Asceticon into Georgian in the tenth century. In Egyptian monasticism there is very little evidence of Basilian influence, although some papyrus fragments have recently been identified as part of the Asceticon. Even Egyptian cenobitism seems to have had a 'respectful distrust'[8] of Basil and in general he is best known as a wonderworker and defender of Nicaea. Any Coptic translation of the Rules has been lost and there is no Ethiopic version, although they were translated into Arabic in the thirteenth century.

It is not surprising that the Asceticon had most direct influence in Byzantine monasticism, although one can not characterise it as Basilian in the same way as that of the West is Benedictine. Cenobitic monasteries tended to look to the Rules for guidance, and Canon 20 of the Second Council of Nicaea (787) suggests that this was especially so in double monasteries of monks and nuns. The monastic renewal begun by St Theodore (759–826) at the monastery of Stoudios at Constantinople involved a return to the teaching of Basil, and Theodore shared Basil's suspicion of the hermit life. In general, though, eremitism was held in high esteem, as was the combination of solitude and community in monasteries known as lavras or sketes. This type of life originated in the Egyptian desert in Nitria and Scetis and became one of the principal forms of Palestinian monasticism in the fifth century. In the cenobia of the Holy Mountains of Asia Minor and Athos and elsewhere in the Byzantine world the Studite interpretation of the Basilian ideal was influential but the actual life lived included a mixture of different elements.[9]

Byzantine monasticism came with the faith to the newly converted Slav nations and the Asceticon was soon translated into Old Slavonic. From the Perchersky Monastery at Kiev, Studite influence spread all over Russia, but in the influential Rule of Iosif Volotsky (1440–1515) we find that much of the Basilian influence comes from spurious works.[10] The hesychast tradition in Orthodox monasticism is in many ways alien to the spirit of the Rules and it is notable that Basil is not present in that influential eighteenth century compilation of spiritual texts, the *Philokalia*. The Asceticon still, however, has an honoured place in the Orthodox monastic tradition.

The Small Asceticon was translated into Latin in 396/7 and had a great influence on Western monasticism. St Benedict both used and recommended it in his Rule and Benedictine cenobitism has a strongly Basilian character. It was also an important element in the *Codex Regularum*, an influential collection of monastic legislation compiled by St Benedict of Aniane (750–821). This ensured Basilian influence in Carolingian monasticism, but in the tenth and eleventh centuries contact with Greek monks in South Italy caused revived interest in Basil and the Greek monastic tradition. The restoration of esteem for monastic manual work in the West in this period was influenced by these encounters.[11] With the schism between East and West these Greek monasteries remained in communion with Rome, and in the fifteenth century became a Basilian Order with a resumé of the Asceticon as their Rule. The Asceticon had earlier been recognised as a Rule alongside those of Augustine and Benedict at the Second Council of the Lateran (1139) and in the sixteenth century it was adopted by a group of Spanish Catholic hermits.[12] There are a number of Basilian Orders in the Eastern Catholic Churches today but these have tended to become conformed to Western models. When Metropolitan Andrew Sheptytsky (1865–1944) formed the Studite monks to restore traditional Byzantine monasticism among the Ukrainian Greek Catholics, a key element in his plan was the translation of the Rules into Ukrainian (1929).

The Rules were never intended to be used as a Rule, but this brief survey has shown how they have influenced monastic developments throughout the Christian world. At the end of his 1913 study, Clark even suggests that Anglican monasticism should develop on Basilian lines.

Modern translations into French (1969), Italian (1974, 1980 and 1993), German (1981), Portuguese (1983), Rumanian (1989), Spanish (1993) and Polish (1994) show a continuing interest in the Rules. There is however a great need for a new critical edition of the Greek text and

a new translation of the Great Asceticon into English. It is hoped
that this small work will encourage a revival of interest in the English-
speaking world and that its presentation of the great themes of
Basilian spirituality will help many to live or at least understand the
great Cappadocian's vision of a life pleasing to God.

NOTES

1. 'Asceticism: a feature review', *American Benedictine Review* 48:3 (Sept. 1997),
   254–65. 'Writing About John Cassian in the 1990s', *ABR* 48:4 (Dec. 1997), 341–6.
   'Feature Review: Three Recent Studies On Early Monasticism', *ABR* 50:1 (March
   1999), 3–11.
2. *Reading Renunciation*, p. 27.
3. *The Cappadocians*, p. ix.
4. Benedicta Ward, *High King of Heaven*, p. x.
5. See the discussion of the changing meanings of the term in the articles 'Spirituality,
   Christian' in *The New Dictionary of Catholic Spirituality* (Collegeville 1993) and
   'Spiritualité', *DSp* 14:1142–73.
6. Rousseau, *Basil of Caesarea*, pp. 279–87. The information on early translations of
   the Asceticon is largely taken from Gribomont, *Histoire du texte*.
7. Basilian influence is noted in Patrich, '*Sabas, Leader of Palestinian Monasticism*',
   pp. 31, 45–7, 178, 182, 227, 295, 353–4.
8. Gribomont, *Histoire du texte*, p. 264.
9. cf. Rosemary Morris, *Monks and Laymen in Byzantium 843–1118* (CUP 1995).
10. *The Monastic Rule of Iosif Volotsky*, tr. David M. Goldfrank (Cistercian Publications
    1983).
11. J. M. McNulty and B. Hamilton, 'Orientale Lumen and Magistra Latinitas: Greek
    influences on Western Monasticism 900–1100' in *Le Millénaire du Mont Athos
    963–1963* (Chevetogne 1963).
12. Lateran II, Canon 26. 'Basiliani Spagnoli' *DIP* 1:1099–1101.

PART ONE

The Background to the Rules

Chapter One

The Family and Formation of a Christian Leader

Now what is the noble birth of Basil?
And what is his country?
His family was intimacy with the Divinity;
and his fatherland, virtue.

St Gregory of Nyssa, *Encomium on St Basil*

Basil was formed by a number of factors including his extraordinary family, his excellent education at Athens, and the influence of the ascetic pioneer of the region, Eustathius of Sebaste. The researches of Jean Gribomont have rediscovered Eustathius' profound influence on the young Basil, an influence obscured by their later theological disagreement. This rediscovery in its turn, together with Basil's massive status in Christian history, can result in a lack of appreciation of the influence of Basil's siblings, especially his sister Macrina and brother Naucratius. Susanna Elm's work has enabled us to form a fairer and more balanced picture of their influence on Basil. The first three chapters will try briefly to present the influences Basil followed and reacted against in developing the teaching he would give in his Rules.

Family background and the young Basil

Basil was born about the year 330 into a rich Christian family which owned land in three provinces.[1] Most of his life was spent in Pontus and Cappadocia, in the centre and north of what is now Asiatic Turkey. This whole area is also called Anatolia or Asia Minor and consists of a central plateau surrounded by mountains which on the north, west and south stretch down to the sea.

Pontus was an independent kingdom until conquered by Rome in the first century BC. By that time it included the Greek colonies along the Black Sea coast. Under the Emperor Diocletian (284–305) it was split into three provinces: Helenopontus, Pontus Polemoniacus with its capital at Neocaesarea, and Armenia Minor with its capital at Sebaste. Pontus was also the name of the civil diocese, sometimes confusingly called Cappadocia, which comprised these provinces together with Cappadocia and the rest of Roman Armenia. Cappadocia itself had been a kingdom before conquest by the Romans and both it and Pontus were thus terms with a wide range of applications, from the area of the civil diocese down to the individual provinces.

In general one can say that Cappadocia is the eastern part of the central rocky plateau and that Pontus includes the wooded mountains and hills running down to the Black Sea coast. Unlike the fertile valleys to the west of Asia Minor, famous to the reader of the Bible for cities such as Ephesus, Laodicea and Sardis, the central plateau is barren and unwelcoming, a 'great earth-sea'. There are few cities and the land is generally flat with isolated mountains. Then, as now, Cappadocia was a land of small, sparse villages set by a stream, on a road or, in the time of St Basil, clustered around the fortified houses of landowners. The soil is difficult and the climate unfriendly with burning heat in summer and a freezing winter. His Homily 8 is entitled 'preached in a time of drought and famine' and in a letter Basil mentions that 'we have been overwhelmed with such a mass of snow, that for two months now we have been lurking in our burrows, buried beneath our very houses.'[2] The economic strength of the region lay in the vast tracts of open countryside. Grain and horses were the characteristic products of the area, although slaves and precious stone were also exported. The economy profited the land-owning families but it produced a great gulf between the rich and the poor, lacking the middle strata of society that urban living develops.

The new religion of Christianity spread early to the area. The First Letter of St Peter in the New Testament, written in the second half of the first century, is addressed 'to the exiles of the dispersion in

Pontus, Galatia, Cappadocia, Asia and Bithynia'. The names of bishops are recorded for both areas in the third century, including the famous pupil of Origen, Gregory the Wonderworker. He was from Pontus and became bishop of Neocaesarea in 240. Through his grandmother, Macrina, who had confessed the faith during persecution, Basil's family was linked to the great Bishop and his disciples. It was from her that he learned the 'doctrines of piety (*dogmata tês eusebeias*)' while growing up at Neocaesarea and he was later to stress this distinguished spiritual ancestry which linked him to the great Origen.[3]

Both Basil's parents were Christians, his father, also called Basil, was from Pontus and his mother Emmelia from Cappadocia.[4] They had nine children, four sons and five daughters. Basil the elder, with all the wealth of his estates behind him, was a rhetor[5] and taught at Neocaesarea. Through him Basil was heir to all the traditions of the Greek *polis*. The eldest three boys, Basil, Gregory and Naucratius, followed in his footsteps with a traditional classical education to prepare them to take their place in public life. This began at home under their father's guidance and, after his death, the younger Basil, then aged about sixteen, went to Caesarea in Cappadocia to continue his education. Two years later he moved to Constantinople, 'Capital of the East and famed at the time for its accomplished rhetoricians and philosophers.'[6] There he was a student of Libanius of Antioch, the famous pagan rhetor who was a defender of the traditional values of the *polis*.[7] In 349 or 350 Basil went to study at Athens, the cradle of Greek philosophy and culture. He was to stay there for about five years. We shall return to this period in the next chapter when we examine his friendship with Gregory Nazianzen. Our present interest is in the other members of his family.

Macrina and Naucratius

By looking at Basil's family and the adoption of asceticism by its members one can see the future author of the Rules both being influenced by them and going beyond them in evolving his own style of Christian living. The family group then becomes a window into the tremendously dynamic development of new forms of living the

Gospel in fourth-century Asia Minor. It is one of the best documented families of late antiquity but this relative abundance of sources can cause problems. The *Life of St Macrina* by her brother Gregory of Nyssa does not mention the influence of Eustathius of Sebaste, whereas in all his writings Basil never mentions the younger Macrina. Gregory however portrays her as the main influence on his brother's adoption of the ascetic life. Later disagreements caused the removal of Eustathius from the history of Basil and his family, but the absence of Macrina in Basil's works is more difficult to explain. The picture of her drawn by Gregory in the *Life* and in *On the Soul and Resurrection* is so striking and impressive that she has recently been referred to as 'the fourth Cappadocian'.[8]

As a bishop Basil seems to have subordinated ties of family and friendship to his intense work for the Church and, as an ascetic, his reforming activities led him in different directions to those followed by his sister. He certainly seems on at least one occasion to have rewritten his past in response to later circumstances.[9] It is perhaps here, as well as to more personal reasons, that we should look for an explanation. Our concern, however, is with the ascetic history of the family. The word asceticism is derived from the Greek word for the physical training an athlete might undertake (*askêsis*). An ascetic can be defined as one who is given to strict self-denial and abstains from worldly pleasures, especially for spiritual reasons.[10] Such attitudes and practices are found in various cultures and times and they have been present in Christianity since its beginning. In Basil's own century they came to special prominence in the Church and transformed the lives of his close family.

On the death, between 341 and 345, of her husband, Emmelia and her eldest daughter Macrina moved from Neocaesarea to the family estate at Annisa in Pontus, in the valley of the River Iris.[11] This was not an unusual move for a landed family of their class. The elder Basil had held a prominent position in Neocaesarea and for various reasons a move to one of their estates might be desirable on his death. The older children would have been formed in the faith by their parents, but once at Annisa the initiative in the education of those still at home passed to Macrina. She had already decided on a life of virginity and adopted the status of a widow[12] after the death, about 340, of the man to whom she had been engaged at the age of twelve. Her life at first followed the traditional model of the household asceticism practised by pious women of her class. Elm[13] compares it to that of the virgin Juliana, who hid the great Alexandrian theologian Origen in her home at Caesarea in Cappadocia during a persecution in the AD 230s.

Gradually, however, Macrina's lifestyle changed and stopped conforming outwardly to social custom. Her mother joined her in the ascetic life, slaves were freed, and a community of virgins formed around her, perhaps the former slaves. She did manual work, a practice alien to women of her status but later a distinctive feature of Basil's teaching. She also practised personal poverty, appointing a local priest to look after her wealth for charitable purposes. This family group, which also included the younger brother Peter who had not had his brothers' classical education, later expanded to accept outsiders. Some were girls orphaned in the famines of 368 and 369, and others rich ladies such as the widow Vetiana and the deaconess Lampadion. The *Life* also indicates that at some time a separate male community evolved under the leadership of Peter (who in 380 succeeded Eustathius as bishop of Sebaste). The traditional pattern of household asceticism had thus been transformed into a regular ascetic community, which was in fact a double community.[15]

Close to Annisa one of Basil's other brothers, Naucratius, slightly younger than him, was also living an ascetic life but of a rather different style. After starting out in his father's footsteps on a brilliant rhetorical career he decided about the year 352 to withdraw to live a poor and solitary life (*monêrês bios*) in the forests near the River Iris with a slave, Chrysaphius.[16] Here, while remaining in close touch with his mother, he looked after a group of old people and supported them by his skill at hunting. His ascetic withdrawal has an archaic flavour to it, recalling Gregory of Nazianzen's description of Basil's ancestors in hiding and living off the wild beasts during the persecutions: 'They betook themselves to one of the forests of the Pontic mountains – these forests are numerous and dense and very extensive . . . Many wild beasts lurk in these mountains.'[17] It is a classical picture, making one think of one of those Byzantine floor-mosaics on the theme of the chase, but it was also a dangerous life. Naucratius and Chrysaphius were both killed on a fishing expedition in 357.[18]

Did Macrina convert Basil to the ascetic life?

With Macrina and Naucratius we have two types of religious life followed in the same family: household asceticism, and withdrawal to the forest. There is also in the background the figure of Eustathius of Sebaste, to whom we will return. He had been condemned for his ascetic ideas at a Synod at Neocaesarea about 339, at the same time and presumably in the same place that Macrina decided to become a 'virgin-widow'.[19] It is reasonable to deduce his influence on the family, but it would also seem that the family had a decisive influence on Basil when he decided to withdraw from his worldly career and live the ascetic life.

In the summer of 355 Basil returned from Athens and during the next year or two was baptised by Bishop Dianius of Caesarea before going off on a tour of the eastern Mediterranean. After his return he went to Pontus and began to live the ascetic life on the other side of the river from Macrina. Elm suggests that he may have settled at Naucratius' retreat (*monê*) with his late brother's companions.[20] The date suggests that this was no coincidence. The example and death of his brother, who had already been living the ascetic life for five years, could have been the impetus needed to start the returned student off on a strict and serious following of the Gospel. There is also the example of his sister, who for over ten years had been living a dedicated life in the same place and who had, at about the time of Basil's return, been joined in this life by her mother whom she helped get over the great shock of Naucratius' death.

Basil thus returned from his studies to find his family home turned into a monastery. Their brother Gregory states that Macrina's influence was decisive:

Basil came home from the Schools where he had had practice

in rhetoric for a long time. He was excessively puffed up by his rhetorical abilities and disdainful of all great reputations, and considered himself better than the leading men in the district, but Macrina took him over and lured him so quickly to the goal (*skopos*) of philosophy[21] that he withdrew from the worldly show and began to look down on acclaim through oratory and went over to this life full of labours for one's own hand to perform, providing for himself, through complete poverty, a mode of living that would, without impediment, lead to virtue.[22]

The situation is not as simple as this, though, and Gregory seems to be repeating a family tradition going back to Macrina. Rousseau makes the interesting suggestion that the 'great upsurge of enthusiastic Christianity during the fourth century', in the wake of toleration in the Empire, was the result of a desire to escape from the traditional style of Christian family life. He points out that the family are only written in to Basil's account of his adoption of the ascetic life in his later writings.[23] When Basil returned from Athens he did not join the family in its pious life; when he finally settled at Annisa it was on the other bank of the river, although writing to Eustathius many years later he does mention frequent meetings at his mother's.[24] This picture of the talented eldest son following his own path should be held in mind when we later come to examine Basil's debt to Eustathius. Having made this reservation one can presume some mutual influence between Basil and Macrina, at least at a later date.[25]

What is clear is that Basil did not take his first steps in the ascetic life in a vacuum. In the lives of those of his family who preceded him in the ascetic life we already see characteristics that are typically Basilian: a combination of withdrawal and community, manual labour, absence of social distinctions and service to the poor. This last-mentioned generosity was singled out by Gregory of Nazianzen as a characteristic of Basil's family when he mentioned, 'their care of the poor, their hospitality toward strangers, ... the dedication of a portion of their goods to God'.[26] We should however note that such praise of the family of the deceased was a standard feature (*topos*) of ancient funeral orations. Just as Basil's family gives one element of the context for his own teaching on the ascetic life, so they themselves were part of a general movement of Christians in Asia Minor towards stricter forms of life. The central figure in this movement, and a direct influence on Basil himself and on his family, was Eustathius of Sebaste. Before turning to him we shall look at Basil's friendship with Gregory Nazianzen and his first years of seclusion in Pontus.

NOTES

1. cf. *Life of Macrina* 5. The provinces were probably Helenopontus, Pontus Ptolemaicus and Cappadocia.
2. Letter 48 to Eusebius of Samosata, written in 371.
3. Letter 204, cf. Letter 210, *On the Holy Spirit* 29 (74), and Gregory of Nyssa, *Life of Gregory the Wonderworker*, PG 46:893–958.
4. For Basil's family and early years see: Gregory Nazianzen, *Oration 43* 'On St Basil the Great'; Gregory of Nyssa, *Life of St Macrina*; Rousseau, *Basil of Caesarea*, pp. 1–26; Elm, *Virgins of God*, pp. 40–42, 61, 78–81.
5. A teacher of rhetoric, the effective use of language and oratory. A very important profession in the classical city (*polis*).
6. Gregory Nazianzen, *Oration 43* 14.
7. Basil's association with Libanius (314–393/404) is shown by Gregory of Nyssa's *Letter 13*, to Libanius, and mentioned by Socrates, *History* 4:26, and Sozomen, *History* 6:26. Much of the correspondence of Basil and Libanius (Letters 335–59) is spurious, see CPG 2900.
8. Pelikan, *Christianity and Classical Culture*, p. 8.
9. Rousseau, *Basil of Caesarea*, pp. 23–6.
10. Recent scholarship on asceticism and the problem of its definition are discussed in Clark, *Reading Renunciation* (1999), pp. 14–42. See also Wimbush and Valantasis, *Asceticism* (1995).
11. Annisa is the name of the whole estate, including both the village and his family home on one bank of the River Iris and Basil's hermitage some distance away on the other side. For the location and name of the site, see the article *Ibora* in DACL 7A:7–9 and *Vie de Sainte Macrine* (*SC* 178), pp. 38–44.
12. Both Widows (cf. 1 Tim 5:3–16) and Virgins were 'orders' (*tagmata*) in the Church, thus Macrina was already living a 'religious' life.
13. *Virgins of God*, pp. 29–30, 133.
14. *Life of Macrina* 37.
15. See Stramara, 'Double Monasticism', pp. 274–7 and pp. 299–300 which suggests that Macrina was the major Superior of both parts of the community. The question of relations between male and female ascetics is discussed in Chapter 15.
16. *Life of Macrina* 8–10.
17. St Gregory of Nazianzen, *Oration 43* 6–7.
18. The *Life of Macrina* only mentions hunting (*thêra*) but three epitaphs on Naucra-

tius by Gregory Nazianzen state that he was drowned after being caught in a net while trying to free it from a rock in the turbulent River Iris. Epigrams 156–8 in *The Greek Anthology*, Book 8.

19. Silvas argues that 'Macrina herself was the first and foremost disciple of Eustathius in her family', 'Tracking the influence of Eustathius', p. 66.

20. *Virgins of God*, pp. 83–4. Stramara, 'Double Monasticism', p. 275 n28, rejects Elm's suggestion that there were fellow ascetics. They were just the poor people Naucratius had looked after. Gregory Nazianzen's *Letter 6* of 359, however, does mention brothers living together with Basil and taught by him. If these were not Naucratius' companions, they had certainly joined Basil very soon after his arrival.

21. Since the second century Christian writers had claimed that the teaching of Christ was the true philosophy. By the fourth century the 'life of philosophy' had come to mean a total commitment to the highest ideals of Christian living, i.e. a life of consecrated virginity.

22. *Life of Macrina* 6, Woods Callahan (1967), pp. 167–8.

23. Rousseau, *Basil of Caesarea*, pp. 17, 23–5, 62–4.

24. Letter 223, written in 375.

25. Rousseau, *Basil of Caesarea*, p. 64, denies any influence, at least of Basil on Macrina. Stramara, 'Double Monasticism', pp. 276–7, on the other hand goes beyond the evidence in saying that Basil joined Macrina's community in 358 and that Macrina is the true founder of Basilian Monasticism. Silvas also emphasises Macrina's role, suggesting that she influenced Eustathius as well as Basil, and calls her 'Mother of Greek Monasticism', 'Tracking the influence of Eustathius', p. 72.

26. *Oration 43* 9.

Chapter Two

Two Friends

'We formed a pair famous throughout Greece.'

Gregory Nazianzen

In the modern calendar of the Roman Church, Basil is commemorated together with his friend Gregory Nazianzen on the 2nd of January.[1] The pair are also often painted with John Chrysostom in icons of the 'Three Holy Hierarchs', and, with Gregory of Nyssa, are known to theologians as the Cappadocian Fathers. Their friendship is one of the more attractive human stories of Late Antiquity and J. H. Newman has drawn a charming portrait of it in his *The Church of the Fathers*.[2] Having explored family influences on Basil's ascetic development, we shall now turn to this friend with whom he shared his first steps in the dedicated life, and with whom he is linked today in image and remembrance.

Gregory of Nazianzus

Gregory was born about the same time as Basil,[3] probably on the family estate of Arianzus near the town of Nazianzus in western Cappadocia. His father, also called Gregory, was ordained bishop of Nazianzus about the year 330, but had originally been a member of a small syncretistic sect called the Hypsistarians.[4] He had been converted five years previously by his wife Nonna who was from a Christian family and who was, from the evidence of her son, an extremely pious lady.[5] They had three children: Gorgonia, Gregory, who was perhaps a little younger than his sister, and Caesarius who entered the service of the Emperor.

After education at Nazianzus, Gregory went on to study at Caesarea in Cappadocia, where he first met Basil, and then to the schools of Caesarea in Palestine and Alexandria. The great theologian Origen had taught at both the latter places in the third century, and this connection seems to have made its mark on Gregory. The place which influenced him most, however, was Athens, to which, at about the age of twenty, he preceded Basil.

Athens

The information that Gregory gives about Athens in his *Oration 43* on Basil and in the poem 'On his own life' is corroborated by other sources and it would appear that at that time it was a lively and rowdy seat of learning.[6] When Basil arrived, Gregory ensured that he was not subjected to the intimidating initiation that students forced on newcomers, and the two swiftly became close friends.[7] He later celebrated this friendship thus:

> God granted me this favour too:
> he took me and attached me to the wisest man,
> the only person, in his life and thought, superior to all.
> Who was this man? No doubt you will easily recognise him.
> It was Basil, the great benefactor of our age.
> With him I shared my studies, my lodgings and
> my thoughts. And if I might boast a little,
> we formed a pair famous throughout Greece.
> All things we held in common and one soul
> united our two separate bodies.
> What particularly brought us together
> was this: God and a desire for higher things.
> For from the moment we achieved such a degree of confidence
> that we divulged to each other even the deep secrets of our
>   hearts,
> we were bound together all the more closely by our longing,
> for shared ideals are a strong incentive to close friendship.[8]

There seems to have been a difference in the two friends reactions to Athens. Both absorbed the traditional classical curriculum under masters such as Himmerius and the Christian Prohaeresius. Both would have felt the tension and connection between their family faith and the Hellenic learning in which they had been brought up. Gregory's attitude to 'Athens, the home of eloquence, Athens, a city to me, if to anyone, truly golden, patroness of all that is eloquent',[9] is generally positive, but it is a Christian appreciation of classical learning, not unaware of its dangers. Basil's attitude is at once more hostile and more ambiguous. In his earliest extant letter, written two years after his return from the city, he said, 'I left Athens, scorning everything there.'[10] The chronology of this period in his life is difficult to determine, but it would appear that on returning home in 355 he put his education to good use and taught for a short time at Caesarea, where his brother Gregory was his pupil.[11] We have seen that the *Life of Macrina* states that on his return, Basil was 'excessively puffed up by his rhetorical abilities'.[12] If this gives us the family tradition, then we can see behind Basil's rewriting of his past that there was not in fact a definitive rejection of Athens and its intellectual culture at the time of his departure from the city. The break came later, connected with his baptism, the tour in search of Eustathius in 356/7, of which more in the next chapter, and his settling at Annisa in 357/8. We are back again to that crucial time in 357: the death of Naucratius and their mother's adoption of the ascetic life.

In practice, however, Basil never rejected his educational inheritance, but rather pressed it into the service of his Christian ideals. One could also say that he tried to transcend its exclusivity in order to teach and shepherd the Christian masses.[13] With his background and abilities he could have risen to prominence in the secular sphere, as did Gregory's brother Caesarius, but he turned to a life of philosophy and his companion in this ideal was his old friend from Athens.

Solitude in Pontus

When Basil left Athens, Gregory was persuaded to stay behind. One suspects that he was, at first, not too sad at this, 'for there is nothing so painful to anyone, as is separation from Athens and one another, to those who have been comrades there',[14] but the loss of his friend and the pull of his ageing parents drew him home to Cappadocia. Even allowing for the distortion caused by later events, it would seem that at Athens they had made plans for a life of philosophical seclusion together. By this time Christian writers had for long used the term philosophy to describe their religion, and it had also gained the narrower meaning of a dedicated life of Christian virtue and asceticism. Their project was not at all at odds with their classical heritage, which had its own, more ancient, tradition of philosophical asceticism and seclusion. If certain of the letters between Basil and Libanius are genuine, it is clear that Basil's old pagan teacher saw this as an admirable thing to do.[15] Basil's later description of a clear break between Athens and Annisa is thus a rewriting of his history:

> Much time had I spent in vanity, and had wasted nearly all my youth in the vain labour which I underwent in acquiring the wisdom made foolish by God. Then one day, like someone aroused from a deep sleep, I turned my eyes to the marvellous light of the truth of the Gospel, and I perceived the uselessness of the wisdom of the rulers of this age who are doomed to pass away.[16]

Another series of letters, this time between Basil and Gregory, give us a privileged insight into the two friends opinions and activities as they made their first steps in this dedicated life. This is particularly important for our purposes as Basil's new lifestyle was to provide the context which produced the Asceticon.

First, in a lost letter written after his return from touring the eastern Mediterranean, Basil reminded Gregory of their shared ideal and invited him to join him. Throughout their friendship the initiative is usually with Basil and Gregory is frequently hesitant and indecisive.[17] He replied:

> I have failed, I confess, to keep my promise. I had engaged even at Athens at the time of our friendship and intimate connection there (for I can find no better word for it), to join you in a life of philosophy (*sumphilosopheô*). But I failed to keep my promise,

not of my own will, but because one law prevailed against another; I mean the law that bids us honour our parents overpowered the law of our friendship and intimacy.[18]

Gregory wanted them to live at Tiberina, near Nazianzus, but Basil decided on a spot near his own family estate in Pontus, later calling Gregory's choice 'that pit of the whole world'.[19]

When Basil arrived at his hermitage (*monê*) at Annisa, which he called the place of his dreams, he wrote to Gregory describing it with rapture:

> There is a lofty mountain covered with thick woods, watered towards the north with cool and transparent streams. A plain lies beneath, enriched by the waters which are ever draining off from it; and skirted by a spontaneous profusion of trees almost thick enough to be a fence; so as even to surpass Calypso's island, which Homer seems to have considered the most beautiful spot on earth . . . What need to tell of the exhalations from the earth, or the breezes from the river? Another might admire the multitude of flowers and singing birds; but I have no leisure for such thoughts. However, the chief praise of the place is, that being happily disposed to for produce of every kind, it nurtures what to me is the sweetest produce of all, quietness (*hêsychia*); indeed, it is not only rid of the bustle of the city, but is even unfrequented by travellers, except the guests who join me in hunting.[20]

Gregory replied saying that, 'the nature of your surroundings would not greatly tend to implant in my soul a desire to live with you until I should learn something of your habits and mode of life.'[21] Basil answered this with his Letter 2, to which we shall return a number of times when discussing the Asceticon. It is of great importance in giving his views on the ascetic life at the time he was just beginning to live it.

It is clear that Basil had made a distinct break with his old life, which he describes in the significant words, 'I have indeed left my life in the city (*astu*).'[22] His new life is Christian; he quotes Matthew

16:24 on taking up one's cross and following Christ and advocates Scripture-reading. There is also a clear connection between the teaching in this Letter and that in the later Asceticon. This is especially so when Basil, living in solitude (*erêmia*), spends many lines describing how the ascetic should speak and comport himself. At the same time, although physically leaving the city, he is still living in the classical thought-world and much of the Letter speaks of contemplation, withdrawal and modes of behaviour in ways comprehensible to the educated pagan.[23] Basil has made a new start in a new abode, but there is also much continuity with his previous life.

Basil and Gregory at Annisa: to luxuriate in hard living

Lured by the life, if not by the scenery, Gregory agreed to join him and the two spent some months together in the hermitage at Annisa. There they lived the life of prayer and work outlined in Letter 2, but in addition to 'the study of the divinely inspired Scriptures' they also composed the *Philocalia*, a selection of texts from the writings of Origen. Such work contrasts with the unlettered wisdom said to have been characteristic of St Antony,[24] but is entirely in accord with what we know of the two friends. As mentioned above, Basil's family were connected to Origen through Gregory the Wonderworker and Basil may have encountered his writings in Alexandria on his tour. Perhaps Gregory, who had studied in the cities where Origen had taught, introduced them to him at Athens? The texts selected are significant, they discuss the interpretation of scriptural texts and how to present the Christian case to unbelievers. The first could have been useful for other ascetics, but the second shows that even in his Pontic solitude Basil was concerned not only with his own devout life but also with the work of the wider Church. It is also possible that the *Moralia*, that carefully ordered selection of 1452 New Testament verses, may have been completed at this time. It too is concerned with the life of the Church as a whole.[25] Their period of life and work together did not last, however, and Gregory returned to his parents.

From his home, probably in 359, Gregory wrote three letters to his friend. The first two paint, in a light-hearted way, a picture of the

hermitage as black as Basil's in Letter 14 is rosy: one can imagine
Gregory rereading Basil's letter with a wry grin on his return from
Pontus.

> For my part I will admire your Pontus and your Pontic darkness,
> and your dwelling place (*monê*) so worthy of exile, and the hills
> over your head, and the wild beasts that test your faith, and
> your sequestered spot that lies under them ... or as I should
> say your mousehole with the stately names of Abode of Thought
> (*phrontistêrion*), Monastery (*monastêrion*), School (*scholê*); and
> your thickets of wild bushes, and crown of precipitous
> mountains ... and your musical birds that sing (but only of
> famine), and fly about (but only about the desert). No one visits
> it, you say, except for hunting: you might add, and except to
> look upon your dead bodies.[26]

> Since you do take my jokes kindly, I send you the rest ... Your
> roofless and doorless hut, your fireless and smokeless hearth,
> your walls dried by fire, that we may not be hit by the drops of
> the mud ... For I remember those loaves and the broth (so it
> was called) ... and if we had not been quickly delivered by that
> great supporter of the poor – I mean your mother – who
> appeared opportunely like a harbour to men tossed by a storm,
> we should long ago have been dead, rather pitied than admired
> for our faith in Pontus. How shall I pass over that garden which
> was no garden and had no vegetables, and the Augean dunghill
> which we cleared out of the house, and with which we filled up
> the garden, when we drew that mountainous wagon.[27]

The third Letter changes tone, and gives a different interpretation of
their life together:

> What I wrote before about our stay in Pontus was in joke, not
> in earnest; what I write now is very much in earnest. O that
> one would place me as in the month of those former days (Job
> 29:2), in which I luxuriated with you in hard living; since volun-
> tary pain is more valuable than involuntary delight. O that one

would give me back those psalmodies and vigils and those ascents to God through prayer, and that immaterial, so to speak, and unbodied life. O for the intimacy and unity in spirit of the brethren who were by you divinised and exalted: O for the contest and incitement of virtue which we secured by written rules and regulations; O for the loving labour in the Divine Oracles, and the light we found in them by the guidance of the Holy Spirit. Or, if I may speak of lesser matters, O for the daily tasks and manual labour; O for the gathering of wood and the cutting of stone; O for the golden plane-tree, more precious than that of Xerxes, under which we sat, not a King enfeebled by luxury, but a monk (*monastês*) worn out by hard life.[28]

As well as giving an impression of the character of the two friends, these letters enable us to reconstruct Basil's way of life and ascetic ideals during this formative time. The image they create is thus important background for our reading of the Asceticon.

At the service of the Church

As the realisation of their Athenian ideal, this period probably saw their friendship at its closest. Basil, however, comes across as a single-minded enthusiast, totally committed to his new way of life. Gregory, on the other hand, seems a gentler creature, torn in different ways and as committed to people as he was to ideals. Basil too had his contradictions, but, rather than the pull of family and friends, it was the affairs of the Church that were to draw him from his hermitage. In the next chapters we shall see how the influence of Eustathius was at work here, but to round off this account of the two friends we should mention how they both emerged into a public role in the Church.

Towards the end of 359, after Gregory's departure, Basil left his hermitage to attend a Synod at Constantinople. At about the same time he was appointed a Reader, a lowly position in the clerical hierarchy. He then returned to Annisa where in early 362 he again welcomed Gregory, who had fled there after being unwillingly ordained priest by his father.[29] Basil's own time for ordination to the presbyterate came later in the year, after Gregory had returned home. Gregory then wrote to him saying that while they both love 'a humble and lowly philosophy' and although it may have been better had it not happened, they must accept the ordination forced upon them for the good of the Church endangered by heresy, and so as not to shame themselves or those who trust in them.[30] One suspects that Basil himself was less affected by the tension between ascetic withdrawal and active involvement in the Church. He stayed at Caesarea after his ordination working with the new bishop, Eusebius, but a disagreement between them led to him returning to Annisa in 363. He remained there until 365 when he made a definitive return to the city of which he was to be ordained bishop five years later.

Basil's episcopal career does not concern us here except to say that it led to a breakdown in relations between the two friends. This culminated in his forcibly consecrating Gregory, with the collusion of his father, bishop of the small village of Sasima. This was because the Emperor Valens had divided Cappadocia, leaving Caesarea the only city in Cappadocia Prima and Basil's See with reduced influence and income. Basil responded by trying to fill the province with friendly bishops; his brother Gregory was made bishop of Nyssa. The new bishop of Sasima pleaded philosophy and fled to the hills, never accepting his new role. The estrangement was eventually healed but even after Basil's death there was still a certain bitterness revealed in Gregory's autobiographical poem of 382.[31]

Gregory's subsequent life illustrates how his character contrasts with that of Basil. He returned to Nazianzus and, after his father's death in 374, reluctantly ran the Church there for about a year before running away again, this time to Seleucia. After Basil's death in 379 he accepted an invitation to shepherd the small group of orthodox Christians in Constantinople. Despite the support of the new Emperor Theodosius, the success of his preaching and his appointment as bishop of the city, he was hurt by hostility and infighting, and resigned during the great Council of Constantinople in 381. Returning to Arianzus, he lived his remaining eight or nine years in a devout and scholarly seclusion, writing many letters and poems.

Although Gregory did not share Basil's talent for public life, one should not ignore his great contribution to the Church. Apart from his five celebrated *Theological Orations*, delivered in Constantinople, one could note his own teaching on the ascetic life and his involvement with local ascetics of all types. A study of his poems and letters would reveal a spiritual doctrine with many connections and contrasts to that of Basil.[32]

Conclusion

The two friends were thus very different characters. Gregory was constantly torn between a life of seclusion and duty to his parents and the Church. Basil, on the other hand, was able to combine philosophy and priesthood in his single-minded commitment to God and the Church. We can, though, trace Basil's ascetic teaching back to the shared enthusiasm for philosophy of the two Christian students at Athens. Their conversations and plans were made concrete in the *monê* at Annisa, and we can thank Gregory for prompting Basil's first expression of his ascetic ideals in Letter 2 and for his own letters and reflections from this period. The friendly badinage of the two friends enables us to get behind the icon-like severity and greatness of the posthumous picture of Basil.[33] Even at this early stage, Basil appears as the dominant party in the friendship. Behind the two friend's first steps in asceticism, though, and behind the influences from Basil's own family stands a shadowy figure to whom the young Basil looked as a Master: Eustathius of Sebaste.

NOTES

1. Before 1969 Basil was commemorated on 14 June and Gregory on 9 May. In the East they are celebrated on 1 and 25 January respectively, and on 30 January, together with St John Chrysostom, as the 'Three Universal Teachers and Great Hierarchs'.
2. Ch. 8, 'Basil and Gregory'. See also ch. 4 of C. White's, *Christian Friendship in the Fourth Century*. Abstracting from their friendship, one could compare the characters of Basil and Gregory to the two Victorian convert Cardinals, Manning and Newman.
3. Various dates have been suggested, but the traditional year of 329 seems correct.

4. The Hypsistarians were monotheists who worshipped God under the title 'the Most High' (*hypsistos*). Their doctrines were a mixture of pagan, Jewish and Christian elements and they seem to have been centred in Cappadocia. Our knowledge of them is derived from Gregory's *Oration 18* and Gregory of Nyssa's *Against Eunomius* 2:6.

5. cf. Gregory Nazianzen, *Orations* 7, 8, 18, and *Epigrams* 24–74.

6. Rousseau, *Basil of Caesarea*, pp. 27–60; Gregory of Nazianzus, *Three Poems*, Introduction, pp. 6–8.

7. Gregory Nazianzen, *Oration 43* 15–17.

8. 'On his own life', tr. White, lines 221–36.

9. *Oration 43* 14. This praise is connected to his meeting Basil, as also is that in *Epigram* 8. cf. Rousseau, *Basil of Caesarea*, pp. 38–40.

10. Letter 1, to Eustathius.

11. Gregory of Nyssa, *Letter 13* 4, to Libanius. Gregory Nazianzen *Oration 43* 25. In his own Letter 210, Basil says that Neocaesarea also invited him to teach there.

12. *Life of Macrina* 6. Elsewhere Gregory always speaks with great respect of his brother, which suggests that this is a true story.

13. The question of Basil's attitude to and use of classical culture is not our concern here, except in its relation to the Asceticon. It is treated in ch. 2 of Rousseau's *Basil of Caesarea*, in Meredith's *The Cappadocians*, and in Pelikan, *Christianity and Classical Culture*.

14. *Oration 43* 24.

15. Basil, Letter 336, cf. the commentary of Rousseau, *Basil of Caesarea*, pp. 57–60, 70–72.

16. Letter 223, written in 375, tr. Jackson.

17. After Basil's death, Gregory revealed this side of his character in his poem 'On his own life' (lines 277–336), where he described how, on returning from Athens, he was pulled in different directions by his parents, a life of action and a life of solitude.

18. Gregory Nazianzen, *Letter 1*. Paul Gallay dates it to 361, but with all the Letters I am following the dating proposed by Rousseau in *Basil of Caesarea*, pp. 66–7.

19. End of Letter 14. Gregory's second Letter, starting 'I do not like being joked about Tiberina and its mud and its winters', is probably earlier than this and implies that Basil is still at Caesarea but about to leave for Pontus.

20. Letter 14, tr. Jackson.

21. Modified from Basil's quotation of it in Letter 2. Gregory's letter is lost.

22. Letter 2. The Athenians called Athens *astu*, as the Romans called Rome *Urbs*. It also means the city as a place rather than a civic body (*polis*). cf. Liddell & Scott, *Greek–English Lexicon*.

23. This is noted by Rousseau, *Basil of Caesarea*, pp. 78–82, and Meredith, 'Asceticism', pp. 325–6.

24. *Life of Antony* 72–80, but a study of his Letters has argued that Antony himself was acquainted with the theology of Origen; Samuel Rubenson, *The Letters of St Antony*.

25. A first version of the *Moralia* could then be the 'written rules and regulations' of Gregory's *Letter 6*. The early date is based on the discussion in Rousseau, *Basil*

of Caesarea, pp. 228–32, but some argue for a later date: Fedwick, 'Chronology', pp. 14–17, and Lèbe, 'S. Basile et ses Règles Morales'.

26. Letter 4.
27. Letter 5.
28. Letter 6.
29. He explained his conduct in *Oration 2* 'In defence of his flight to Pontus'. Over twenty years later in his poem 'On his own life' (lines 337–85) he still writes of this episode with emotion.
30. Letter 8.
31. 'On his own life', lines 386–485. In *Oration 43* on his old friend he was more balanced and gracious, cf. Rousseau, *Basil of Caesarea*, p. 238.
32. A brief examination relating to female ascetics is found in Elm, *Virgins of God*, pp. 151–8. She notes: 'It is a rare coincidence that two authors complement each other as perfectly as do Basil of Caesarea and Gregory of Nazianzus. Basil has provided us with structures and regulations, and Gregory has filled the regulations with names, allowing us at least a glimpse of the individuals affected by them' (p. 158). Meredith, *The Cappadocians*, pp. 42–50, gives an outline of Gregory's contribution to theology and spirituality, and the latter is also discussed in Bouyer, *The Spirituality of the New Testament and the Fathers*, pp. 341–51.
33. This picture is certainly rooted in reality, but it was also fostered by the orthodox party in texts such as Gregory's *Oration 43*, and Gregory of Nyssa's *Encomium on his Brother Basil* which seems designed to establish an annual commemoration in his honour.

Chapter Three

Eustathius and the Wider Ascetic Scene

I prayed that I might find some one of the brethren
who had chosen this way of life,
so as to traverse with him life's brief flood.

St Basil, Letter 223

Basil did not compose the Asceticon in a vacuum. He was not the founder of monasticism in Cappadocia and Pontus but rather inserted himself into a tradition of Christian asceticism. It was his reform of that tradition and his subsequent fame as a champion of orthodoxy that elevated him into the most prominent place in Anatolian monasticism, pushing those who had preceded him into the shade. Eustathius and his followers provide the immediate context for Basil's ascetic teaching, but it is worth first setting even him into context and briefly looking at the Christian ascetic tradition and the origins of monasticism.

Ascetic tradition and the New Testament

From the first we find an ascetic element in Christian teaching. This is so with many of Jesus' sayings in the Gospels, for example, 'If any one would come after me, let him deny himself and take up his cross and follow me.'[1] It is also the case with the letters of St Paul, who writes, 'every athlete exercises self-control (*enkrateuomai*) in all things. They do it to receive a perishable wreath, but we an imperishable ... I treat my body with severity and subdue it, lest after preaching to others I myself should be disqualified.'[2] Such texts reflect teaching and practice in early Christian communities and they were constantly resorted to as that practice developed and new situations were faced. From the beginning, inspired by the examples of Jesus and Paul, dedicated celibacy was a feature of the Christian movement. This survived the disappointment of hopes in an imminent Second Coming and early sources note that the presence of celibates was characteristic of the young Church. The Letter of Clement at the end of the first century mentions them as an accepted part of the community but also warns of the danger of pride: 'He that is pure in the flesh, let him be so and not boast, knowing that Another has bestowed his continence (*enkrateia*) on him.'[3] This problem was to be echoed in Basil's lifetime at the Synod of Gangra.

Ascetic elements in contemporary Jewish texts and the sect of the Essenes indicate that the roots of this Christian phenomenon may lie in the Jewish milieu of Jesus and his disciples. Evidence including the Dead Sea Scrolls suggests that at least some of the Essenes, a sect like the Pharisees and the Sadducees, were celibate and that they lived a life devoted to the Law which was strikingly similar to the Christian monks of later centuries.[4] The Jewish writer Philo of Alexandria also mentions a similar community in Egypt called the Therapeutae. His description of these Jewish contemplatives is so similar to Christian monasticism that the Church Historian Eusebius states that they were Christian monks from the time of the Apostles.[5]

There is much scholarly debate on the place of asceticism in the New Testament and the Apostolic Church. Some writers have suggested that under Greek influence an entirely new emphasis on asceticism and celibacy entered the post-Apostolic Church, attaching ascetic meaning to texts written in a different context. With a better understanding of asceticism in the Judaism of the time of Christ, however, many scholars stress the continuity in attitudes to these subjects, with some even suggesting that, 'monasticism was always simply there in the life of the Church . . . and Christian monasticism was a continuation of Jewish monasticism.'[6] There is a long and strong line of Christian ascetic tradition through the period of persecutions to which Basil is heir. Among the prominent teachers in this tradition was Origen, in whose writings can be found much of the later Greek vocabulary of monastic spirituality.

Basil himself, though, believed that his teaching in the Asceticon was either simply scriptural or a reasonable deduction from scriptural premises.[7] In studying his use of Scripture, it is necessary to bypass the historical–critical method of biblical analysis and avoid its narrow concern with the author or redactor's intention. As the Fathers differentiated the literal from the spiritual meanings of Scripture, so modern theorists speak of supplementary levels of meaning added to or drawn out of a text.[8] Each Christian author, and Christian asceticism as a whole, thus produces a portfolio of scriptural texts, each laden with a meaning which itself develops as the tradition progresses. Successive Jewish and Christian interpretations of the Song of Songs give a good example of this type of process. The scriptural canon is closed but, especially for Christians who believe that tradition is the life of the Spirit in the Church, out of it can develop new meanings as well as old. It is not helpful to approach the Asceticon with the idea that each verse of Scripture has its own closed package of meaning sealed in the first century. Two factors can therefore help a fruitful reading of the Asceticon: an awareness of Basil's place in Christian ascetic tradition and an attentiveness to Basil's own use of scriptural texts.

The origins of Christian monasticism

We are still left with the question of when and how Christian monasticism began. The traditional model is that it began with St Antony in Egypt and from there spread throughout the Christian world during the fourth century. Basil fits well into this picture: inspired by his family and Gregory to live a life of Christian devotion, he visited Egypt and other centres of the new monastic movement. On returning home, influenced by the cenobitic communities established in Egypt by Pachomius, he founds the first monastery in Asia Minor at Annisa. The Syrians also believed that their monastic tradition originated from Egypt, in the person of the wandering monk St Awgen and his 70 companions, who came from the desert of Nitria to found a monastery on Mount Izla, near Nisibis. Such ideas, however, do not stand up to scrutiny.

While Egyptian influence was perhaps decisive in Latin-speaking areas, in the eastern Mediterranean it seems that monasticism emerged independently in different areas and that only then was there cross-fertilisation. As a result of this and of the paradigmatic nature of Egyptian monasticism, other areas then sought an Egyptian lineage. The different forms of monasticism, however, are marked by the social and geographical circumstances and the native religious traditions of their local area. To explain this diffuse development, historians tend to emphasise the continuity between fourth century monasticism and the earlier Christian ascetic tradition.[9] This is important, but there was also something new that emerged in the fourth century after the Emperor Constantine's recognition of Christianity. In the momentous period for Church and Empire between then and the reign of the orthodox Emperor Theodosius I (379–95), we find that organised monastic life becomes an important feature of the Christian scene. The ancient ascetic tradition of the Church, while still retaining its own vigour, produces monastic communities and hermits who are separated as never before from normal society. The part played by Athanasius, Basil, Jerome and Augustine in this process shows that the separation was nonetheless relative, and it also shows the central position of this new phenomenon in the life of the Church.

Basil was born during the reign of Constantine and died just before the accession of Theodosius. We have seen how there were various forms of asceticism practised in his family and how his own adoption of an ascetic lifestyle was partly influenced by the classical philosophical tradition. He is also one of the great figures in early monasticism and so in studying his teaching we are observing the transition from older models of ascetic practice to monasticism proper. He was not, however, the founder of monasticism in Asia Minor. Whatever the influence of Gregory and his family, the young Basil stepped into an existing tradition and attached himself to an older man, already familiar to Emmelia and her children. His guide and master as he adopted the dedicated life was the experienced ascetic leader and controversial bishop of Sebaste, the *éminence grise* of Cappadocian monasticism: Eustathius.

Eustathius and the Council of Gangra

Eustathius was born just before AD 300 and was the son of Eulalius, probably bishop of Sebaste in Armenia. The historians Sozomen and Socrates tell us that as a young man his father rebuked him for his outlandish and unclerical attire, a characteristic of the ascetics.[10] Sozomen calls him the founder of monasticism in north-east Asia Minor, although he did not create the ascetic movement.[11] Basil, speaking of his own early days mentions his 'thick cloak and the belt and the sandals of untanned hide'.[12] After leaving Sebaste he tried and failed to join the clergy in Antioch, but in the 330s he was accepted into the clergy at Caesarea in Cappadocia. After a brief stay in Constantinople he returned to Pontus and Armenia where he again got into trouble and was condemned by a Synod at Neocaesarea about 339. Some years later, possibly in 341 or perhaps as late as the mid 360s, he and his followers were again condemned, this time at the Council of Gangra. As he left no writings, an idea of his teaching can be gained from the Canons of this Council.[13]* The twenty Canons condemned:

a) Those who *condemn marriage*; (1, 9); and abandon their husbands for this reason (14); those who overesteem virginity against it (10); and refuse Communion from married priests (4).

b) Those who *overturn the social order* in other ways: slaves who rebel against their masters on the pretext of the Christian life (3); those who condemn meat-eating (2), or wear unusual clothes (12); women who dress as men (13), and shave their heads (17); those who neglect their children (15), or parents (16).

c) Those who *separate themselves from normal Church life*; (5, 11); who abhor gatherings at Martyr's shrines (20); celebrate liturgies outside Church and without priests (6); offer alms and tithes outside episcopally approved structures (7, 8); and do not follow the Church's rules of fasting (18, 19).

This is a hostile source which should be treated with some caution.

---

* See Appendix: The Canons of the Council of Gangra.

It is likely that Eustathius's views became more moderate after he became a bishop, the period in which he influenced Basil. From Gangra, though, one can gain some idea of the radical concepts of Christian living that were in the air as the children of the elder Basil and Emmelia were growing up.

Doctrine and life: Homoiousian asceticism

As well as his ascetic activities Eustathius was also involved in the ecclesiastical and theological conflicts of the time. In the late 340s one of his disciples, Macedonius, became bishop of Constantinople, and another, Marathonius, succeeded to the important see of Nicomedia. Both of these men had founded monasteries for men and women and also hospices for the poor and the ascetics had supported their attempts at episcopal office. When Eustathius himself became bishop of Sebaste about 356, he too founded a hospice in his see-city. The significance of this group of bishops can only be understood against the background of the long and bitter theological conflicts of the fourth century. Such conflicts may seem strange to us today when most people see religion as a private option. Then, not only was it a question of imperial policy, but the debates were about what people held most dear: their Saviour, Christ, and their own salvation.

The first Ecumenical Council of Nicaea (AD 325) condemned the teaching of Arius, an Alexandrian presbyter, that the Son (Christ) was a creature and not eternal, being of a different and inferior nature to the Father. It taught that the Son was of the same nature (in Greek 'homoousios') as the Father. From then until the second Ecumenical Council, at Constantinople in AD 381, the Church was torn by conflict between the supporters of Nicaea, such as Athanasius of Alexandria, who held 'homoousios' to be the touchstone of orthodoxy, and various groups who rejected the *homoousion* as unsuitable for theological use or even opposed it.

The politics and constantly shifting groupings of the conflict are very complex and were made more so by the interventions of the emperors. In the 350s there was a revival of Arian fortunes. A group led by Aetius and Eunomius openly opposed the *homoousion* and

taught that the Son was unlike (*anomoios*) the Father: the Anomoeans. The more moderate contented themselves with saying that the
Son was like (*homoios*) the Father. Another group, this time from
the theological centre ground, went further than these Homoeans
in the direction of Nicaea. They have been called 'Homoiousian' as
they held the Son to be similar in being (in Greek *homoiousios* or
homoios kat'ousian) to the Father. Heavily influenced by the theology
of Origen, and the theological heirs of Eusebius of Caesarea, they
distrusted the novelty and ambiguity of *homoousios* and believed that
their formula better safeguarded the traditional doctrine about Christ.
Among the protagonists of this party were Macedonius of Constantinople, Basil, bishop of Ancyra in Galatia from 336 to 358,
and Eustathius of Sebaste.[14] It was here in this grouping that the
young Basil found his first theological home.

In connection with this group Susanna Elm has identified what she
calls 'Homoiousian Asceticism':[15] communities of men and women,
usually situated in episcopal cities, involved in charitable work and
intervening in church politics. They were inspired by the teaching of
Eustathius and a presentation of their ascetic doctrine is found in
Basil of Ancyra's treatise 'On Virginity',[16] which thus supplements the
hostile Canons of Gangra. By the late 340s these ascetics had been
firmly integrated into Church structures. Gribomont notes that Eustathius was the first 'monastic' founder to orientate the movement's
resources to the care of the poor and sick.[17] This moderation and
integration did not please all the Eustathians and at least one radical
group, under an ascetic called Aerius who had been responsible for
one of the hospices for the poor, repudiated Eustathius and fled to a
freer life in the wilds. Basil of Ancyra's 'On Virginity' seems to show
reaction against such extremists, just as a similar moderation is found
in our Basil's later Asceticon.

Basil the disciple

When Basil returned from Athens to devote himself to philosophy, it
was to these circles around Eustathius that he attached himself. They
were no strangers to each other, in Letter 244 Basil notes that he had

'ministered to' Eustathius from childhood (*ek paidos*). His first extant letter is to Eustathius, called 'the philosopher', and states that, 'owing to the repute of your philosophy, I left Athens, scorning everything there'.[18] He travelled around the ascetic centres of the eastern Mediterranean, Egypt and Alexandria, Palestine, Syria and Mesopotamia, following but not meeting Eustathius. While it seems that Eustathius was the greatest lure for the journey, Basil's later letters suggest that it was also motivated by a desire to visit the ascetics whom he had heard, probably from Gregory, dwelt in these areas.[19] In one of these letters, to Eustathius, he remembers this time and says, 'I prayed that I might be given guidance to introduce me to the teachings of religion (*eusebeia*) . . . I prayed that I may find some one of the brethren who had chosen this way of life.'[20] His prayers were answered in the person of Eustathius and it was under his guidance that Basil made his first steps in the ascetic life at Annisa. The letter goes on:

> Ask yourself: How often did you visit us in the retreat (*monê*) on the River Iris, when, moreover, our most divinely favoured brother Gregory (of Nazianzen) was present with me, achieving the same purpose (*skopos*) in life as myself? . . . And how many days did we spend in the village opposite, at my mother's, living as friend with friend, with conversation astir among us both night and day?

This and the previous chapters hopefully give an idea of the young Basil in the context of family, friends and the Church of his time. When the spotlight is taken off him and a softer lamp illumines the ascetic landscape of Asia Minor, one can begin to understand the background of the Asceticon. Although this may seem to diminish Basil, a new appreciation of his greatness emerges when we see what he does with the tradition he inherited. There is a unity in Basil's espousal of both the theological and ascetic views of Eustathius. Basil's favoured word '*eusebeia*' – piety – which we will find used again and again in his writings to describe the ascetic life, also means 'orthodoxy, right belief' in patristic usage. The knowledge that he was originally a Eustathian enables one to have a better understanding of Basil's Asceticon.

As in theology he was to break with the Homoiousians and, with the two Gregories, formulate that 'Cappadocian theology' of the Trinity which triumphed in the Council of 381, so in ascetic spirituality he was to develop his own synthesis along Eustathian lines and formulate an impressive body of spiritual teaching. In the next chapter we shall see how this happened.

NOTES

1. Matt. 16:24. Other examples include Matt. 19:21; Luke 9:57–62; Luke 14:26–7, 33; and on celibacy, Matt. 19:10–12, Luke 20:34–6.
2. 1 Cor. 9:25–7. Clark describes 1 Cor. 7 as 'probably the most ascetically charged chapter of the New Testament', *Reading Renunciation*, p. 13, cf. ch. 10 of the same work: '1 Corinthians 7 in early Christian exegesis'.
3. Clement, *To the Corinthians* 38. Other texts include: Ignatius of Antioch, *To Polycarp* 5:2 and Justin Martyr, *Apology* 1:15:6. The second-century non-Christian writer Galen also notes that celibates have a prominent place among the Christians (Arabic quotation from his lost summary of Plato's *Republic*, translated in Stevenson, *A New Eusebius* (1963), p. 133). Many apocryphal Acts and Gospels also stress celibacy, the evidence is reviewed in Peter Brown, *The Body and Society*, Part One; 'From Paul to Antony', pp. 3–209.
4. There has been much debate about the community described in some Scrolls and its relation to the Essenes and the settlement at Qumran. There is however other contemporary evidence of Essene communities from Josephus, Pliny and Philo.
5. Eusebius, HE 2:17.
6. J. C. O'Neil, 'The Origins of Monasticism', p. 270, in *The Making of Orthodoxy* (1989) ed. Rowan Williams. Cf. also Brian J. Capper, 'With the Oldest Monks: Light from Essene History on the Career of the Beloved Disciple', *Journal of Theological Studies* NS 49:1 (1998), pp. 1–55. A discussion of all these issues is found in Clark, *Reading Renunciation*, pp. 18–22. She notes that arguments for Christian asceticism being an alien import often originate from Protestant circles.
7. cf. *Moralia* 26:1, the start of Letter 22, and especially SR 1.
8. cf. Clark, *Reading Renunciation*, pp. 5–10.
9. cf. Guillaumont, A., *Aux origines du monachisme chrétien* (1979). It is interesting to note that while Cousin, *Précis d'histoire monastique* (1956), starts with St Antony after five pages on the origins of monasticism, Desprez, *Le monachisme primitif* (1998), has four chapters on the antecedents of Christian monasticism before it reaches Antony.
10. Socrates, HE 2:43, Sozomen, HE 2:24; cf. Gribomont, 'Eustathe de Sébaste', *É&É* 1:95.
11. Sozomen, HE 3:14.
12. Letter 223.
13. The full text in English with a commentary is in *The Seven Ecumenical Councils*

NPNF2: 14, pp. 87–101. The presiding bishop was Eusebius, probably Eusebius of Nicomedia who was then bishop of Constantinople. For the date see Gribomont, 'Le monachisme en Asie Mineure', *É&É* pp. 26–9. This date has been challenged, see Fedwick, 'Chronology', p. 4 n14 and p. 14 n81. He suggests mid or late 360s when the bishop could have been Basil's predecessor, Eusebius, bishop of Caesarea AD 362–370.

14. Much has been written about the Arian controversy and there are a variety of conflicting views concerning it. A broad survey of the crisis is found in R. P. C. Hanson, *The Search for the Christian Doctrine of God. The Arian Controversy 318–381* (Edinburgh 1988).

15. *Virgins of God*, chs. 4, 6.

16. Formerly attributed to Basil of Caesarea, this text is found in *PG* 30:670–810. It is discussed in Elm, *Virgins of God*, pp. 113–24, 132–3.

17. Gribomont, 'Eustathe de Sébaste', p. 106.

18. Gribomont shows that this is Eustathius of Sebaste in 'Eustathius le philosophe', *É&É* 1:107–16. A different view is given by Peter Brown, *The Body and Society*, p. 302, who thinks that the Eustathius of this letter is a pagan diplomat and philosopher.

19. Letter 223 and also Letter 207, but see Rousseau, *Basil of Caesarea*, p. 73 n53. Gregory had studied in Alexandria and Palestine.

20. Letter 223 (written *c*.375).

Chapter Four

Basil Develops his own Teaching

We who have been entrusted with the ministry of the Word should always be zealous for the perfecting of your souls.

St Basil, Preface to the Shorter Rules

The influence of Eustathius, Gregory and Macrina shaped Basil's understanding of the ascetic life. It is, however, as misleading to merely record his dependence as it is to ignore it. The historians who present Basil as a founder do have a point, although his real position was as a reformer of an existing movement. His life is strongly marked by the charism of leadership and the aim of this chapter is to chart his development from the eager young disciple of Eustathius to the confident spiritual Master of the Asceticon. He also developed the teaching he inherited and we shall briefly look at this, while leaving further examination to later chapters. Thus in asceticism, as in theology, he diverged from the position of Eustathius and it is not surprising that there was a public end to their relationship.

Basil the leader

In his continuation of Eusebius's *Church History*, Rufinus compares Basil and Gregory Nazianzen to the two olive trees by the lampstand in Zechariah 4:11–14. In this comparison Gregory comes out best and Rufinus makes the strange point that he forced Basil to give up the practice of rhetoric and come with him to a monastery. Written in the West in the year 402, the source may be a lost life of Gregory or it may be Evagrius of Pontus, who left Basil to join Gregory and later met Rufinus.[1] The surviving letters, however, suggest that Basil was the dominant partner in their ascetic experiment. He persuaded

Gregory to return to their ascetic ideal when he had returned home, and he persuaded him to come to Annisa rather than Tiberina. It is also indicative of his character that Basil followed his own path and did not join his mother, Macrina and the young Peter in their community.

It seems clear that, even if he did not inherit former companions of Naucratius, Basil had other ascetics besides Gregory with him at his *monê* from an early date. The mention of visiting hunters in the early letters suggests that this was not so,[2] but Gregory's more serious letter states that there were other brothers (*adelphoi*) and that Basil was the leader. The same letter speaks of that leadership made concrete in 'written rules (*horoi*) and regulations (*kanones*)' which, like the *Philocalia*, they both composed. While the Rules of the Asceticon are referred to as *horoi* in the printed editions, this was not what Basil himself called his answers. We have already suggested that this phrase refers to the *Moralia*,[3] but Elm thinks that it is Basil's Letter 2.[4] This, however, rather than a joint composition, is a letter from Basil to Gregory outlining his vision of the ascetic life. It is also addressed to one who has not yet decided to join Basil in living the life described. What is significant here is that from the start of his ascetic life Basil was writing, thus effectively teaching, about asceticism. Also, as will be noted in the commentary on the Rules, the doctrine taught is remarkably consistent between the early texts and the Asceticon.

One final question is who these other ascetics were. We do not know for certain, but as Letter 1 shows that Basil was in contact with Eustathius from the start of his ascetic life, it can be assumed that they were, like Basil, part of the wider Eustathian movement. The mention in Letter 223 of Eustathius' visits to the *monê* on the River Iris confirms this.

Church and priesthood

Socrates connects Basil's foundation of several monasteries in Pontus to his desire to counteract the Arian heresy.[5] This is probably not true but it does reveal a real connection. Rousseau explains it thus:

'his ascetic life was combined not only with a growing sense of pastoral vocation but also with a growing interest in the religious conflicts that lay at the heart of church affairs at that time.' He also says, 'the chronology of (Basil's) commitment to the clerical order is completely interwoven with his explorations in the ascetic life: each forces us to reassess the significance of the other.'[6] Given the picture of Homoiousian asceticism outlined in the last chapter this is not surprising. Recalling Basil's ordination and that engagement in ecclesiastical politics mentioned in Chapter 2, we shall be able to understand how this enabled the teaching first formulated at Annisa to reach a wider audience.

The first thing to note is that this engagement happened very soon, about two years after he returned to Pontus. During these two years contact with Eustathius would have kept him informed of developments in the Church: the rise of the Homoean party under the patronage of Constantius II (sole Emperor 353–61), the emergence of the neo-Arian Anomoeans, and the vigorous counter-attack of the Homoiousians starting from their synod at Ancyra in April 358. At the twin councils of Seleucia and Rimini in 359, however, the bishops of East and West accepted a Homoean formula and the synod at Constantinople in January of the following year was to be the crown of this success. It was to this council that Basil came as an insignificant associate of Dianius of Caesarea and the Homoiousians. Constantinople confirmed the Homoean triumph and many bishops were deposed. As well as Athanasius of Alexandria who defended the *homoousion*, these included Eustathius, Basil of Ancyra and Macedonius of Constantinople. The radical Anomoeans also suffered for a while.

Our Basil returned to Pontus and eventually broke with Dianius who had subscribed to the decrees of Constantinople. He was reconciled with Dianius on his deathbed in 362 but significantly the 'Nazarites' of Caesarea, whom Elm identifies as urban Homoiousian ascetics, campaigned for Basil to become bishop. Their support continued even after the election of Eusebius to the see, and as a result Basil, after being ordained presbyter in 362, returned again to Annisa in 363.[7] In the correspondence of Gregory of Nazianzus there are letters from this period to Basil and Eusebius trying to get Basil back into the city. He eventually returned after 18 months in 365.[8] Even during his period away from Caesarea, Basil was still involved in the affairs of the Homoiousian party. On the way to the Synod of Lampsacus in 364, Basil prepared some notes for Eustathius to use against the Anomoeans which became his first theological treatise: *Against Eunomius.*

All this involvement in ecclesiastical conflicts is of relevance for our study of the Rules. It is probable that the first version of the Asceticon, the Small Asceticon, was prepared while Basil was a priest. His travels in the Homoiousian interest would have given many opportunities for meetings with ascetics at which questions might be asked and his answers recorded. Letter 22, in itself a mini-Rule, may date from this time.[9] The fact that the Eustathian party was characterised by ascetic involvement and the glimpse of Basil as the chosen leader of the Nazarites suggests that his rise to prominence in Homoiousian circles was parallel to his emergence as a leader among the ascetics of this party. His leadership would have filled the vacuum caused by the absence of Eustathius, who was in exile in the Balkans in 360 and journeyed to the West a few years later.

The Asceticon itself may first have taken shape in Pontus. A sixth-century editor of the Asceticon recorded in his scholia (editorial comments) that he found the oldest manuscript there[10] and that the Small Asceticon first took shape before Basil became a bishop when he was asked questions by the ascetics around him (*peri auton*).[11] The historians also associate Basil's ascetic activity with the area.[12] Given Basil's increasingly prominent position in Eustathian circles, it is unlikely that his questioners were only from the community at Annisa. His answers never present him as a local Superior. It is even possible that they included the Nazarites of Caesarea and other Cappadocian ascetics. Just as different collections of the *Sayings of the Desert Fathers* were built up in individual communities, so we can, on the basis of the two sources of the sixth-century edition, posit a distinctive Basilian ascetic tradition in Pontus which was transferred to and developed in Caesarea after his definitive move to the city in 365.

Basil of Caesarea

Basil's commitment to the life of the wider Church began in an ascetic context and, while involvement in public life and the fight against heresy took up more and more of his time, he remained involved with the ascetic movement throughout his life. As bishop from 370 he was part of a distinct Eustathian tradition which united these elements.

The event of his episcopate which has most caught the imagination of subsequent generations is his confrontation with Arianism and the civil power in the persons of the Prefect Modestus and the Emperor Valens.[13] Yet despite the religious difference between the Emperor and Basil, the former gave his support to Basil's great project to assist the poor of his city: the Basileiados. We have already noted how Eustathius directed the energies of the ascetics to practical charity. This inheritance combined with the traditional paternal and social role of the bishop is shown in Basil's reaction to the famine of 369,[14] but the Basileiados best illustrates how important such activities were in his ascetic teaching. It is significant that in *Oration 43* Gregory Nazianzen describes this 'new city' immediately after his account of Basil's monastic activities.[15] In Basil's own Letter 150 he associates this poor-house (*ptôchotropheion*) with ascetic teaching. The evidence, including some of the Rules, suggests that at least some of the staff were ascetics and that he saw serving the poor and sick not just as a good work for monks and a service to society but as an integral part of the ascetic life itself, related to the commandments of Christ.

It was at the Basileiados that the erudite Byzantine author of the sixth-century scholia found his Caesarea manuscript with its extra Shorter Rules. During his episcopate Basil continued visiting and teaching the communities of ascetics and he revised and augmented the collections of his answers. At one point, possibly in 376/7,[16] he added the *Moralia* and various Prefaces to the Rules to form a collection which he called the *Hypotyposis Askêseôs* (Outline or Pattern of Asceticism) which was the source of the scholiast's Pontus manuscript. Perhaps Basil sent a copy back to his old communities? The Preface to the Hypotyposis is strange in that it describes the short works that precede the Rules in some detail, but mentions the Rules almost as an afterthought.[17] Another ascetic work from this period is his brother Gregory's earliest known work, 'On Virginity'. Gregory had married but seems to have written this work in 371 under Basil's influence to give a theoretical foundation to the ascetic life different to that provided in the Longer Rules. It starts and ends with allusions to the unnamed Basil and the last chapter begins with what looks like a reference to the Asceticon or *Moralia*.[18] Thus it is clear that Basil's ascetic activities continued throughout his episcopate, together with other work for the Church such as his interventions in Antioch where there was a schism. This period also saw him move away from the Homoiousian position in theology and break with his old friend and mentor Eustathius. First, however, we shall return to the wilder fringes of the ascetic movement.

Messalians, heretics and enthusiasts

The settled and disciplined life of the brothers at the Basileiados was part of Basil's reform of asceticism, but his letters show that wilder forms of ascetic enthusiasm retained their popularity. Even in the Rules, where the word *spoudê* (zeal or enthusiasm) is common, there are traces of such views in the questions. The Canonical Letters show Basil engaging critically with deviant ascetic groups such as the Manichaeans and Encratites,[19] but Letters 169–171 give a vignette of him dealing with a particular situation. They are actually by Gregory Nazianzen[20] and deal with the errant Deacon Glycerius, whom he had ordained. Glycerius neglected his duties, assumed unusual dress, gathered a group of virgins and young men and, at a festival, led them off to live in the wilds. Gregory was very annoyed and expected Basil, who had 'collected' the group, to deal with them. Elm has shown that this group was following a common ascetic pattern of the period[21] and it is significant that Basil seems to have received them in a sympathetic manner. The communities with which he dealt were thus not all of a settled Eustathian type and the background to the Rules was one of spiritual and ascetic ferment. Basil's great achievement, as a man of the Church and a man of the Spirit, was to unite these potentially schismatic currents of enthusiasm with the official Church, as was to happen in the thirteenth century West with the Franciscans.

The groups called Messalians (Syriac for 'those who pray'), condemned by Ephrem of Nisibis (*c.* 373), Epiphanius of Salamis (374 and 377) and then at the end of the fourth century at the Synods of Side and Antioch, may have been a continuation of this current of asceticism. Certainly, some called them 'Eustathians'.[22] They were characterised by a great emphasis on direct inner experience in prayer and a rejection of work and Church structures. There are indeed clear connections between the beliefs and actions of the Eustathians condemned at Gangra, enthusiasts such as Glycerius the Deacon and Eustathius' former disciple Aerius, and the Messalians. The Glycerius incident happened in 374 at the same time that Epiphanius was penning his first condemnation of the Messalians. Elm says that, 'what distinguishes Eustathius' followers condemned at Gangra from the Messalians condemned around 390 at Side appears to be little else than the interim of sixty years.'[23]

The whole question of Messalianism is complex and is an academic minefield with a variety of contradictory opinions held and disputed by scholars. The Pseudo-Macarian texts are at the heart of the Messalian controversy. They are a collection of spiritual writings attributed to 'Macarius', formerly identified with Macarius the Egyptian (*c.* AD 300–390) but probably written in the region of Antioch in the period AD 385–430. It would seem that they are the same as the *Asceticon* written by Symeon the Messalian, which was used by the Fathers of the Third Ecumenical Council at Ephesus in 431 who renewed the condemnation of the movement. They were later to influence the spiritual movement called Hesychasm in the Greek East and Protestant Pietism and Methodism in the West. The author, like Basil, seems to have been attempting to moderate the extremists. Columba Stewart has shown how this work comes out of a Syriac milieu and how the condemnations are in part the result of the meeting of Semitic and Greek ways of thinking.[24] Scholars have discovered close links in themes and vocabulary between Basil and Pseudo-Macarius, and certain works of his brother Gregory of Nyssa show even stronger parallels. His 'On the Christian Mode of Life' is thought to be dependent on the *Great Letter* of Pseudo-Macarius, and one can see his relations with the Messalians to be very similar to those of Basil with the enthusiasts around Eustathius. The author of the Pseudo-Macarian synthesis is however to the 'left' of Basil and to some extent justifies Messalian views.[25] Where we find 'pre-Messalian' questions in the Asceticon, such as Shorter Rule 238 on uninterrupted spiritual activities, Basil's responses are always discouraging.

The Messalians were a Syrian phenomenon and Basil had close contacts with the area beginning with his tour after returning from Athens. Syria had a long ascetic tradition[26] and as well as the extreme ascetics chronicled by Theoderet of Cyrrhus (*c.* AD 393–466) in his *Religious History*, Syrian monasticism also had a strongly cenobitic character. James of Nisibis (dd. 337/8), who became a bishop and engaged in charitable activities, can be compared with Basil. This is a theme which would repay further attention.

The break with Eustathius

Friendship, for Basil, was always secondary to what he saw as the will of God and the greater good of the Church. We have seen how this damaged his relationship with Gregory. His friendship with Eustathius eventually ended in recrimination and theological divergence and his ascetical mentor was edited out of his biography like a purged Soviet General from a picture of a May Day parade.

Eustathius helped Basil set up the Basileiados and two of his disciples, Basil and Sophronius, went to Caesarea as part of this programme. In late 371 they were in conflict with Basil, partly over ascetic matters, and fled the city. This caused friction between him and Eustathius.[27] The main cause of their breach was, however, theological. The differences became worse after talks at Sebaste in 373 and were made public in Basil's Letter 223 in 375. Eustathius had moved towards a position which seemed to deny the divinity of the Holy Spirit and his followers became known as *Pneumatomachoi* – those who fight the Holy Spirit (*Hagion Pneuma* in Greek). Basil fought against this position, notably in his *On the Holy Spirit*, and the

Homoiousian party split, with one party attaching itself to Basil's 'Neo-Nicene' group and another following the opinions of Eustathius. The party around Basil and the two Gregories held that God is one in nature (*ousia*) and at the same time three Persons (*hypostaseis*), Father, Son, and Holy Spirit, all equally God but all distinct from each other. This was the teaching which, after the deaths of Eustathius and Basil, would be recognised as orthodox by the Second Ecumenical Council at Constantinople in 381, and which remains to this day the normative faith of Christians.

The theological and personal division was accompanied by a division among the ascetics. Elm points out that Homoiousian monasteries continued,[28] but from this time onwards Basil's ascetic doctrine triumphed just as his theological position had been recognised as orthodox. Eustathius was thus pushed into the heretical twilight and official history came to regard Basil as the founder of monasticism in Asia Minor.[29] The conflict with Eustathius thus had an ascetic dimension and the exaltation of Basil in his brother's 'On Virginity', together with his own later versions of the Asceticon, are perhaps part of a strategy to promote his views among the ascetics. Gregory writes of his brother, without mentioning his name, saying, 'Look to this man as the model (*kanôn*) of your life. Let this one be for you as the goal (*skopos*) of the divine life as the fixed stars are for the pilots.'[30]

A comparison of Basil's position with the Eustathian position condemned at Gangra, though, confirms his position as a reformer. In this he follows Eustathius himself who seems to have moderated his position as he became more involved in Church affairs. Celibacy is not a prominent theme in the Asceticon and *Moralia* 73 shows Basil as a supporter of marriage, but there and in Longer Rule 12 he allows separation from one's partner, even against their will, to live the ascetic life. It thus seems that he saw consecrated celibacy as a higher state than matrimony. Likewise with slaves who flee to the communities, Basil takes a moderate position and advocates their return, unless an evil master is causing the slave to transgress the commandments.[31] In this case it may be right to accept him and bear the consequences. This contradicts Canon 3 of Gangra but, at the same time as displaying independence of social conventions, Basil is careful to situate the issue at the level of the commandments, the fundamental teachings of the Gospel.[32] Concerning unpaid taxes, in Shorter Rule 94 he teaches that if a brother has made a full renunciation of property these should not trouble him or those who received him. He has nothing of Caesar's to render unto Caesar. Other issues such as clothing and abstinence will be discussed in subsequent chapters.

In examining relations between the sexes we shall see how Basil fundamentally changed the Homoiousian model but the overall impression is that Basil is firmly in the Eustathian tradition and sympathetic to the wider variety of ascetic enthusiasts. At the same time, while preserving the radical nature of their commitment, he aimed to bring this way of living the Gospel firmly within the Church. Thus he does follow in the footsteps of his old master, but the definite and lasting achievement is Basil's.

NOTES

1. Gribomont, *Histoire du Texte*, p. 260. On Rufinus and Evagrius see Clark, *The Origenist Controversy*, pp. 188–93.
2. Basil, Letter 14; Gregory Nazianzen, Letter 14, where the plural dead bodies (*nekrous humas*) in a section in the second person singular may imply companions.
3. Gribomont, *Histoire du Texte*, p. 257 notes that Basil uses the word *horos* of the *Moralia* in his Preface 'de Fide', CPG 2886. The word for written, *graptos*, may also mean 'scriptural'.
4. *Virgins of God*, p. 46 n19, although on p. 66 she says that the letter 'reflects the contents of these regulations and canons'.
5. Socrates, HE 4:26.
6. Rousseau, *Basil of Caesarea*, pp. 84–5.
7. Gregory Nazianzen, *Oration* 43 26–9. If we accept from Sozomen, HE 2:43, that the Synod of Gangra was held in the 360s, this conflict may supply both the context and an Eusebius in conflict with the Eustathians.
8. Gregory Nazianzen, *Letters* 19 to Basil, and 16, 17 and 18 to Eusebius.
9. cf. the discussion of this text in Gribomont, 'Les Règles Épistolaires', and the date given in Rousseau, *Basil of Caesarea*, p. 193 n4.
10. Scholia 3, 7. The text of the Scholia is edited in Gribomont, *Histoire du texte*, pp. 152–6.
11. Scholion 2.

12. Rufinus, HE 11:9, Socrates, HE 4:26, Sozomen, HE 6:15, 17. It is possible that Pontus here may refer to the whole civil diocese.
13. Gregory Nazianzen, *Oration 43* 44–57; Gregory of Nyssa, *Against Eunomius* 1:119–46. It was emphasised by the historians: Rufinus, HE 11:9, Socrates, HE 4:26, Sozomen, HE 6:15, Theodoret, HE 4:16. The theme is prominent in the popular iconography of Basil and forms the frontispiece of the 1721 edition of his works: Fitzgerald, 'Notes on the iconography of St Basil the Great'.
14. Gregory Nazianzen, *Oration 43* 34–36; Basil, Letter 31, and 3 Homilies: CPG 2850, 2852, 2853.
15. *Oration 43* 63, he describes Basil's care for the suffering in terms reminiscent of his teaching on this subject in the Rules.
16. Fedwick, 'Chronology', p. 17.
17. PG 31:1509–13. The ninth-century Patriarch and scholar Photius does the same in his comments on the Asceticon in *Bibliotheca* 191.
18. *Traité de la Virginité* (*SC* 119) 23:1:6, pp. 134–7, note connections with Basil's ascetic teaching.
19. Letter 188, Canon 1; Letter 199, Canon 47.
20. Gregory Nazianzen, *Letters* 246–48 (*CPG* 3032).
21. *Virgins of God*, pp. 188–95. She notes that the anarchic nature of such groups usually settles into a structured pattern. This can be compared with the development of institutions revealed in the Rules.
22. cf. Gribomont, 'Le Monachisme en Asie Mineure', pp. 40–41; Meyendorff, 'Messalianism', p. 206; Elm, *Virgins of God*, pp. 189–99.
23. Elm, *Virgins of God*, p. 193.
24. Stewart, *Working the Earth of the Heart*.
25. See Gribomont, 'Monachisme au sein de l'Église' 22; 'Monachisme enthousiaste' section IV: Basile et Macaire; 'Monachisme en Asie Mineure' 414–15.
26. cf. Brown, *Body and Society*, 101, 195–7, 329–38.
27. Basil, Letter 119 to Eustathius.
28. *Virgins of God*, pp. 221–2.
29. On the other hand, Sozomen records a tradition that Basil's Asceticon was in fact by Eustathius, HE 3:14.
30. 'On Virginity' 23.
31. LR 11, quoting the Letter of Paul to Philemon.
32. See Elm, *Virgins of God*, p. 103, which notes that Basil, unlike Macrina and the two Gregories, never questioned the *institution* of slavery. It was very much part of the fabric of society at that time, as unremarkable then as shop assistants are today, and one should note that, despite their questioning, both Gregories owned slaves.

Chapter Five

The Asceticon: Text and Life

Then, besides the Conferences of the Fathers, and their Institutes and their Lives, there is also the Rule of our holy father Basil. For observant and obedient monks, all these are nothing less than tools for the cultivation of virtues.

Rule of St Benedict: Chapter 73

The last chapter has given some suggestion of how the Asceticon was composed. Even during Basil's lifetime there were a number of versions in circulation as a result of additions to the text and his own revisions. If one adds later recensions, edited after his death, and translations into other ancient languages, it is clear that the transmission of the text of the Asceticon is a very complicated issue. The work of a number of scholars, notably Jean Gribomont OSB and Paul Jonathan Fedwick,[1] has clarified the situation, and to help in understanding the Rules some of their conclusions will be briefly outlined here. The text also raises other questions such as its genre (the type of work it is) and the original situation in which the answers were given. Finally it is worth asking how Basil defines the style of life he is advocating and those who live it.

The most common version of the Asceticon: the Vulgate recension

The text used in this book is that edited by the Maurist Benedictines in eighteenth century France. Volume 2 of the complete works, including the Asceticon, was published in 1722 and reprinted by Migne in his *Patrologia Graeca*. The English translations by Clarke and Wagner, and almost all versions in modern languages, are from this edition. It has 55 Longer Rules (*horoi kata platos*) and 313 Shorter

Rules (*horoi kat'epitomên*) which form the Asceticon proper, to which are joined various other ascetic works, only some of which are by Basil.[2] Although this is the most easily available version, the Greek manuscripts on which it is based only go back to the work of the sixth-century Byzantine author of the scholia mentioned in the last chapter. Gribomont called this recension the Vulgate – from the Latin *vulgatus* (common/popular), a term used to describe Jerome's Latin Bible – because it is the most commonly used recension.

The problem with it is that while the text is by Basil, its arrangement is not. The scholia reveal that it is based on the Pontus manuscript which went up to Shorter Rule 286, with the remaining Shorter Rules taken from the Caesarea manuscript associated with the Basileiados. The division into 55 Longer Rules seems to have been the scholiast's own work, his oldest manuscript only had 18 sections which were each headed by a real question. The Shorter Rules in the Vulgate are rearranged in ten thematic sections followed by an appendix and the Caesarea addition. Within each section the earlier material has been placed first:[3]

1) Repentance and conversion: 3–20.
2) Sin: 21–84.
3) Poverty: 85–95.
4) Duties of Superiors: 96–113.
5) Obedience: 114–25.
6) Fasting: 126–40.
7) Work: 141–56.
8) Interior dispositions (*diatheseis*): 157–86.
9) Family: 187–90, and virtues recommended by Scripture: 191–238.
10) Moral exegesis of Scriptural texts: 239–78.
11) Series without internal unity: 279–86.
12) Caesarea addition: 287–313.

The Small Asceticon

In the Latin West, the *Rule of St Benedict* (mid sixth century) begins
and ends with St Basil. Its Prologue begins with an allusion to a tract
then believed to be by Basil, the *Admonition to a Spiritual Son*, and
the final chapter includes in its recommendations for further
reading 'the Rule of our holy father Basil'. The Great Asceticon, of
which the Vulgate is one form, was only put into Latin about the
year 1300 by the Spiritual Franciscan, Angelo Clareno (1245–1337),
who was exiled to Greece. The Rule of Basil mentioned by Benedict
must thus be the *Instituta Monachorum* translated by Rufinus of
Aquileia in 396/7 for Urseius, Abbot of Pinetum near Ravenna.[4] This,
however, has only 203 Rules in one series. W. K. L. Clarke's solution
to this problem was to say that Rufinus abbreviated the Greek text,[5]
but it is now known that the text he translated was the Small
Asceticon (*mikron askêtikon*) mentioned in scholion 2.

This was the first edition of the questions and answers, formed
while Basil was still a priest (it is called 'R' by Gribomont and
recension A or Asceticon 1 by Fedwick). It now exists only in the
Latin of Rufinus and an even earlier Syriac translation. In both of
these the original text has, as far as we know, been modified to suit
the ascetic situation of the intended audience. Translation was not a
mere mechanical transmission. Fragments of papyrus from Anti-
noopolis in Egypt have been shown to be from the lost Greek text
of the Small Asceticon.[6] It is possible that a copy of the Small
Asceticon was taken to the monastery on the Mount of Olives with
which Basil was in contact. Rufinus was in Jerusalem from 380–97
and could easily have obtained a transcript of this work, which could
also have been transmitted to Egypt.[7] The Syriac version with 186
answers, entitled 'Questions of the Brothers', may have been translated
in Basil's lifetime. It is an early version of the Asceticon and he
was in frequent contact with Syria as shown by the correspondence
with his friend Eusebius of Samosata. An argument against this,
however, is that it is commonly cited in Jacobite monastic texts but
not in Nestorian.[8] This suggests that it may have been translated after

the fifth century schisms in a Monophysite milieu, but before 534, the date of the earliest witness to the text.[9]

As the Small Asceticon is the earliest, one can presume that the Rules that only occur in the Great Asceticon are later than those in both. There are various versions of this Great Asceticon which has its origins in editions of the Rules produced by Basil while he was a bishop.

The Great Asceticon

We have seen how a number of different versions of this larger collection of Basil's answers were compiled and collected in his lifetime. There is the scholiast's manuscript from Caesarea and his Pontus manuscript, which was called the Hypotyposis. The scholia also mention consulting texts from the East (*anatolê*) which probably meant the civil diocese of Oriens. This included Syria and parts of South-East Asia Minor.

Gribomont studied over 150 manuscripts from before the fifteenth century and identified six main recensions, or families of manuscripts, of the Great Asceticon. This has been confirmed, with certain modifications, by Fedwick's later research, although he reclassified the recensions. All these recensions have roughly the same contents as the Vulgate version but arranged in different ways and with various numbers of Shorter Rules. Some of these arrangements go back to Basil himself but others, like the Vulgate, are the work of later editors.

One recension goes back to a text used in the ninth century at the famous monastery of Stoudios at Constantinople. It is, however, much older than this and is the source of an Armenian version translated before the mid fifth century. It has a single series of 350 Rules of which the first 41 correspond to the Longer Rules of the Vulgate. Although scholion 4 says that the Caesarea manuscript divides the Longer Rules into 32 sections, it also had all the Rules in one series and Gribomont has shown that the Studite manuscript was a direct descendant of that from Caesarea. This in turn was probably a copy of an older text going back to Basil's time.[10] Fedwick calls this recension 'K' (*Kaisareia*) as he calls the Vulgate family, based on the Pontus manuscript, recension 'P'.

The scholiast states that the oriental manuscripts divide the Longer Rules into 20 and have 252 Shorter Rules. No extant manuscript has exactly this number but one family, recension 'O', has the division into 20 Longer Rules. A manuscript of this type was used by Severus of Antioch (dd. 538) and the recension is thus associated with the diocese of Oriens.

One recently discovered manuscript from the Ecumenical Patriarchate at Constantinople differs from the other recensions and has a single series of 357 Rules. The Shorter Rules are not collected in thematic sections and Fedwick believes that this is closer to Basil's own arrangement. He suggests that this text originated at the Basileiados and so calls it recension 'B'.

Two other families of manuscripts are the result of later editorial work. One, with 20 Longer Rules, was created by monks in the Greek-speaking areas of Southern Italy out of earlier recensions in the ninth or tenth century. Fedwick calls this recension 'I'. The final family of manuscripts is called the misogynous recension, 'M', as it removes all reference to female ascetics.[11] As manuscripts are often modified to suit the audiences for which they are copied, Fedwick suggests that its place of origin is Mount Athos, where from the beginning no female ascetics were allowed.[12]

The origin of the Rules

St Benedict calls the Asceticon the 'Rule of St Basil', but this is not a good description. It is not a Rule like the *Rule of St Benedict*, a quasi-systematic body of regulations, but rather a series of questions and answers. In this book these are consistently called Rules, which is the term used in the Vulgate, or Answers, to differentiate Rules from the Small Asceticon. Modern scholars use the word '*erotapokrisis*' (from the Greek for question, *erôtêsis*, and answer, *apokrisis*), but while this gives a more exact description, Rule is less cumbersome and is also the traditional term used in English.

In his Preface to the Hypotyposis Basil describes them as 'all the answers I gave to the brothers' questions about the common ascetic discipline (*sunaskêsis*) of the godly (*kata theon*) life'.[13] He gives a fuller description of this context in the Preface to the Shorter Rules (which is part of the Preface to the Small Asceticon):

> It is necessary that we who have been entrusted with the ministry of the word should always be zealous for the perfection of your souls. Sometimes we must bear witness publicly before the whole Church, at other times we may allow ourselves to be consulted privately at his pleasure by any one who may come to question us concerning that which belongs to sound faith and the true method of right conduct according to the Gospel . . . Seeing that God has brought us here together . . . let us not turn aside to any other work . . . but rather pass the hours of the night that remain in careful thought and in searching out that which is needful.[14]

This nocturnal gathering of committed Christians has nothing to indicate a 'monastic' or 'institutional' character. Rather than an Abbot speaking to his monks the text sounds more like the active members of a modern parish gathering on a Sunday night for an exchange with a visiting preacher.

Letter 223 mentions 'visiting the brotherhoods and spending whole nights with them in prayer, always speaking and hearing opinions about God', but a different situation for the questions is presented in Longer Rule 54. Speaking of a regular meeting of the superiors of different brotherhoods, it says that they should 'report to one another any untoward happenings and difficult problems concerning conduct, and how they have settled each one, so that if any has fallen into error it may be clearly unfolded to the judgement of the many and that right decisions may be confirmed by their collective testimony.' Some of the Rules, especially those dealing with the Superior, seem to come from this context, with Basil answering questions from the assembled leaders. This more institutional setting is suggested by Rules of later date and so one can suggest a change in context from the questions as the communities develop towards a more settled institutional structure.

From what is known of the wider ascetic context, though, it is too simplistic to have a model of linear progression from the loose association of ascetics to an institution. Throughout his life Basil encountered many varied forms of ascetic life and the various communities would have evolved in distinct ways at different times.

Answers to the brothers' questions: the genre of the Rules

One can now ask what genre the Rules represent. Their form as question and answer, as already noted, is also their genre: *quaestio-responsio* or *erotapokriseis*. This is found in classical literature but, as Paul Blowers notes in his study of Maximus the Confessor's *Quaestiones ad Thalassium*,[15] it also had a rich development in the Christian tradition. He mentions two versions of this genre in patristic works: questions relating to difficult passages of Scripture, as in Eusebius' *Quaestiones evangelicae ad Stephanum*, and 'the spiritual–pedagogical tradition of monastic questions and responses'. The Rules are clearly of the second type and although many questions ask about the interpretation of scriptural texts, only a few involve those difficult issues, *aporiai*, characteristic of the first. This monastic genre is found in the *Sayings of the Desert Fathers*, the *Conferences* of Cassian, and the works of Pseudo-Macarius, Mark the Monk, Isaac the Syrian, Barsanuphius and John, Maximus and Anastasius of Sinai.

Blowers' brief survey of the tradition[16] shows that it is rooted in a particular monastic way of spiritual teaching and so was never a purely literary form. He says that it first emerged in the *Sayings of the Desert Fathers* (*Apophthegmata Patrum*) and then evolved through various forms such as dialogues, homilies and discourses.[17] While he situates Basil within this evolution, it is unlikely that he was influenced by the Egyptian Apophthegmata.[18] Basil's classical education may have inclined him to the genre, but one suspects that its real roots are in the way of spiritual teaching practised in Eustathian circles. As such it could be that the Rule stands together with the Apophthegmata at the source of this monastic literary genre.

While being rooted in an oral monastic culture, though, the genre could be transformed into an artificial literary technique as was the case with Cassian's *Conferences.* As we have seen, Basil's ascetic teaching was from the start both oral and written. The Shorter Rules all give the impression of being responses to genuine questions, which were then written down – although some may be the result of written correspondence between Basil and ascetics in Pontus after he became bishop of Caesarea.[19] Sometimes we find Basil giving short answers as if impatient or angry, as in Shorter Rule 111:

> *If the senior has ordered something to be done among the sisters without the knowledge of the senior sister, is the senior sister justified in being angry?*

to which Basil replies simply '*kai sphodra*' (most certainly).

While the Longer Rules probably had their origin in such questions, the extensive reworking of those which are found in both Small and Great Asceticons show that Basil intended them to form a more systematic exposition of the fundamental elements of the ascetic life. Thus while the division into 55 Longer Rules is the work of later editors, their existence as a distinct group of answers does go back to Basil.[20] In the Rules we thus see the transition of this genre from a way of teaching to a literary technique.

Another genre is dialogue, as used by Plato. Gregory of Nyssa wrote his *On the Soul and Resurrection* in this style with himself and Macrina as the protagonists, and Basil discusses different forms of dialogue in his Letter 135. Although the Rules do not fit this literary genre, their original context is dialogue in the wider sense. The quotation from the Preface and Longer Rule 54 show a situation where there was discussion and we shall see the same circumstances described at the head of the first Longer Rule. Basil also, throughout his ascetic works, puts great stress on the right use of speech and so one can presume that the communities were places of spiritual dialogue. This then provided the context for the individual questions and answers which are the Rules. A dialogue is not necessarily between equals, but one should distinguish a dialogue with a teacher from a teacher's discourse or sermon. It is likely that a similar context produced many of the Egyptian Apophthegmata, some of which are themselves mini-dialogues.[21]

The life of the Christian

Having discussed the text of the Asceticon and the situation in which it was produced, it seems useful, before we go on to study the Rules themselves, to ask how Basil defines the life his audiences seek to live.

The most common definition of the life is one of *eusebeia* – piety or religion. He also uses *theosebeia* as a synonym, as in the word *theosebountes*, 'godly men' (SR 74). These are much stronger words than the modern use of 'piety'; that they can be applied to the life Basil describes is proof of that. A similar description is that it is a life *kata theon* (according to the [way of] God).[22] He speaks of the *askêsis* (exercise) of *eusebeia* (LR 38) and the work of *eusebeia* (LR 32). Ascesis is an important term for Basil. He speaks of the brothers as *askoumenoi* (LR 19) and similar ideas are invoked when he refers to them as 'athletes of the Commandments of Christ' (LR 17) and engaged in the *gymnasia* of eusebeia (LR 19). The use of the word *synaskêsis* gives a characteristically Basilian stress on community (the preposition *syn* means 'together with').[23] The individual effort of the monks of Egypt and Syria here becomes a community activity.

'The ascesis of being well-pleasing (*euaristêsis*) to God according to the Gospel of Christ' (LR 5) illustrates another key concept: pleasing God, which is opposed to men-pleasing (*anthrôpareskeia*, SR 50) and self-pleasing (*autareskeia*, SR 118). One becomes pleasing to God by keeping the commandments and fulfilling his will while renouncing one's own will. A life pleasing to God is one of strictness or exactness (*akribeia*, LR 22), 'the strict life of the knowledge of God (*theognôsia*)' (LR 10). As such it is a life dominated by a purpose and with a clear aim, *skopos*. This must be one of the most frequently used words in the Asceticon: 'The life of the Christian is consistent (*monotropos*) and has one aim (*skopos*) – the glory of God.'[24] Here we see the key description of the ascetic: he is a Christian, no more and no less. He is called by the New Testament title *adelphos* (brother) and the community is called *adelphotês* (brotherhood).

The final and essential definition is that it is a scriptural life. One recalls the character of the *Moralia*, that many of the questions concern the meaning of scriptural texts, and that even the language of the Asceticon is heavily scriptural. Basil, as a competent teacher, often uses biblical characters to provide 'icons' of the ascetic life, or of deviations from it.[25] In Longer Rule 16 on self-control (*enkrateia*) he says, 'All the Saints were famous for self-control. The life of all the Saints and holy men (of the Bible), and the example of the Lord himself when he sojourned in the flesh, will help us in this respect.' Thus the Christian should live in a scriptural thought-world, surrounded by a great cloud of witnesses as he attempts to conform his life to the Commandments of God revealed in Scripture.

In his Funeral Oration on his old friend, Gregory of Nazianzen applies this use of biblical figures to Basil himself: 'There have been many men, we know, in the Old Testament and the New, remarkable for piety, as lawgivers, generals, prophets, teachers, men brave to the shedding of blood. Let us compare our Basil with them and thereby obtain a full appreciation of his worth.'[26] The long list goes from Adam to the Apostles and is an example of a common way of glorifying the saints. On a personal level, as one reads the Rules one is able, as it were, to look at the Scriptures with the eyes of St Basil, to share some of his insights into the meaning of the text.

On examining these definitions one thing is clear: none of them clearly defines those with whom Basil is dealing as against 'ordinary Christians', as the word 'monk' does today. Certain texts imply a boundary, but the main boundary, as in Longer Rule 32 on the parents of brothers, is between those who live '*kata theon*', who are devout, and the worldly. In the Asceticon, composed over two or three decades, we can see various situations and a gradual development of institutions and hardening of boundaries, but Basil's ascetic teaching, which was also given in all its rigour in Homilies addressed to wider audiences, was addressed to *all* Christians. It was only in the context of later developments that the Asceticon came to be seen as a purely *monastic* document.

NOTES

1. Gribomont, *Histoire du Texte* (1953). Fedwick, *Bibliotheca Basiliana Universalis* 3 (1997).
2. *Moralia; On the Judgement of God; Concerning Faith*: (authentic). *Preliminary Sketch of the Ascetic Life; On Renunciation of the World; On Ascetic Discipline; Two Ascetic Discourses; Epitimia* – an ascetic penal code; *Ascetic Constitutions*: (possibly or certainly unauthentic). The two books *On Baptism* and certain letters are also sometimes found with the Asceticon. See *CPG* 2875–98 and the discussions in the works by Gribomont and Fedwick just cited.
3. This is Gribomont's 'series X', *Histoire du texte*, pp. 166–78, 193–208.
4. Ed. Zelzer (1986). Mentioned by Rufinus in his HE 11:9. See the commentary in de Vogüé, *Histoire littéraire du mouvement monastique* 3, pp. 247–94.
5. Clarke (1913). Appendix B, pp. 162–7.
6. Sever J. Voicu, 'P. Antin 111: Un testimone ignorato delle *erotapokriseis brevius tractatae* di Basilio'.
7. Basil, Letters 258, 259. Cf. Fedwick, *Bibliotheca Basiliana Universalis* 3, p. 2.
8. The Nestorians split from the Catholic Church after the Council of Ephesus in 431 and the Jacobites or Monophysites after the Council of Chalcedon in 451. Both disputes were about the person of Christ but cultural and political differences played a large part in the divisions.
9. Gribomont, *Histoire du Texte*, pp. 144–6.
10. Gribomont, *Histoire du Texte* pp. 161–3.
11. LR 33, SRs 82, 108–11, 153–4, 220, and the last section of the *Moralia* are omitted and SR 281 is put into the masculine.
12. Fedwick, *Bibliotheca Basiliana Universalis* 3, p. 164.
13. *CPG* 2884, *PG* 31:1509–13, with the reading *sunaskêsis* noted by de Vogüé in *Histoire littéraire du mouvement monastique* 3, p. 248.
14. Clarke (1925), p. 229. Rufinus' translation of the same passage from the Prologue to the Small Asceticon (3–11) is found in Zelzer (1986), pp. 5–6.
15. Blowers, *Exegesis and Spiritual Pedagogy in Maximus the Confessor*.
16. op. cit., pp. 28–94.
17. op. cit., p. 36.
18. Burton-Christie notes that only by the end of the fourth century were small written collections of Apophthegmata in circulation. *The Word in the Desert*, p. 79.
19. Suggested by Elm, *Virgins of God*, p. 68. In his correspondence Basil sometimes replies to questions, e.g. Letters 233 and 234 to Amphilochius.
20. As noted in scholion 6.
21. Burton-Christie calls these 'snatches of early monastic conversation'. *The Word in the Desert*, p. 78.
22. e.g. LR 22, SRs 2, 107.
23. e.g. LR 26 and the Preface to the Hypotyposis.

24. LR 20.
25. Tsichlis, 'Monastic Themes', pp. 292–3. Cf. Heb. 6:12.
26. *Oration 43* (On Basil) 70–76. The same technique is found in Gregory of Nyssa's *Encomium*.

PART TWO

The Life of the Commandments:

A COMMENTARY ON THE FIRST SEVEN
LONGER RULES ILLUSTRATING THE KEY IDEAS
OF BASIL'S SPIRITUAL TEACHING

Introduction to Part Two

So let us also who boast of Basil as our teacher, show by our lives his instruction, becoming that which made him celebrated and great in the eyes of God and man, in Christ Jesus our Lord, to whom be glory and power for ever and ever. Amen.

St Gregory of Nyssa: *Encomium on his Brother*

There are 55 Longer Rules in the Vulgate recension of the Asceticon. These are the result of the subdivision of Basil's original 18 or 20. Following Adalbert de Vogüé,[1] one can divide them into seven thematic sections:

1) Separation from the world and common life: LRs 1–7.
2) Renunciation (*apotagê*): LRs 8–15.
3) Mastery over appetites: (*enkrateia*) LRs 16–23.
4) Good order in the community (*eutaxia*): LRs 24–36 (None after LR 23 are in the Small Asceticon).
5) Work: LRs 37–42.
6) Duties of Superiors: LRs 43–54.
7) LR 55 on the use of medicine.

In the first section Basil provides the basic foundation of his whole ascetic system in a sustained reflection on the double commandment of love.[2] These Rules introduce most of the major themes of Basilian spirituality and they are the subject of this second part of the book.

A note on method

In commenting on the Rules, it is first of all important to situate each answer within the Asceticon as a whole and, if it occurs in the Small Asceticon, to see how the text has been developed. One can then connect it with the wider context of Basil's life and times examined in Part 1 and seek for possible influences from earlier writers. Comparison with other Basilian texts can also be illuminating, but those of dubious authenticity are generally avoided because, as shown in modern discussions of his attitude to homosexuality, they can give a misleading impression. It is also helpful to look at the writings of the two Gregories, but while a sustained comparison with works such as Gregory of Nyssa's 'On Virginity' would be useful, it is beyond the scope of this book.

When Basil died, the Asceticon did not only have a history, it also had a future. Such a text, like Scripture, exists as part of a developing tradition. While aiming to avoid anachronism, one can gain a deeper understanding of Basil's teaching by asking how later monastic writers developed it or responded to the same problems with similar resources from Scripture and tradition. The commentary thus attempts to set Basil firmly in the early monastic tradition. One sees much divergence within this tradition, such as that between Basil and his former disciple Evagrius of Pontus, but it is also sufficiently homogeneous to be spoken of as one tradition. The same can be said of Catholic Christianity as a whole and so one feels justified in using concepts of nature and grace and original sin to understand Basil's teaching. While these have been more extensively developed in the Latin West, the realities with which they deal are an essential part of the Christian tradition as a whole.

Chapter Six

The Commandment of Love

Since God's word has given us permission to ask questions, we ask first of all to be taught if there is any order (taxis) or sequence in the commandments of God, so that one comes first, another second and so on; or whether all are interdependent and all may be regarded as equally important as far as making a start goes, so that one who so desires may be safe in beginning at any point he likes in the circle?

Your question is an old one and was put forward long ago in the gospels, when the lawyer came to the Lord and said, 'Teacher, which is the first commandment in the Law?', and the Lord answered, 'You shall love the Lord your God with all your heart, and with all your soul, and with all your strength and with all your mind. This is the first and great commandment. And a second is like it, you shall love your neighbour as yourself.'* The Lord himself then gave this order to his commandments. He defined the commandment of love towards God to be the first and greatest; and second in order and like it, or rather completing the first and depending on it, the commandment of loving one's neighbour. Thus from what has been said, and from other similar passages contained in the inspired Scriptures it is possible to learn the order and sequence of all the Lord's commandments.

Commentary

The first thing to notice about this 'Rule' is its structure. It is a question and an answer. Whether the question was originally spoken

---

* Matt. 22:37–9.

or written, it is clear that we are not in the presence of a distant authority composing a textbook. We are rather admitted into the circle of Basil's disciples and able to listen to their dialogue with their teacher. This is obviously not a dialogue of equals, Basil teaches with authority, but the initiative in proposing the question does lie with the disciple. The diversity of questions reflects the interests of Basil's disciples, but it is clear that he has marshalled this raw material into some sort of order. Retaining the Question–Answer structure does mean, however, that Basil did not wish to stray too far from the original situation of his teaching.

The commandments and good order

Having said this, the arrangement of the questions has been carefully worked out. It is significant that we start with *this* question. Why should Basil want to start this important work with a rather arcane question about the order of the commandments? Would it not be better to follow the example of the preaching of Christ and John the Baptist and start with repentance, surely the true foundation of the Christian ascetic life? Basil starts with the call to repent in the *Moralia*, but here he clearly wants to stress the primacy of love, the first and greatest commandment. He is speaking to a group who have passed beyond their first conversion to a desire for a closer following of Christ. Both approaches have their use, just as we learn the teaching of Christ from both John and the Synoptic Gospels.

Basil thus wants to start with love, but he also wants to start with the commandments. What he is discussing in the Rules as a whole is life lived according to the commandments: in the seventeenth Longer Rule he speaks of his audience as 'athletes of the commandments of Christ'. The Shorter Rules also start with a discussion of the commandments, referring to Christ the sun of righteousness, 'who illumines us with his commandments as with rays'.[3] The commandments in question are thus Christ's, but just as Jesus draws his two greatest commandments from the Law of Moses,[4] so Basil does not separate the Old and New Testaments. It is the same Lord who speaks in both. A modern reader might think first of Moses when he hears the word 'Commandment', but Basil instinctively turns to Christ.

Although we can easily see that love and the teaching of Christ are important, the concern shown by the questioner to find out the order of the commandments seems rather strange and artificial. It is like subjecting the freedom of the gospel to military discipline. It may be that Basil used the imperfect questions of his disciples as a springboard for more elevated thought, but it is clear from his answer that he took this desire for order very seriously.

The question of the disciple is really quite simple and practical: where do you start? That Basil put it first is significant because good order, in Greek *eutaxia*, is one of the central themes of his teaching. The Longer Rules can be divided in half after Longer Rule 23. The Rules in the second half, not in the Small Asceticon translated by Rufinus and thus probably later in date, are primarily concerned with the organisation of communities. Longer Rule 24 on 'the manner of our life together' starts with the programmatic text 'let all things be done decently and in order' (1 Cor. 14:40). Both sections of the Longer Rules therefore start with this concern with order, order in personal spirituality and order in community spirituality. Without this discipline and structure the Christian life can easily degenerate and Basil was too experienced a pastor not to realise this.

To go beyond the commandments? Evagrius and Maximus

Later ascetic writers such as Evagrius of Pontus (345–99) and Maximus the Confessor (*c*.580–662) also show a concern with order in personal spirituality and write with great psychological insight on the interrelationship among the virtues and between various evil thoughts.[5] Although Maximus significantly modifies Evagrius' teaching and is equally indebted to other teachers, we shall here concentrate on the common elements in their teaching as compared to that of Basil. He shares their concern with structure but it is significant that his subject matter is the scriptural commandments.

The commandments do also have their place in the spiritualities of Evagrius and Maximus but they are part of the preliminary stage.

Evagrius states that, 'ascesis consists in keeping the commandments',[6] but this ascesis is not enough: 'the effects of keeping the commandments do not suffice to heal the powers of the soul completely. They must be complemented by a contemplative activity appropriate to these faculties, and this activity must penetrate the spirit.'[7] In the Evagrian system there is a profound treatment of the ascetic life and the struggle against the passions, but the dynamism is always towards contemplation. For Basil the accent on the practical is stronger and more orientated to community, and prayer appears, as we will see, in a different guise.

Evagrius and Maximus both agree that the purpose of the commandments is to reach a state transcending or integrating the passions which is called in Greek *apatheia*.[8] *Apatheia* then brings to birth love (*agapé*), but for them love is not the sole end of the spiritual life. St Maximus, using the same double commandment as Basil, teaches: 'The whole purpose of the Saviour's commandments is to free the mind from hate and a lack of self-control (*akrasia*) and bring it to the love of him and of one's neighbour, from which there springs the splendour of holy knowledge in all its actuality.'[9] Even if knowledge (*gnôsis*) here is just an aspect of love rather than a separate stage, it is clear that we are in a different thought world to that of Basil.

The double commandment of love

Although Basil was trained in philosophy and had studied at Athens, his teaching is profoundly scriptural and less indebted to the theories of the Greeks. Speaking with the voice of an authoritative Teacher, he takes the questioner first of all to the Gospel. He is first and foremost a Minister of the Word. As such he does not start with an abstract discussion of the commandments or open up a vista to a higher *gnôsis*, but rather he begins with a programmatic text: the two commandments of love in Matthew 22. It is here, from the Lord himself, that we get our *taxis*, our order. Scripture is thus central to Basil's discussion, not just a convenient quarry of proof-texts with which to buttress his argument. We see this again and again throughout the Asceticon and it must have been the fruit of many years reading and pondering the sacred text until it became the subconscious medium of his thoughts. In the case of Basil, as with the other Fathers such as Augustine, this meditative reading of Scripture, which we call *lectio divina*, was surely a fundamental practice of his spiritual life.

In the *Moralia* he groups together collections of texts, but here he comments on the texts he quotes. In fact the whole of the Longer Rules can be seen as a commentary on these two commandments. In particular the first seven Rules, which form a distinct unit, develop the commentary on this text. The connecting theme of this unit could be expressed as separation from the world (to love God) and community (to love neighbour). The second Rule deals with love of God and the third with love of neighbour. The sixth advocates retirement to establish an environment suitable for the remembrance of God and the seventh rejects the strictly solitary life on the basis of the law of love. This question has clearly been put first for very good reasons.

Basil comments on the text at hand but he is not afraid to go beyond it. The second commandment to love not only follows the first but *completes* it. This theme is taken up in the third of the Longer Rules where he moves beyond even this close relation between them to teach, in language reminiscent of Trinitarian theology, what could be called a coinherence of the two commandments: 'In keeping the first commandment one keeps also the second; and through the second one returns again to the first.' One loves the neighbour in God, and God in the neighbour. This simple question is already pointing us to the heights of the Christian life.

The answer ends with a rather ambitious statement that from what has been said and other similar passages one can, 'learn the order and sequence of all the Lord's commandments'. This is rather a daunting task and in fact Basil does not follow it up, but it does show his confidence in Scripture as the source of knowledge for the Christian. His brother, Gregory of Nyssa, was less optimistic when writing on a similar theme: 'Concerning the parts of virtue, what sort one must consider the greater, which ones we must pursue rather than the others, what the order of them is, it is not possible to say.'[10]

Is love first or last?

One final point which highlights the importance of this Rule emerges in comparison with the ascetic works of John Cassian (*c.*360–430), whom St Benedict groups with Basil in his suggestions for more advanced reading at the end of his Rule. While Basil puts it first, Cassian makes no use of this double commandment of love.[11] This is because for him, following his master Evagrius, love is at the end of the process of spiritual and ascetic growth which includes the commandments. The Evagrian approach is not as rigidly compartmentalised into stages as one might at first suppose.[12] The stages are not a strictly temporal sequence and can coexist, but for Evagrius, as for Cassian, love is the perfect virtue which casts out servile fear. It is thus, in that sense, not first but last. Benedict draws from both these approaches: love is at the summit of his Ladder of Humility in Chapter Seven: 'Now, therefore, after ascending all these steps of humility, the monk will quickly arrive at that perfect love of God which casts out fear', but at the start of his list of the tools of good works in Chapter Four, 'First of all, love the Lord God with your whole heart, your whole soul and all your strength, and love your neighbour as yourself.'

NOTES FOR INTRODUCTION TO PART TWO AND CHAPTER SIX

1. de Vogüé, 'The Great Rules', p. 52.
2. This is noted by Gribomot, *Histoire du texte*, p. 240 and Fedwick, *Bibliotheca Basiliana Universalis 3*, p. 48.
3. SR 1, which is the twelfth rule in the Small Asceticon, coming after LR 23 (R11).
4. Matt. 22:37–9 is based on Deut. 6:5 and Lev. 19:18.
5. For example: Evagrius, *Praktikos* 6–39 ; and Maximus, *Centuries on Charity* 3:20.
6. *Praktikos* 81.
7. *Praktikos* 79.
8. See, for example, *Praktikos* 81, which Maximus follows in *Centuries on Charity* 1:2.
9. *Centuries on Charity* 4:56, cf. Evagrius, *Letter to Anatolius*.
10. *On the Christian Mode of Life*, tr. Woods Callahan, p. 150.
11. de Vogüé, *Doctrinal and Spiritual Commentary*, p. 85.
12. Evagrius sets out the three stages of the spiritual life in the first chapter of his *Praktikos*: 'Christianity is the dogma of Christ the Saviour. It is composed of

praktikê, of the contemplation of the physical world, and of the contemplation of God.' A discussion of these stages is given by Bamberger in the introduction to his translation of *The Praktikos and Chapters on Prayer*, pp. lxxxi–xciv.

Chapter Seven

Our Natural Desire for God

LONGER RULE 2
CONCERNING LOVE TOWARDS GOD, AND THAT THE INCLINATION AND POWER TO KEEP THE LORD'S COMMANDMENTS ARE IN MEN NATURALLY

(Part 1)

Speak to us first then of love towards God. For we have heard that one ought to love, but we seek to learn how this may successfully be done.

Love of God cannot be taught. For we have neither learnt from another person to rejoice in the light and to cling to life, nor did anyone else teach us to love our parents or those who brought us up. In the same way, or much more so, the learning of the divine loving desire (*pothos*) does not come from outside; but when the creature was made, I mean man, a certain seminal word (*logos spermatikos*) was implanted in us, having within itself the beginnings of the inclination to love. The pupils in the school of God's commandments having received this word are by God's grace enabled to exercise it with care, to nourish it with knowledge, and to bring it to perfection. Therefore we also, welcoming your zeal (*spoudê*) as necessary for attaining our end (*skopos*), by God's gift and your assistance of us with your prayers will strive (*spoudazô*) to stir up the spark of divine loving desire (*pothos*) hidden within you according to the power given us by the Spirit. You must know that this virtue, though only one, yet as regards power accomplishes and comprehends every commandment. For, 'the one loving me', the Lord says, 'will keep my commandments'* and again, 'on these two commandments hang all the law and the prophets'.† And we shall not now try to survey the whole field accurately (for we would miss the whole meaning of the commandments by concentrating

---

* cf. John 14:23.
† Matt. 22:40.

on details) but in so far as it is in our power and befits our present purpose (*skopos*) we shall remind you of the love (*agapê*) due from us to God.

But let me say this first: As regards all the commandments given us by God, we have already received from him power to keep them, so that we may neither feel discontented as though anything strange were demanded of us, nor be elated as though we paid more than was given us. And by this power, if we work rightly and fittingly, we fulfil in godly manner the life of virtue; but if we corrupt its working we are carried away into vice. This is a definition of vice – an evil use, and one contrary to the command of the Lord, of things given us by God for good. Similarly the virtue required by God may be defined as the use of them with a good conscience according to the commandments of the Lord.

This being so, we may say the same about love. Having received a commandment – to love God – we possess the power to love implanted in us at the moment that we were formed. The proof of this is not external, but anyone can learn it from oneself and within oneself. For by nature we desire beautiful things, though we differ as to what is supremely beautiful; and without being taught we have affection towards those near and dear to us, and we spontaneously show goodwill towards all our benefactors.

Now what is more marvellous than the divine beauty? What thought has more charm than the magnificence of God? What loving desire (*pothos*) of the soul is so keen and intolerable as that which comes from God upon the soul which is cleansed from all evil and cries with true affection (*diathesis*), 'I am wounded with love'?* Wholly indescribable and inexplicable are the flashes of the divine beauty: speech cannot express them, hearing cannot receive them. Though you speak of the rays of the morning star, of the brightness of the moon or the light of the sun, all are worthless in comparison with its glory and fall short as far, compared with the true Light, as the deep shades of a moonless night compared with the glow of the noonday sun. This beauty is unseen by fleshly eyes, and comprehended only by the soul and mind when, if at all, it has illumined one of the saints, and left in them the sting of intolerable loving desire (*pothos*). Saints like these, weary of the present life, cried, 'Woe is me, that my dwelling is prolonged',† 'When shall I come and appear before the face of God?'* and, 'To depart and be with Christ, for

---

* Song of Songs 2:5.
† Ps. 120:5, this quotation is not in Rufinus.
* Ps. 42:2.

that is far better'† and 'My soul thirsts for God, the strong, the living One'‡ and 'Lord, now let your servant depart'.§

Oppressed by this life as if it was a prison, those whose souls were touched by the divine loving desire (*pothos*) could hardly restrain their impulses. Yes, they had an insatiable desire to behold the divine beauty and prayed that their contemplation of the sweetness of the Lord might last on into life eternal.

So then, men naturally desire beauty. But the good is properly beautiful and lovable. Now God is good, and all things desire good. Therefore all things desire God.

Commentary

This second Longer Rule follows on from the first and deals with the greatest of the two commandments of love. The next Rule discusses the commandment which is 'second in order and power'. In the Latin Small Asceticon and in some recensions of the Great Asceticon, however, both of these, together with the fourth, fifth and sixth Longer Rules, all make up a very long second answer. This long text, more like a lecture on the commandments than Basil's usual direct responses, was probably the original shape of his answer. This is shown by the fact that, of the group of Longer Rules into which it is split up, only this one has a question at its head. The first seven Longer Rules do, however, make a coherent section in theme and language, which is broken with the opening of the eighth. With this complex structure and history, it does not seem wrong to split this long text into two for the purposes of commentary.

The school of God's commandments

On reading this first part, one is struck by the beauty of Basil's prose and the richness of the teaching and imagery. He was obviously not one of those who keep the best until last, and we can see why he had such a hold on the minds of the ascetics of Cappadocia and Pontus. His role is clearly defined in the first paragraph. He is filled

---

† Phil. 1:23, not in Rufinus.
‡ Ps. 42:2
§ Luke 2:29, not in Rufinus, who adds an allusion to Ps. 26:4.

with the power of the Holy Spirit and, as a spirit-filled Elder, his task is to stir up the spark of divine loving desire that his hearers have within them. We are in the world of the enthusiasts who posed such a problem for the Hierarchs of that age. Basil's language confirms this. He welcomes their zeal, in Greek *spoudê*, and he uses the related verb, *spoudazô*, in the same sentence. These were words of self-definition for the enthusiasts and Basil is thus identifying himself with them. He certainly helped reconcile these zealot groups with the mainstream Church, but our text implies that he did not do this from the outside.

The audience are in the school of God's commandments, where God teaches both through the commandments themselves and through his Spirit working in Basil. One is reminded of the key phrase of the Prologue to St Benedict's Rule, which he takes from his main source the *Rule of the Master*, 'Therefore we intend to establish a school for the Lord's service'.[1] Unfortunately the mention of the school is missing from Rufinus' translation, which omits the first few sentences of the Greek text, so we cannot posit a direct influence.

Logos spermatikos

Turning to the content of Basil's teaching, we still have the commandments discussed in the first Rule, but we seem to have moved out of the biblical thought world into that of Greek philosophy. The antithesis drawn in the commentary on the previous Longer Rule between the biblical spirituality of Basil and that of his former disciple Evagrius will need to be modified. How does Basil use these Hellenistic ideas?

The key concept of the first section, which answers the question of how we love God and gives the reason why love can't be taught, is *logos spermatikos* – 'seminal reason' or 'a seed consisting of the word'. This is not biblical but philosophical, of Stoic origin, where it is usually plural, and also found in Plotinus (*c.* AD 204–270). It was however taken up by Christian thinkers such as Justin Martyr, Origen, Methodius of Olympus, Athanasius, and later Augustine, and modified to their purposes. Basil is in good Christian company and so one must not judge him on the basis of a fundamentalist biblicism as having abandoned revelation for speculation. As in the case of the Fathers of the Council of Nicaea, who used the non-biblical word *homoousios* to defend biblical teaching, it is important to investigate how he uses the term.

The Stoics taught that everything in the Universe is endowed with a life which derives from a material fiery air or spirit (*pneuma*) which is also reason (*logos*). This is immanent in all things as *logoi spermatikoi* which give the parts of the Universe their individual structure and vitality according to their natures. *Logos spermatikos* is thus a generative principle of individual substances by which things are what they are, an undivided part of or participation in the Universal Logos.

Given the identification of Jesus as the Word (*Logos*) of God in the Gospel of John, it is not surprising that Christian writers were interested in the *logoi spermatikoi*. The term is sometimes used by them broadly in the Stoic sense without assimilation to Christ the Logos, for example as 'generative principles' in Origen's discussion of the virgin birth,[2] or as 'the logos which has no life of its own and which is innate in every creature' contrasted by Athanasius with the living, uncreated Logos of God.[3] In other cases the term is developed in a Christian direction. Justin in his *Second Apology*, Chapters 8 and 13, would seem to use the adjective *spermatikos* in an active sense, thus 'the seed-sowing Word'. For him the 'seeds of the word' are a sort of immanent revelation of which all men partake and which is perfected in Christianity. He used this in dialogue with the philosophers, anticipating modern discussion of the relation between Christianity and other religions.

The universal nature of this phenomenon is a point of contact with Basil's use of the term, in distinction to Origen who implies in his *Commentary on the Gospel According to John*, when discussing the 'seed of Abraham' (John 8:37), that not all men have these 'generative principles'.[4] Origen also uses this Stoic idea in his discussions of the identity of the earthly body and the risen body, based on Paul's image of the seed and the plant in 1 Corinthians 15. Just as the seed has a principle of growth and individuation which makes it become a plant, so there is a similar *logos* in our earthly bodies which will, after death, grow into the glorious body of the resurrection.[5] These earlier Christian writers thus modify the meaning of the term according to the text or question with which they are dealing. Basil, in discussing our love of God, does the same.

If Basil uses *logos spermatikos* with Justin's active meaning, and he does use it in the singular, one could give the following as an alternative translation of the appropriate passage above:

> ... a certain seed-sowing Word was implanted in us, having from his store the beginnings of the inclination to love. The pupils in the school of God's commandments, having received him, are by nature and God's grace disposed to cultivate these beginnings with care, to nourish them with knowledge, and to bring them to perfection.

There is in this case a clear allusion to the parables of the Sower and of the darnel in Matthew 13, 'he who sows the good seed is the Son of Man' (Matt. 13:37). It is more likely, however, that Basil's use of the term is closer to the original idea of a dynamic constitutive principle placed in creatures by the Creator. Lampe's *Patristic Greek Lexicon* singles out *logos spermatikos* in this passage from the Rules as having a distinctive meaning, 'an innate principle in all men by virtue of which we love God'.

Basil thus develops this philosophical term in a specifically Christian direction, as do Justin and Origen in their different contexts. He establishes this new meaning in relation solely to human beings and to their natural tendency to love God, which the Creator placed in them at their creation. Connected to this specific use of *logos spermatikos*, the theme of seeds is important in the Asceticon, for example in Longer Rules 3 and 8. Although Basil would have encountered these concepts in his general education, one can surmise that the main influence would have been his study of Origen during the years of seclusion in Pontus. Although Basil's use is different from those of Origen mentioned above, it is closer to Origen's teaching in his *Homilies on the Song of Songs* (II:9) where he says, 'When the maker of the universe created you, he sowed in your hearts the seeds of love.'

Basil thus, following earlier Fathers, profoundly Christianises this Hellenistic idea and integrates it into his own scheme based on love and the commandments. It is also not merely an abstract theory but explains an anthropology based on experience: no one taught us to love our parents.

Basilian maximalism: nature and grace

It is clear from the text that Basil has a very positive view of human nature and its potential. To practise virtue is to use things rightly according to our conscience and the commandments. This is a right use of our natural inclinations, whereas vice is a turning away from what is natural, or rather treating a lower good as if it were the highest. Virtue is natural and our nature is from God, we have received at creation the power to keep the commandments.

Anthony Meredith writes of certain passages in the Rules which point to a weak doctrine of grace and the absence of a doctrine of original sin. In commenting on this text he says: 'The sentiment expressed, if not the actual words chosen, is so like certain passages in Plato and Plotinus that the only difference between Basil and them is in the realm of grace, and even here it is possible to overstress the cleavage between Christian and pagan.'[6] In Shorter Rule 224, we find in the case of Cornelius, the Centurion of Acts 10, the 'natural tendencies' acting as a kind of preparation for the Gospel. Nature can thus work for our salvation but it does need the help of grace.

It is not surprising that the Greek Fathers can sound semi-Pelagian when compared with the overpowering stress on grace in the Latin Augustinian tradition. In Shorter Rule 271 Basil speaks of almsgiving blotting out sins but insists that we need, 'primarily, the mercy of God and the blood of Christ'. He is speaking here of a 'synergy', the theological term for the human will and the Holy Spirit working together, although he doesn't use the actual word *sunergeia*. We can therefore, by God's power given to us both through nature and by grace, keep *all* the commandments. This is Basilian maximalism: his high view of human nature is combined with a high view of what we must achieve, and this applies to all, not just an elite of ascetics.

If we fail, the fault is entirely ours, an evil use of a good thing. This implies a high doctrine of the power of the free will, a necessary precondition for asceticism.

It is possible for our natural tendencies to be led astray by our own will or even, as we shall see later, by external evil powers. Basilian maximalism is not just naturalism: the power to love comes from God, it is 'by God's gift' that the sparks are enkindled, and it is 'by God's grace' that we may nurture the seeds. Grace is thus present but usually in an unexplicit way. In the second part of this Rule the stress is on God's generosity as our benefactor and his constant benevolent initiative towards us throughout history. Perhaps the mistake is for the reader to approach Basil with Western pre-conceptions of a strict distinction between nature and grace. For Basil, although the natural human will has been weakened, the two are really just two aspects of the divine initiative and work together to assist man to reach his goal.

The sting of intolerable loving desire: Christian Platonism

The stress on love is a sign of the scriptural nature of Basil's teaching, even when he is speaking the language of the philosophers. The situation is, however, not as clear as it would appear from the English translation. The question at the head of the Rule uses the character-istic New Testament term for love, *agapê*, and the related verb, *agapaô*, and Basil replies that the love (*agapê*) of God can not be taught. In the next sentence, however, he is speaking about something else, *pothos*, which is here translated 'loving desire'. The context shows that the same reality, our love for God, is meant by both words. With *pothos* we are outside the scriptural vocabulary as it appears neither in the New Testament nor in the Septuagint. In Greek literature it usually means desire or longing, and it can sometimes be translated as love. Here, then, it indicates a desiring form of love and we can presume that Basil uses it instead of *agapê* because of this dynamic emphasis. It is a rare word in the Asceticon and this fact reinforces the idea that Basil is using it for a deliberate purpose. The theme of desire, however, is a frequent one in the Rules, for example in Shorter Rule 259:

> *Who is aglow with the Spirit?**
> He who with fiery eagerness, insatiable desire (*epithumia*) and tireless zeal (*spoudê*) does the will of God in the love of Christ Jesus our Lord according to what is written, 'in his commandments he will desire greatly.'†

It is this desire that Basil wishes to stir up in his hearers, and which has as its object the divine Beauty. We are back again to the philosophers, because for Plato and Plotinus *erôs*, which also means loving desire, is the means of ascent to Beauty or the One.[7] This Platonic theme was developed by Origen who identified this passionate, desiring love with the biblical *agapê*: 'So you must take whatever Scripture says about charity as if it had been said with reference to passionate love, taking no notice of the difference of terms, for the same meaning is conveyed by both.'[8] Origen also teaches that every human being feels the passion of love for something[9] and that this desire was implanted by God at the first spiritual creation. Basil's extensive study of the works of Origen is probably behind his words here. One wonders if he used the word *pothos* deliberately to avoid the multitude of ideas associated with *erôs* while maintaining the idea of a passionate, desiring love.

It is entirely in keeping with Basil's high view of nature that he should follow Origen and the Platonists in giving this natural, desiring love a central place in the human response to God. If Origen's *Commentary on the Song of Songs* is a source for this passage, it is not surprising that Basil quotes the Song, 'I am wounded with love'. There is however a difference in that while Origen speaks of being wounded by the dart that is the Word of God himself, he associates it with the beauty of the creation rather than the Creator. Basil's prose soars towards mystical poetry in this section when he speaks of the intolerable desire which fires the pure soul struck by the divine

---

* Rom. 12:11.
† Ps. 111:1.

Beauty. His insistence on the commandments and the organisation of community life can give the impression of a dry, this-worldly moralism. This use of the language of desire and beauty shows the limitations of the criticism.

A second criticism is that in taking up this language he is selling out the faith to pagan Greek philosophy. The relationship between the two is much disputed and is much more subtle than a direct antithesis. For the world that Basil inhabited, a marriage of Hellenism and the Gospel was a desirable proposition.[10] It might be better to ask, as we did with the *logos spermatikos*, how Greek thought is used? A study of the most passionate paragraph shows that he is speaking within the framework of revelation. His subject is the reality expressed in the quotations from the Song of Songs, the Psalms and the New Testament. He does not follow Plato and Plotinus in relating the loving desire to the god Eros but uses their language in a Christian context where the impersonal Good or Beauty has become the personal God of the Bible. The Rule as a whole does strongly resonate with Hellenistic philosophy and ends this section with a syllogism, but it is led captive to Christ by the chains of love. The Philosopher's question 'Can virtue be taught' is referred to love and the *logos spermatikos* has 'the beginnings of an inclination to love'.

Christianity and Hellenism: a new synthesis in the Great Asceticon?

Towards the end of this extract there is a section, not in Rufinus' translation, which speaks of the saints oppressed by this life as if it was a prison and desiring to contemplate the divine beauty. Prison evokes the Cave in Plato's *Republic*, but it is the word contemplation (*theôria*) which strikes the attention as it is not a common topic in the Asceticon, in strong contrast to the works of Evagrius. In Rufinus we find a free quotation of Psalm 26:4 in the same place in the text, which probably suggested the idea of contemplation when the Small Asceticon was reworked: 'And again he said, blazing with the fires of this flame, my soul thirsts for the living God, and having an insatiable urge towards his desire he prays that he might see the will of the

Lord and be protected in his temple.'[11] It is strange that here, and also in the first paragraph before the words 'You must know that this virtue . . .', the passages added in the Great Asceticon are profoundly Hellenistic in tone. The first introduces the *logos spermatikos* and twice uses the word *pothos*. This word would seem to be missing from the Latin at its third mention in the text above, and only possibly translated by *amor* in the fourth, although it is probably behind desire (*desiderium*) in the section just given. This is strange in that from the early Letter 2 to the later *Moralia* and Rules there is a move away from a Hellenistic mystical vocabulary to one much more scriptural. Here, in the change from the earlier Asceticon to the later, we find such language returning although not to dominance. Does this indicate a move from antithesis to synthesis in the mature mind of the Bishop?

A more characteristic Basilian theme is the memory of God and in the second section we find a practical example of the recollection of the divine action in salvation history, which reminds the reader that love of God is both necessary and natural.

LONGER RULE 2

(Part 2)

So then, whatever is done rightly by free choice is also in us naturally, as long as our thoughts have not been led astray by evil. Love of God is therefore demanded of us as a necessary debt, which to the soul that cannot pay is the most intolerable of all evils. For alienation from God and rejection is more intolerable even than the punishments that await us in hell, and more oppressive to the one who experiences it than deprivation of light is to the eye, even though there is no attendant pain, or deprivation of life to the living creature. But if there is a natural affection (*storgê*) of children for their parents, and this is proved both by the habits of animals and the disposition (*diathesis*) of human beings in early youth towards the mother, shall we not seem more stupid than infants, even wilder than beasts, if we remain loveless and alienated as regards our Maker? Even if we have not known his nature from his goodness, we ought to have an extraordinary love (*agapê*) and affection (*storgê*) for him from the very fact of having been made by him, and to cling continually to his memory as children cling to their mother.

A benefactor, though, ranks higher than those who are loved naturally. And this sentiment (*pathos*), attachment to those who have given some good, is not only characteristic of humans but also of nearly all animals. 'The ox knows its owner and the ass its Masters crib', but God forbid that the next part be said of us, 'but Israel does not know me, and my people does not understand'.* Concerning the dog and many similar animals I do not need to say what great goodwill they show towards those who feed them. But if we naturally choose goodwill and affection towards our benefactors, and endure every labour to pay them back for what they have already done, what words can worthily describe the gifts of God, which are so many as to be innumerable, and so excellent that one alone is sufficient to make us render all thanks to the Giver? I will leave out the rest, which, though in themselves of surpassing greatness and grace, are outshone by the greater gifts, as stars are by the rays of the sun, and in themselves display a less resplendent intrinsic grace. For I have no time to leave the surpassing gifts and to measure the goodness of the Benefactor (*euergetês*) by the lesser.

Let us then pass over in silence the risings of the sun, the circuits of the moon, the varying temperatures of the air, the changes of the seasons, the water descending from the clouds or springing forth from the earth, the sea itself, the whole earth and what grows in it, the inhabitants of the waters, the tribes of the air, the myriad varieties of animals, everything in fact that is ordered to the service of our life. But that supreme benefit we could not neglect even if we wished. To be silent about it is absolutely impossible for anyone with a sound mind and reasoning power (*logos*); but to speak of it worthily is still more impossible.

For God made man in his own image and likeness, made him worthy of knowledge of himself (i.e. God), adorned him with knowledge beyond all other creatures, allowed him to luxuriate in the inconceivable beauties of Paradise and made him ruler of all earthly things. Then when he had been deceived by the serpent and fallen into sin, and through sin into death and all it entails, God did not reject him; but first gave him a law as a help, set angels to guard and care for him, sent prophets to reprove vice and teach

---

* Isa. 1:3.

virtue, frustrated the impulses by threats, stirred up eagerness for good by promises, made clear in advance the end of virtue and vice by the frequent example of many persons who served as a warning for others, and, in addition to these and others like them, he did not turn away from those persisting in disobedience. For we were not neglected by the goodness of the Master, nor even did we hinder his love for us, even though we had insulted our Benefactor (*euergetês*) by callous indifference to his gifts. On the contrary, we were called back from death and made alive again by our Lord Jesus Christ himself. In him even the manner of the benefit given is a greater wonder: 'Being in the form of God, he did not count equality with God a thing to be grasped, but emptied himself, taking the form of a servant'.*

He took our weaknesses and bore our diseases, and was wounded on our behalf, that by his wounds we may be healed.† And he redeemed us from the curse, having become a curse on our behalf,‡ and underwent the most dishonourable death, so that he might bring us to the life of glory. He was not satisfied merely to make us alive when we were dead, but he bestowed the dignity of divinity, and prepared eternal resting-places surpassing all human thought in the greatness of their delight. What then shall we render to the Lord for all that he has given us?§ He is so good as to ask for no repayment, but is content merely with being loved in return for his gifts.

When I think of all this – let me speak freely of my personal feelings – I fall into a fearful shuddering and terror, lest perhaps through carelessness of mind or absorption in vain things I should fall from the love of God and become a reproach to Christ. For he that now deceives us and is eager to make us forget our Benefactor, using every trick and worldly enticements, jumping on us and attacking us to destroy our souls, he will one day offer our carelessness as a reproach to the Lord and will boast of our disobedience and apostasy. He neither created us nor died for us, but despite this he kept us following his disobedience and neglect of God's commandments. This reproach against the Lord and this boasting of the enemy seem to me harder to bear than the punishment of hell, namely that we should become to the enemy of Christ a subject of boasting and an opportunity for pride against

* Phil. 2:6–7.
† Isa. 53:4.
‡ Gal. 3:13.
§ Ps. 116:12.

him who died for us and rose again, to whom for this reason we are more abundantly debtors as is written.*

Let this be enough about the love of God. For my purpose (*skopos*) is not to say all – for that is impossible – but under various headings to implant brief reminders in your souls, which shall stir up the divine loving desire (*pothos*).

Commentary

Basil does not just want to discuss our love for God, he aims to inspire it, to stir up loving desire (*pothos*) in his hearers. Again one sees that his concern is practical and springs from a pastoral situation.

God is our Benefactor

Our love for God is explored by analogy with natural affection for parents and the special love one has for a benefactor. God too is our maker and benefactor and must be loved as such, but Basil does not just equate parent and Creator, benefactor and Redeemer. Love of God is as natural as that of a child for his mother, but the higher love one has for a benefactor is also given to God as Creator. Basil discussed the creation of the world in his sermons on the beginning of the Book of Genesis, the Hexameron, and he evokes its wonders in the third paragraph, but the supreme benefit is the creation of man in the divine image and likeness. This benefit is not just creation as a single act but God's continual care for human beings despite their turning away from him. Here Basil situates the ascetic life firmly in the context of salvation history. It is not just a case of the individual realising the potential of the seeds of divine love within himself and ascending from the earth to heaven, the Christian's personal spiritual drama is played out as part of the great dramatic story of God's dealing with the human race.

God plays the part of Benefactor (*euergetês*) and this has a significant connection with Basil's life and social context. The society of Late Antiquity was based on webs of patronage in which those with

---

* cf. Rom. 8:12.

power and wealth acted as benefactors. Origen was supplied with what was in effect a secretariat and publishing house by his rich benefactor Ambrose, whom he had converted from heresy. Bishops such as Basil acted as Patrons, both directly towards the poor and as mediators between the citizens and central government.[12] Just as images from contemporary society such as Emperor or Philosopher were used to understand Christ, so the use of benefactor language concerning God would evoke many associations for Basil's audience, whatever their social status.

Basil continues to emphasise the natural character of our love for God. The *logoi spermatikoi* are a philosophical and internal justification of this and the comparisons with children and animals reinforce his argument from external examples. The example of the dog and its master who feeds it is not in Rufinus, and one can only speculate why the thought of dogs impressed itself on the episcopal mind. When he says that a Benefactor is ranked higher than those loved naturally, one could think of the gift of divine grace but there is no development here of the distinction between nature and grace. The word grace (*charis*) is used, except in the first inserted passage, in the non-theological sense as loveliness or beauty of form, and we have already noted the unexplicit doctrine of grace in Basil's theology. The positive appreciation of nature and its tendency towards God is thus part of the same system as the gifts of God given in history. The same divine Benefactor is the source of both.

The Anaphora of St Basil

The section where Basil recounts the history of God's dealings with his human creation is important in that there are very close similarities between it and the Anaphora, or Eucharistic Prayer, of St Basil used in the Byzantine Liturgy. It is probable that this text does go back to him and it may represent a reworking by Basil of an existing Anaphora, although the question is very complex.[13] Basil was actively involved in the development of the Church's worship, as shown by the liturgical legislation in Longer Rule 37, the defence against the charge of liturgical innovation in his *De Spiritu Sancto* and Letter 207, and the brief mention in Gregory Nazianzen's Funeral Oration that he had composed prayers while a presbyter of Caesarea.[14] There is not an exact verbal correspondence between the Rule and the Anaphora but the subject matter is so close that there must be a direct connection between the two texts. The following part of the Anaphora, which occurs after the Sanctus, illustrates the similarities:

> Having made man, in taking dust from the earth, and having honoured him with your image, you had placed him in the Paradise of delight, promising him immortality of life and eternal good things in the observance of your commandments. But when he disobeyed you, the true God who created him, and was led astray by the deception of the serpent and was put to death by his own transgressions, you cast him out in your righteous judgement, O God, from paradise into this world and you caused him to return to the earth from which he was taken, providing for him the salvation of regeneration in your Christ himself. For you did not totally reject your creature, which you had made, O Good One, nor did you forget the work of your hands, but you visited him in manifold ways because of your tender mercy, you sent him the prophets, you wrought wonders through your saints who were pleasing to you in each generation, you have spoken to us through the mouth of your servants the prophets announcing beforehand the salvation to come, you have given us the law to help us, you appointed angels as guardians. But when the fullness of time came you spoke to us in your Son himself, through whom you had also created the ages, he who is the splendour of your glory and the form of your substance, and upholding all things by the word of your power, did not count equality with you, O God and Father, a thing to be grasped, but being God before the ages he was seen on earth and lived among men, and having taken flesh from a holy Virgin, he emptied himself taking the form of a servant.[15]

One can see here the characteristically Basilian themes of the commandments, saints living lives pleasing to God, and the remembrance of the benefits of God. Perhaps in this Rule he was freely recalling the liturgical text with which he was familiar. This liturgical echo in the Rules is a significant sign of the ecclesial and corporate nature of the type of life he was building up among the ascetics.

Cosmic drama: the influence of Satan

The last part of this Rule is centred on the work of Christ and the Christian's response and it leads Basil into revealing his own personal feelings in a paragraph not found in Rufinus. Having taught that the love of God is natural for us, he fears that he should fall away from it through distraction. We will see later how important a single-minded and undistracted attention to God is in Basil's spiritual teaching. This falling away recalls a controversial aspect of Origen's theological speculations. The great Alexandrian taught that, before the creation of the material world, rational beings originally lived a life of contemplation with God. They fell from this through a type of boredom (in Greek *koros*), some becoming embodied human beings in this world, others becoming angels or demons. The aim of these beings was then to return to their original state. The Church later recognised that this doctrine of the pre-existence of souls was not in accord with the true faith.[16] Basil's fall recalls this primal fall in Origen's cosmology, but it is significant that Basil is speaking of a personal and not a cosmic fall. For him the latter was caused by the serpent as mentioned above. In addition to Christ, the Devil puts in a major appearance in this penultimate paragraph.

He is presented as the deceiver and enemy of our souls who is always trying to distract the Christian, enticing him first into careless-ness and then to apostasy and neglect of the commandments. In comparison with other early ascetic literature, the Asceticon gives much less attention to the threat from Satan and the demons in the spiritual life. Compared with the 'Life of Antony' it is partly a ques-tion of genre, but in general Basil does tend to situate the movement to evil solely in one's own will (*idion thelêma*), possibly as a conse-quence of his high view of human nature. In his sermon *That God is not the Author of Evils*[17] he teaches that evil comes from our own perverted wills which turn away from God through lack of interest in him. The word he uses is *koros*, the same as used by Origen in his account of the primal fall.[18] Again we see Basil using the ideas of the great Alexandrian, but separated from his controversial cosmology. In addition to his dominant interest in human nature, the relative lack of interest in evil spirits may also have been a reaction to excessive views of demonic influence current among the enthusiasts.[19]

The presence of the Devil here is significant, though, as it situates the ascetic life, as part of Basil's re-telling of Salvation History, in the context of the cosmic drama of war between good and evil. The Devil was disobedient and neglected God's commandments and he encourages us to do the same. The ascetic's work is contrary to that of Satan in that it is one of obedience to the commandments. Despite all the positive anthropology mentioned above, the presence of the Evil One means that our salvation is not assured.

The scope of Satan's influence on us is explored in Shorter Rules 75, 'Whether it is right to say that Satan is the cause of every sin, in thought, word and deed', and 275, 'Does the passage, "I Paul wanted to come again and again but Satan hindered us" (1 Thess. 2:18), imply that Satan can hinder the purpose of a Saint?'. Both of these are present in the Small Asceticon, numbers 195 and 202. In these it is said that he can use natural tendencies (*physika kinêmata*) and forbidden lusts to lead us to evil deeds, but that he has no access into the soul itself. Shorter Rule 75 also points out that we ourselves can be the source of evil when through carelessness we 'leave uncultivated the natural seeds of good' (*ta physika tôn agathôn spermata*).

Thus, with neglect and malign influences, 'natural' things can lead to evil. In our present circumstances they are in need of training in the school of the commandments. This does not nullify the fact that throughout his works Basil upholds the naturalness of a serious devotion to Christian virtues. There is no overthrowing of nature by grace, as in certain forms of Protestantism, nor is there a supernatural order overlaid on less elevated natural virtues, as in a decadent scholasticism. On the other hand, St Basil's teaching is not mere naturalism. Shorter Rule 309 on whether one should approach Holy Communion after a 'customary natural mishap', a nocturnal emission of semen, teaches that he who has been buried with Christ in Baptism is superior to nature and custom. In this case what is natural, *kata physin*, is not helpful to the life of piety and must be overcome by grace. Basil teaches that this overcoming of nature is possible: ' "Those who are of Christ have crucified the flesh with its lusts and passions" (Gal. 5:24) and I know that this has been attained both in men and women by the grace of Christ through genuine faith in the Lord.' The rooting of the life of piety in Baptism is as characteristic for him as rooting it in our created nature. Here in the realm of sexuality is a hint at a nature that is fallen, but this late answer is not typical of the Asceticon as a whole. Philip Rousseau is probably right in saying that nature 'is the key to his thought',[20] although it is a nature that is informed by love and raised above itself.

An end of eternal punishment?

Connected with the presence of the devil in the text is the explicit mention of hell or gehenna. Both of the occurrences are in passages not in Rufinus and the context is rather strange. In Christian Greek writings gehenna is the place of torment, hell, whereas hades, although sometimes synonymous with gehenna, is usually the abode of the dead to which Christ descended. Basil says that alienation from God and being a reproach to Christ are worse than the punishment of gehenna. This may be just a figure of speech, exaggerating to express how terrible this would be, but one may wonder if it is a hint at Origen's suggestion that the punishments of gehenna are temporary and remedial[21] and thus not as ultimately terrible as the normal Christian teaching on the eternity of hell. This is unlikely as elsewhere Basil, in contrast to his brother Gregory, explicitly teaches the everlasting nature of the punishments of hell.

In Shorter Rule 267, 'If one man shall be beaten with many, another with few blows (Luke 12:47), how do some say that there is no end of punishment?', he explicitly teaches from Scripture that the punishments of gehenna will never end: 'for if there is ever an end of eternal punishment, eternal life too will surely have an end.' His interpretation of this text from Luke rather suggests different degrees of eternal punishment. The question shows that Origenist views were present among the enthusiasts but Basil's answer shows that he is in the mainstream of ecclesial opinion. It is possible that he was maintaining the principle of reserve and withholding the 'higher doctrine' of universal restoration from the multitude. He says that belief in an end of punishment allows people to 'sin more boldly' and thus the concept of eternal punishment could have a prophylactic function. This is, however, unlikely as it does not fit with the general run of his teaching, and so one may conclude that the language in the text above is figurative. If it had been in the Small Asceticon and omitted from the Great one could suspect a development away from Origen's opinions, but the compilation of texts from Origen in the *Philocalia* shows that from the start of his ascetic life Basil seems to deliberately avoid the controversial opinions of his master.

One should not end with the devil, hell and controversy, but rather note the passionate loyalty to Christ and appreciation of the glorious works of God that Basil shows in this passage. It is clear that, concerning the love of God, his teaching springs from his own experience and life of devotion.

NOTES

1. *Rule of St Benedict*, Prologue 45.
2. *Contra Celsum* 1:37.
3. *Contra Gentes* 40.
4. *Commentary on John* 20:5
5. cf. *Origen*, Crouzel, p. 254 and, for example, Origen's *Contra Celsum* 5:22–3.
6. Meredith, 'Asceticism', p. 327. He also notes that the optimism here concerning the uncorrupted nature of the soul is more muted than that in the *Life of Antony* 20.
7. See for example Diotima's speech in Plato's *Symposium* and Plotinus' commentary on the *Symposium* in *Ennead* 3:5.
8. *Commentary on the Song of Songs* Prologue 2. This text only survives in Rufinus' Latin translation and in this text he uses the words *caritas* and *amor*, which presumably translate *agapê* and *erôs*. Cf. James W. Zona, ' "Set Love in Order in Me" Eros-Knowing in Origen and Desiderium-Knowing in St Bernard', *Cistercian Studies Quarterly* 34:2 (1999).
9. *On the Song of Songs*, Prologue 2.
10. See *The Cappadocians*, Anthony Meredith, pp. 114–24: 'The Cappadocians and Hellenism'.

11. *Basili Regula*, ed. Zelzer, 2:23–4, p. 12. Fiery imagery is prominent in this section of the Small Asceticon.
12. See 'Social Patronage and Political Mediation in the Activity of Basil of Caesarea' by Marcella Forlin Patrucco, in *Studia Patristica* XVII, pp. 1102–7; and *Basil of Caesarea*, Rousseau, pp. 159–62.
13. The important study of the Liturgy of St Basil by Hieronymus Engberding (1931) identified an original shorter form of the Anaphora, used by the modern Coptic Church in Egypt, and an amplified version used in the Byzantine Liturgy with variant Syriac and Old Armenian recensions. Later writers have shown that the added passages in the longer text are almost certainly the work of Basil himself. Other writers, including Louis Bouyer in *Eucharist* (1968), have suggested that Basil had also worked on the shorter Egyptian recension. John Fenwick in *The Anaphoras of St Basil and St James: An Investigation of their Common Origin* gives an account of previous scholarship on the question and, after studying the different versions, concludes that Basil may have left his mark on the shorter form of the Anaphora before becoming bishop in 370, that he inserted material to create the longer versions during his episcopate, and that the Syriac and Armenian recensions represent distinct stages of this work. The development of this passage in our text from the Small Asceticon to the Great may reflect this process.
4. Gregory Nazianzen, *Oration 43* 34.
15. Translation modified from *The Divine Liturgies*, ed. J. N. W. B. Robertson (London 1894). This also gives the Greek text.
16. cf. Crouzel, *Origen*, ch. 11, 'The Church of the Pre-Existence and the Fall', pp. 205–18.
17. *PG* 31:329–53.
18. See Meredith, *The Cappadocians*, p. 122.
19. As noted in Part 1, the later Messalian groups were accused of teaching that a demon dwells in each person since birth, cf. Stewart, *Working the Earth of the Heart*, pp. 55–6, 59–61.
20. *Basil of Caesarea*, Rousseau, pp. 221–4, see also pp. 331–47.
21. For the idea of an end to 'eternal' punishment see Crouzel, *Origen*, pp. 242–7, and on the question of Origen's teaching on the Apokatastasis, the restoration of all things at the end of time, see pp. 257–66. This question continues to fascinate theologians, for example: *Dare we Hope that all Men may be Saved* by Hans Urs von Balthasar, and 'Dare we hope for the Salvation of All' by Kallistos Ware in *Theology Digest* 45:4 (1998).

Chapter Eight

Love of Neighbour and the Fear of God

LONGER RULE 3
CONCERNING LOVE TOWARDS ONE'S NEIGHBOUR

To discourse on the commandment which is second in order and power will come next.

We have said above that the law is the cultivator and nurturer of those powers which have been implanted in us from the beginning like seeds (*spermatikōs*). But since we have been commanded to love our neighbour as ourselves, let us learn whether we have power from God to fulfil this commandment too. Who does not know that man is a tame and sociable animal, and not a solitary and fierce one? For nothing is so characteristic of our nature as to associate with one another, to need one another and to love our kind. So the Lord himself first gave us the seeds of these things, and accordingly demands their fruits, saying, 'A new commandment I give to you, that you love one another'.* And wishing to stir up our souls to keep this commandment, he demanded as a proof that we are his disciples, not signs and miracles – and yet he granted the working of these too in the Holy Spirit – What does he say? 'By this all will know that you are my disciples, if you have love for one another.'† And he links these commandments in such a way that he transfers to himself benefits conferred on one's neighbour, for he says, 'I was hungry and you gave me food . . .' and so on.‡ To which he adds: 'As you did it to one of the least of these brothers of mine, you did it to me.'§

Therefore in keeping the first commandment one also keeps the second: and through the second one returns again to the first. And the one who loves

---

* John 13:34.
† John 13:35.
‡ Matt. 25:35.
§ Matt. 25:40.

the Lord also, so it follows, loves his neighbour. For, 'the one who loves me', said the Lord, 'will keep my commandments.'* And 'this,' he says, 'is my commandment, that you love one another, as I have loved you.'† But again the one who loves his neighbour fulfils love towards God, since God accepts the favour as conferred on himself. For this very reason Moses, the faithful servant of God, showed such love towards his brothers that he chose to be blotted out of God's book in which he had been entered, unless the people were forgiven their sin.‡ And Paul was bold enough to pray that he might be accursed from Christ on behalf of his brothers, his own flesh and blood, wishing that he himself might be accepted as an exchange for the salvation of all, after the pattern of the Lord.§ Though he knew all the time that it was impossible for a man to be alienated from God who has sacrificed the grace of God because of his love for God in order to keep the greatest of the commandments. He also knew that for this very reason he would receive very much more than he gave. What we have already said is abundant proof that the Saints reached this measure of love towards one's neighbour.

Commentary

In subject and content, this Rule follows on naturally from Longer Rule 2. They are, as we have seen, one answer in the Small Asceticon, but there is a clear break in subject matter between equivalent sections. This occurs between verse 57,[1] 'And let this be enough about the love of God . . .', which is the last paragraph of Longer Rule 2, and verse 58, 'Consequently now is the time to explain also that commandment which we have said is second in order and power', which corresponds to the first sentence of the present Rule. One can understand why they have been divided here, but it is important not to neglect the continuity between them. They both expound the double commandment of love introduced in the first answer.

This continuity is made plain by the mention of the seeds or powers which enable us to love God, and it is shown that we have, in the same way, the power to love our neighbour. To do so is natural

---

* John 14:23.
† John 15:12.
‡ cf. Exod. 32:32.
§ cf. Rom. 9:3.

because God has given us the seeds and he demands, in the new commandment from St John's Gospel, the fruit. Here Rufinus has the language of seeds (*semina seminavit*), but the earlier words in our text describing the powers as 'like seeds' are not present in his version of the Small Asceticon. Basil probably added the adverb *spermatikôs* to recall the earlier passage he had inserted in the Great Asceticon about the *logos spermatikos*. The text of the Great Asceticon also has two other inserted passages, the sentence on miracles beginning, 'And wishing to stir up . . .', and the last part on Moses and Paul beginning, 'For this very reason . . .'

Why love your neighbour?

The ground of our love of neighbour is in our nature as created by God. Such love is natural and we have already noted the importance of nature in Basil's positive anthropology. The philosophical character of his teaching is maintained, this time recalling Aristotle's words on the basically social nature of man: 'Man is by nature a political animal, and so even when men have no need of assistance from each other they none the less desire to live together.'[2] Basil's definition of man as a sociable animal also connects with the Stoic influence on his anthropology.[3] Anthony Meredith detects here the influence of the Stoic principle of *oikeiôsis*, the natural attractiveness of beings of the same class to each other. This natural inclination has the same end as the scriptural commandments quoted here, and he notes that 'Basil does not see love of neighbour as a challenge to nature but as its fulfilment.'[4] The primary challenge of Christ, to love one's enemy, is not present here.

This omission does not necessarily mean Basil taught that we should only love those we like. The commandment of Christ to love one's enemies[5] is given in *Moralia* 5:1, 'That one ought to be pure from all hatred towards all people, and to love one's enemies.' It is perhaps better to understand Basil's teaching as meaning that we should not solely love those we like, but rather love those whom we are like, that is those who share our common human nature. Love of the neighbour who harms one is taught in Shorter Rule 163,

'In what way can one attain love towards one's neighbour?', although here the neighbour is a 'brother'. Does this term mean a fellow ascetic, a fellow Christian, or a fellow human being? A similar ambiguity is found in the first letter of St John with its great stress on loving one's brothers. In the context of this Letter's dualism between the community and the world, and parallel to the Qumran literature, the exhortation to love one's brother could express exclusivism and separation and refer only to the community.[6] Although he does not quote it,[7] Basil's teaching is very similar to that of the Letter with its stress on commandments and mention of God's seeds in 1 John 3:9, which are, however, only in those 'born of God'. Reserve about its place in the New Testament Canon may have led Basil not to quote 1 John in his Ascetica, but it does seem to be an influence on his teaching here.

Basil was concerned to divert the energies of the ascetic movement towards charitable activities, as in his great foundation of the Basileiados. Clarke, however, notes that Basil's 'philanthropy was based on passages from the New Testament other than those of the Sermon on the Mount which appeal most today'.[8] An example is Shorter Rule 155 which deals with ascetics working in these charitable institutions:

> We who serve the sick in the hospital are taught to serve them with such a disposition as if they were brothers of the Lord. Now if the man who receives our service cannot be given this title, how ought we to attend to him?

Basil's answer teaches that if the sick remain persistent in their sins despite exhortation from the Superior, then they should be expelled from the hospital (*xenodocheion*). It is clear from this answer that his motive was not primarily that of social utility, human solidarity and compassion. It was rather rooted in a piety which gives meaning to solidarity and compassion. Another Shorter Rule, however, shows that he was not only concerned for the elect. Love for the ungodly is expressly taught in Shorter Rule 186, 'We are taught to show love unto death on behalf of both the righteous and sinners, making no distinction.' His teaching on love of neighbour is thus more complex than at first sight, but while the emphasis is different in different texts he does not completely ignore the love of those who are not 'brothers' in the strict sense.

Man is not a solitary animal

Basil's teaching on man as a sociable animal also, if one is attentive to the language used, suggests another aspect of his thought. 'Who does not know that man is a tame and sociable (*koinōnikon*) animal, and not a solitary (*monastikon*) and fierce one? For nothing is so characteristic of our nature (*physis*) as to associate (*koinōnein*) with one another, to need one another and to love our kind.' Gribomont notes that this pejorative use of *monastikos* with the same meaning as *monios*, a solitary wild animal (as used in Ps. 79:13 [LXX] for the solitary wild boar), seems to be proper to Basil who also uses it to describe the lion in Homily 9 on the Hexameron.[9] Basil's rejection of solitude as unnatural implies a rejection of much of the ascetic tradition of Egypt and Syria. Monk (*monachos*) and related words are connected to the idea of singleness and solitude, especially with relation to celibacy. In the Pachomian literature *monachos* is used of a monk who lives in community but Basil avoids monastic terminology throughout the Asceticon. Perhaps this was because he associated it with solitude. It was not because he was not familiar with such language: he uses it elsewhere, for example in his Canonical Letter 199. His hostility is to the life of the isolated hermit and our text prepares the way for the more developed rejection of the solitary life in the seventh Longer Rule where he teaches that 'the love of Christ does not allow us each to be concerned solely with our own interests'. Here again it is both nature and revelation together which point the Christian in the right direction.

The natural and Christian alternative to the solitary life is life in community, in *koinônia* (fellowship). *Koinônikos* is only used once in the New Testament and there it has the meaning 'generous'.[10] The related verb and the noun are more frequent, with *koinônia* being an important element in the definition of that Apostolic community (Acts 2:42) which Basil takes as his ideal at the end of Longer Rule 7. In Pachomian monasticism it was a technical term for the monastic community as a whole.[11] This use of the word 'monastic' shows that we have a problem. Today in the West, after centuries of dominance by the Rule of St Benedict, this term is usually applied to communities. One must always bear this in mind when saying that Basil rejects monastic terminology. The difference in meaning allows one to speak of the bishop of Caesarea as one of the great monastic legislators, and anyone trying to live the monastic life today will recognise his teaching as profoundly monastic, if this word is understood in the sense of 'monastic community'. Any stress on the 'non-monastic' nature of his teaching thus needs to be heavily qualified.

Love in the Scriptures

The fruit of the natural seeds of love of neighbour is demanded by the Lord in texts from St John's Gospel. Gribomont devoted a paper to Basil's use of the Johannine tradition,[12] and it is noticeable that in the first eight Longer Rules all the Johannine quotations are in the first five which are more theoretical, whereas in Longer Rules 6, 7 and 8 on the practicalities of separation, renunciation and community, the accent is on Paul and the Synoptics. One of the Johannine quotations here is not in the version of Rufinus, John 13:35 has love as the sign of a true disciple. In the first inserted passage Basil notes that Christ does not demand signs and miracles as an authenticating mark of discipleship. This may have its roots in a situation where Basil had encountered certain enthusiasts who put great emphasis on miracles and other charismatic phenomena as the mark of a true Christian. Basil does not reject these manifestations, and clearly accepts miracles as an effect of the working of the Holy Spirit, but he firmly subordinates them to love just as Paul does in 1 Corinthians 13. These additions to the text are thus valuable in revealing the development of Basil's thought and hint at later experiences in his ministry among the ascetics.

Basil's next move is very clever in that, using the two texts from Matthew, he unites the two commandments so that in keeping one we also keep the other. This suggests, as has already been noted, a coinherence of the commandments. It also gives a scriptural basis for his concern with directing the energies of the ascetics towards charitable work. In serving the poor and sick they are serving Christ. Such activity is thus not a distraction from prayer and undistracted attention to the Lord, as was argued by certain contemporary enthusiasts. There are hints at this controversy in the Rules, for example in Longer Rule 37.

Finally, we move to the Saints as extreme examples of the love of neighbour in action: Moses and Paul who wish to be lost to save their brethren. The last inserted passage recalls and surpasses Basil's key ideal of obedience to the commandments even to death.[13] We have already noted that Basil uses the saints as 'icons' of the ascetic life, just as St Athanasius provided a literary icon for monks in the *Life of Antony*. A striking example of this is in Basil's early Letter 2 where speaking of Joseph, Job, Moses and David, he writes that in the Scriptures are found:

> ... the lives of saintly men, recorded and handed down to us, which lie before us like living images (*eikones*) of the godly way of life (*politeia*), for our imitation of their good works ... Just as painters in working from models constantly gaze at their exemplar and thus strive to transfer the expression of the original to their own artistry, so too he who is anxious to make himself perfect in all the kinds of virtue must gaze upon the lives of the saints as upon statues, so to speak, that move and act and must make their excellence his own by imitation.

In this final section a characteristically Basilian concern for practicality and moderation is seen when he explains Paul's gesture in Romans 9, saying that he knew all the time that he couldn't be lost. In loving his brethren he was loving God and thus keeping both great commandments at the same time. Similarly in Shorter Rule 190 he explains this same gesture of Paul against those who claim that it justifies a preferential love for one's relations according to the flesh. This time he notes that it was done for spiritual reasons and because of the incarnation of the Lord, not because of ties of fleshly kinship. Different aspects of the same text are thus emphasised in different contexts.

As when discussing the first great commandment, Basil here touches on other more specific issues to which he will return later in the Rules. We are given an impression of a teacher with coherent views constructed on a rational and scriptural basis, who is able to use them in speech and writing in response to a myriad of questions. His views do develop over time, but, like Paul of Tarsus, the coherence remains.

LONGER RULE 4
CONCERNING FEAR OF GOD

For those who are just being introduced to piety, instruction through fear is more profitable, according to the advice of the most wise Solomon who said, 'The fear of the Lord is the beginning of wisdom.'* But you who have passed the stage of infancy in Christ, and no longer need milk but are able to be perfected in the inner man by the solid food of doctrine, require the more important commandments, in which the whole truth of love in Christ is accomplished; taking care, obviously, lest the abundance of God's gifts become a cause of ingratitude towards your Benefactor. For, he says, 'when someone is entrusted with much, of that person even more will be expected.'†

Commentary
This is one of the shortest of the Longer Rules and seems rather out of place here. The other Rules in the first section are all about the commandment to love and how one can carry it out, but here we have the theme of fear and a personal reference to the audience. Even in Rufinus, where it is just part of the second Answer, it forms a brief aside between the discussions of love of neighbour and the importance of the remembrance of God in the practice of love. It does however fit in with the general flow of this answer as it poses the question of the relation between love and fear. It is also a valuable witness to the nature of Basil's original audience and their relation to the Church as a whole.

---

* Prov. 1:7, Ps. 110:10.
† Luke 12:48.

To be perfected by the solid food of doctrine

The language used here is significant. The word translated, 'those who are being introduced', *eisagomenoi*, was used in the early Church of catechumens, those who are preparing for baptism. The other category mentioned, those 'who have passed the stage of infancy in Christ', are described as capable of being perfected. The verb used, *teleioô*, to perfect, is also used of Christian baptism. The background to this passage is thus Christian initiation. Hebrews 5:12, which provides the language about milk and solid food, was also written in a similar context and the following verses use the same language of perfection (*teleios, teleiotês*): 'You need milk, not solid food; for everyone who lives on milk is unskilled in the word of righteousness, for he is a child. But solid food is for the mature (*teleiôi*), for those who have trained their faculties by practice to distinguish good from evil. Therefore let us leave the elementary teaching (*logos*) of Christ and go on to maturity (*teleiotês*)' (Heb. 5:12–6:1). The Letter to the Hebrews is thus one source of Basil's teaching here.

The word for doctrine, the plural *dogmata*, is also significant as Basil uses it in his Treatise *On the Holy Spirit* of the esoteric or interior tradition of the Church as opposed to that which is proclaimed in public, *kêrugma*: 'dogma is one thing, kerygma another; the first is observed in silence, while the latter is proclaimed to the world.'[14] In this Treatise Basil's examples of traditions handed down in silence, on which *dogmata* are based, are all from the liturgy. These can only be explained to the baptised because the experience to which they refer is proper only to the baptised. This Church-esotericism, in which all the baptised are 'on the inside', is the context of Basil's teaching in this Rule. In it *dogma* is related to the 'solid food' of Hebrews and thus contrasts with the milk or 'elementary teaching'. It indicates a more advanced teaching characterised by the words 'perfection', 'more important' and 'whole truth of love'. The baptismal language shows that, while his hearers have not just been baptised, there is a close parallel with the doctrine taught to catechumens in pre- and post-baptismal catechesis. While there may not be a conscious secrecy involved, there is a certain esotericism in this Rule.

This recalls texts in Clement of Alexandria and Origen, among others, which have been used to speak of a 'discipline of the secret' or a 'principle of reserve'. An example is Origen's *Homily on Leviticus* 13:3:4, on the shew-bread:

> Every word of God is a loaf but there is a difference in loaves. For there is a certain word which can be delivered in the common hearing and which can teach the people about the works of mercy and of all kindness . . . but there is another which contains secrets and speaks about the faith in God or the knowledge of things.

In Origen there are thus hints of a secret knowledge beyond that imparted to the baptised. In Basil's disciple, Evagrius of Pontus, this higher knowledge is hardened into a system and given expression in his *Gnostic Chapters*. Basil, however, would seem to be following a different path, closer to the Gospel where Jesus had his inner circles of the twelve and the three. There are 'more important commandments' but they concern 'the whole truth of love' rather than gnostic speculations. He is not speaking of baptism when using the language of perfection with his audience, but his use of baptismal language certainly roots this more mature Christianity in Christian initiation.

What we seem to have here is a group of the more committed and more mature who are still part of the Church but can be distinguished, perhaps by their zeal, from the great mass of Christians. One is reminded of Basil's Preface to the Shorter Rules taken from the prologue to the Small Asceticon, which is quoted in Chapter 5. There Basil says he 'should always be zealous for the perfection' of the souls of his small nocturnal audience.

Gribomont notes that in this Rule we find 'the point of distinction between monks and the bulk of Christians, with a formula which is neither that of the vows nor that of counsels.'[15] This is important as during Basil's lifetime we see a gradual development of ascetic institutions and distinct 'monastic' communities. Basil is also a significant figure, as we will see later, in the emergence of monastic vows. This development is revealed in the Rules, with those later Answers not in the Small Asceticon often presupposing structured communities.

Even in the Small Asceticon itself, certain responses such as the advice on seating at table in the tenth Answer imply an increasing separation. The recommendations about clothing in the eleventh Answer, while addressed to all Christians, would inevitably produce a distinct group.

In Longer Rule 4 we can thus see, in the distinction described, the origins of a separate ascetic community. It would be a mistake, though, to read the existence of such communities back into all the earlier Rules.[16] In this sense Basil is not 'monastic' but witnesses to the evolution of 'monasticism'.

Does perfect love cast out fear?

The distinction between infants in Christ and those who can 'be perfected in the inner man by the solid food of doctrine' is also important in that it is connected with the place of fear in the spiritual life. The key text here is from Proverbs or Psalm 110, 'The fear of the Lord is the beginning of wisdom', and this is the only time it is used in the Rules.[17] From this text Basil deduces that fear is profitable at the start of the Christian life, but that those who have advanced to 'the solid food of doctrine' need 'the more important commandments', those of love. One thus grows out of fear and this explains the stress on love found at the start of the Longer Rules. They are addressed to these more advanced Christians.

It is possible that Basil is here responding to the claim of his audience to be 'more perfect' and leading them on to a more balanced and less elitist view of the spiritual life. Desprez speaks of 'tendencies of a Messalian type to interior perfection'[18] manifested in this Rule. It is true that references to the 'interior man' are rare in Basil's works and that he addresses his words to Christians in general, but the Preface to the Small Asceticon shows that his hearers were a group of the more devout within the congregation. Rather than defining different types of Christian, it is more a question of a progression which, at least in theory, is for all Christians. This does not necessarily mean that Basil was not using his interlocutors own terminology, but, if he was, he did so for his own purposes. The warning against ingratitude to the Benefactor who gave such gifts, picking up a theme in the second Rule, could be a corrective to spiritual pride among those who view themselves as spiritually mature. The words of Jesus from Luke, not in Rufinus, reinforce this theme.

The real question which emerges from this Rule is the place of fear and love in the life of the Christian. It is this which justifies its creation as a separate entity in the Great Asceticon. The text from Proverbs is used to show that the 'fear of the Lord' is appropriate only at the beginning, during infancy in Christ. This echoes the Preface to the Longer Rules in the Great Asceticon, not in Rufinus, where Basil describes the three dispositions that lead to obedience:

> Either from fear of punishment we turn away from that which is evil, and so are of a servile disposition; or seeking to profit by the reward, we fulfil the commandments for our own benefit, and are accordingly like hirelings; or else we do good for the sake of the Good itself and for love of him who gave us the Law . . . and so we have the disposition of sons.

The fear here is good, as it says later, 'it is not possible for those who fear to neglect any of God's orders', but it is still a fear of punishment. Love and not fear characterise the third disposition, just as in the fourth Longer Rule the Christian, as he is being perfected, moves on to the 'more important commandments' which relate to love. It is thus a progression from fear to love, and we return to the world of the first letter of John, 'Perfect love casts out fear' (1 John 4:18). Notice that both in the Rule and in St John, love is associated with perfection. Despite Basil's reservations about the canonical status of 1 John, we can again see its influence behind the text.

Cassian and 'the more sublime fear of love'

This, however, is only part of the biblical teaching on fear. In the Old Testament and parts of the New the fear of the Lord is a lasting and necessary disposition, not alien to love and perfection. An example is 2 Corinthians 7:1, 'make holiness perfect in the fear of God'. Cassian in his eleventh Conference, the first of Abba Chaeremon, allows for both these types of fear. Chaeremon starts by teaching that three things restrain us from vice: fear of hell, hope for heaven and love of virtue or a disposition for the Good itself.[19] These correspond closely to Basil's three dispositions that lead us to obey, quoted above. Cassian's friend Germanus objects, as we have done, that in this scheme fear is imperfect (as is hope), whereas certain scriptural texts suggest otherwise. In his response Chaeremon quotes 1 John 4:18 but goes on to speak of:

> . . . the more sublime fear of love, which is begotten not by dread of punishment or by desire for rewards but by the greatness of one's love. It is with this anxious disposition that a son fears his very indulgent father, or a brother his brother . . . inasmuch as they are afraid not of blows or insults but of the slightest offence against love.[20]

He distinguishes between this filial fear and that imperfect servile fear 'which is called the beginning of wisdom' and is cast out by perfect love. Filial fear is thus part of the third disposition of love given by both Basil and Cassian.

In his *Institutes*, however, Cassian proposes in the words of Abba Pinufius the same scheme that Basil uses in our Rule, using the same text from Proverbs.[21] We ascend from the fear of the Lord to that love which casts out fear. This is the text which lies behind St Benedict's Ladder of Humility in Chapter 7 of his *Rule* which also culminates with the quotation from 1 John on perfect love casting out fear. In Cassian, then, we do have these two types of fear but the servile type, which is cast out by love, can be taught on its own with no reference to the other. There is such a close connection between the teaching of Basil and Cassian that there would seem to be a direct dependence. If Longer Rule 4 is followed by the teaching given in the *Institutes*, and is only a part of the biblical doctrine of fear, can we find evidence in the Asceticon that Basil also teaches something approximating to Cassian's filial fear?

Does Basil teach this filial fear?

In Basil's warning about ingratitude at the end of the Rule Desprez sees a hint of the need for this filial fear.[22] Without it one can easily become ungrateful. Thus the whole point of his teaching here is that those who see themselves as advanced and spiritual and having passed the stage of fear in fact need it to avoid the fatal sin of pride. If this is true, though, it is not explicit, and one needs to look elsewhere in the Asceticon to see if Basil has a more elevated conception of the place of fear.

One need not look far, as towards the end of Longer Rule 5 fear is mentioned in the context of the memory and presence of God. Basil is here clearly speaking to the same type of mature Christian as in Longer Rule 4. He says that doing every action in the knowledge that one is seen by the Lord will lead to the presence of an 'enduring fear' which hates iniquity, and to the perfection of love. The fear is a lasting one, it is not just the first stage, and it is associated with the perfection of love. Thus the 'whole truth of love' mentioned above does not exclude the presence of fear. A second example of this higher fear is found in Longer Rule 44. Here one of the criteria used by the Superior in questioning a brother returned from a journey is whether 'he has completed every day and night living in the fear of God'. Basil is very strict about whom he allows to travel and fear of God is obviously expected to be an attribute of these mature brethren. Again it is implied but not stated that this is a fear, like Cassian's, 'of the slightest offense against love' rather than a servile fear of punishment.

The situation in the Asceticon is thus not unlike that in Cassian where he seems to contradict himself between the *Institutes* and the *Conferences*. In Basil, however, the concept of a higher fear which coexists with love is much less developed than it was to be by Cassian. This is not surprising, but the evidence from both writers shows that one needs to read any passage in the context of the whole work.

Fear in the Asceticon: does Basil's teaching develop?

There does remain a problem, however, in explaining the place of fear in Basil's teaching using the extracts from Longer Rules 5 and 44. Neither is found in the earlier version of the Asceticon translated by Rufinus. Did Basil's spiritual doctrine have an original coherence, inspired by the first Letter of St John, where fear was left behind by those on the paths of love? If so, our text would be a remnant of this earlier stratum, rather than just one aspect of the full picture as the comparison with Cassian has suggested.

The first thing to note is that most references to fear are common to the two recensions. Apart from the two Longer Rules already mentioned, texts proper to the Great Asceticon include Longer Rule 10, where it says concerning new entrants that 'fear of God masters every defect of soul',[23] and Shorter Rule 138, where the ascetic who does his own will in fasting is told to fear the judgement of God on Eve in Genesis 3:16. Longer Rule 10 is similar to Longer Rule 4 in placing fear at the start of the dedicated life and in giving the 'more perfect precepts' to those who are already living a good life. In other texts proper to the Great Asceticon, such as Shorter Rules 81, 114 and 260, the theme of fear is mentioned in a scriptural quotation and not developed by Basil. We also find references to fear in the Small Asceticon which are not in the Great, for example R 7 (=LR 15) on the reception of new members and R 123 (=SR 16) where 'compunction of the fear of God' becomes plain 'compunction' in the later version. This implies that Basil had no burning new insights on the place of fear in the spiritual life by the time he came to compose the Great Asceticon.

In the Small Asceticon *timor* occurs 16 times and the verb *timere* nine. Although fear is connected with the beginnings of the ascetic life in answers 7 and 117, it is clear from the majority of references that fear remained a fact of life for the brethren and was not, as implied in the second answer,[24] left behind on commencing a stricter, more mature Christian life. Answer 138, 'How are we able to fear the judgements of God?'[25] is just one example of this and the occurrence of fear language in six of the questions asked shows that this disposition was of practical concern to his audience. If fear remains even in the Small Asceticon, then what sort of fear is it? Does it fit into Cassian's two-fold scheme?

The dominant theme in the texts is a fear of the judgement of God.[26] This is often expressed, with reference to a text from Scripture, as fearing the *sententia dei*.[27] This fits well with the scriptural nature of the life dealt with in the Rules, but the ambiguities of the word *sententia* indicate a certain ambiguity in Basil's teaching here. *Sententia* can mean a text or maxim, for example a scriptural quotation, but it can also mean a judgement or an opinion. The corresponding Greek word in the Great Asceticon is *krima* which means judgement or condemnation. Is the fear here one of punishment, which lingers beyond the first steps in the life of piety, or is it a fear of offending our loving Father? It would seem to be the former, but the latter may perhaps be behind the quotation of Ephesians 5:21, 'be subject to one another in the fear of Christ'[28] in answer 12 (=SR 1), and filial fear could be behind answer 15 (=SR 98) where the Superior giving orders should fear lest he do anything contrary to the will of God or Scripture. The concept of mature filial fear would also seem to be found in question 116, 'If one who is less distinguished is saddened because he sees one who surpasses him in fear of the Lord being preferred to himself, how should we treat him?' Here it is the advanced brothers who have fear of the Lord, and the quotation from Psalm 14:4, 'he glorifies those who fear the Lord', in Basil's answer confirms that he is speaking of a mature fear. It is notable that in the parallel Shorter Rule 171 of the Great Asceticon 'one who surpasses him in fear of the Lord' has become 'one who is more devout', showing that this mature fear is assimilated to devotion and piety.[29] Thus, even in the Small Asceticon, the teaching that fear is for beginners is only part of the picture. The evidence also suggests that, while it had its place, fear was not a major element in Basil's spirituality. Love is the dominant theme.

It is here that the limitations of comparing Basil with Cassian become evident. For the former, in both major recensions of the Asceticon and despite the plain words of our Rule, fear of God remains a feature of the spirituality of the brethren. While one can find texts suggesting both of Cassian's types of fear, the distinction was not an issue for Basil. Filial fear of offending God and fear of punishment are just two aspects of the fundamental disposition. Thus, while utilising Cassian has been of value in clarifying Basil's teaching, one must beware of retrojecting subsequent distinctions. For Basil, fear, whatever the internal motivation, is primarily a fear of transgressing the commandments and is subordinated to love and piety.

This small Rule thus raises some major questions concerning Basil's spiritual teaching. In the next Rule we turn from the commandments to be kept and how we can fulfil them, to the practicalities of doing so.

NOTES

1. Verse numbering from the Zelzer edition

2. Aristotle, *Politics* 3:4:2, tr. H. Rackham (Loeb 1932).

3. Gribomont notes of LRs 2 and 3 that 'there is clearly here a use of Stoic insights on the role of nature'. 'Les règles épistolaires', *É&É*, p. 171 n35.

4. *The Cappadocians*, p. 29.

5. Matt. 5:44.

6. cf. *The Theology of the Johannine Epistles*, Judith Lieu (1991), pp. 68–71. J. A. T. Robinson, in *The Priority of John*, pp. 329–39, argues against this that, 'brother here simply means fellow man'. It is the same ambiguity as in our text.

7. The few quotations from 1 John in the Basilian corpus are noted by Gribomont in 'La tradition johannique chez saint Basile' in *É&É*, pp. 219–20. The Letter is only quoted 13 times, mainly in the homilies. It is strange that it does not occur in the 1500 New Testament verses given in the *Moralia*. Gribomont notes Basil's reserve regarding the canonical status of 1 John and the Apocalypse in pp. 225–7.

8. Clarke, *Ascetic Works* (1925), p. 286 n7.

9. 'L'Exhortation au renoncement attribuée à saint Basile' in *É&É*, p. 375 n1.

10. 1 Tim. 6:18. For *koinônia* and related words see *Exegetical Dictionary of the New Testament*, Vol. 2, pp. 303–5.

11. cf. Pachomian texts translated by Armand Veilleux in *Pachomian Koinonia*, 3 vols (1980–82).

12. 'La tradition johannique chez saint Basile', *É&É*, pp. 209–28.

13. As in SR 116.

14. *On the Holy Spirit* XXVII:66 (translation of David Anderson, 1980). The meaning of the distinction *dogma/kêrugma* has been hotly debated, see 'Ésotérisme et tradition dans le traité du Saint-Esprit de S. Basile' in Gribomont, *É&É*, pp. 446–80.

15. In the discussion at the end of 'Commandments du Seigneur', *É&É*, p. 317. Rousseau warns against putting a monastic or elitist interpretation on this text, using

Rufinus to interpret Basil, *Basil of Caesarea*, p. 199, but it is clear from the distinction drawn in the text, in Greek *men . . . de*, that he was speaking to a group of the more committed. LR 4 would seem to confirm this.

16. This process of development is skilfully examined in Rousseau, *Basil of Caesarea*, pp. 195–205.
17. *Basilius von Caesarea: Die Mönchsregeln*, tr. Frank, p. 405.
18. Quoted in *É&É*, p. 316.
19. *Conferences* 11:6:1.
20. *Conferences* 11:13:1.
21. *Institutes* 4:39 and 43.
22. Quoted in *É&É*, p. 316.
23. The mention of fear is absent from the parallel sixth answer in the Small Asceticon.
24. LR 4 = R 2:70–73.
25. cf. Ps. 118:120. This is the same as Shorter Rule 209.
26. Answers 61 (SR 35), 67 (SR 117), 100 (SR 169), 112 (SR 47), 134 (SR 172), 138 (SR 209), 174 (SR 220) and 203 (SR 274).
27. Answers 67.1, 100.1, 174.3, 203.1 (2.70).
28. Eph. 5:21 is also present in the question of Shorter Rule 114, but it is absent from the corresponding question 13 in Rufinus.
29. R 116 '*qui in timore domini praecedit*': SR 171 '*eulabesteros*'. In later Judaism we find fear of the Lord becoming synonymous with religion or piety: cf. Sirach 1:11–20 and the use of the term 'god-fearer' of sympathetic and devout gentiles.

Chapter Nine

The Heart of Basilian Spirituality: *Diathesis* and the Undistracted Memory of God

LONGER RULE 5
CONCERNING THE AVOIDANCE OF DISTRACTION (*ameteôriston kata dianoian*)

This must be recognised, that we cannot succeed in keeping any commandment at all, nor in the actual love towards God and our neighbour, if our minds are wandering now in one direction, now in another. For it is impossible to gain an accurate knowledge of any art or science if one is always starting on fresh subjects; nor even to master one, without having recognised what befits the end (*telos*) in view. For it is necessary that actions should correspond with the aim (*skopos*) since nothing right is accomplished by inappropriate methods. It is impossible to master the perfection (*telos*) of the smith's art through the works of pottery; nor are athlete's crowns won by enthusiasm (*spoudê*) for playing the flute. But for each end (*telos*) a proper and fitting labour (*ponos*) is demanded. So also we practice successfully the art (*askêsis*) of being well-pleasing (*euaristêsis*) to God according to Christ's gospel, by retirement (*anachôrêsis*) from the cares of the world and complete estrangement from distractions.

Therefore the Apostle, although he had allowed marriage and considered it worthy of blessing, contrasted its preoccupations with the cares that are concerned with God, as if the two were inconsistent, saying: 'The unmarried man is anxious about the affairs of the Lord, how to please the Lord; but the married man is anxious about worldly affairs, how to please his wife.'* So also

---

* 1 Cor. 7:32–3.

the Lord bore witness to his disciples as regards their sincere and undistracted (*ameteôriston*) disposition (*diathesis*) saying, 'You are not of this world.'* On the other hand he testified that it was impossible for the world to receive the knowledge of God, or the Holy Spirit. 'Righteous Father', he says, 'the world has not known you.'† And, 'the Spirit of truth, whom the world cannot receive.'‡

The one, then, who would truly follow God must be loosed from the chains of attachment to this life. Now this is secured by complete retirement (*anachôrêsis*) and forgetfulness (*lêthê*) of former habits. So that, unless we exile (*apoxenoô*) ourselves from relations according to the flesh and worldly society (*koinônia*), migrating as it were to another world in our habit of mind, as the Apostle said, 'our homeland is in heaven'§ – it is impossible that we should succeed in the aim (*skopos*) of being well-pleasing to God, for the Lord said clearly, 'So every one of you who does not renounce all that he has cannot be my disciple.'‖ Having done this, it is fitting for us to keep our hearts with all watchfulness (*phylakê*), so as never to lose the thought of God, or to defile the memory of his wonders with imaginations of vanity; but to bear about the holy thought of God with continual and pure memory imprinted on our souls, like an indelible seal. For thus we gain love towards God, which both stirs us up to the practice of the Lord's commandments and is in its turn preserved by them in permanence and security. And this the Lord shows, saying in one place, 'If you love me, keep my commandments,'¶ and in another, 'If you keep my commandments, you will abide in my love', adding with still more insistence, 'just as I have kept my Father's commandments and abide in his love'.**

By these he teaches us to keep always before us as the aim (*skopos*) of the work set us, the will of the one who gave the order, and to direct our effort (*spoudê*) towards him, as he says elsewhere, 'I have come down from heaven, not to do my own will, but the will of him who sent me.'†† For as the arts of daily life, having set before themselves certain proper objects (*skopos*),

---

* John 15:19.
† John 17:25.
‡ John 14:17.
§ Phil. 3:20.
‖ Luke 14:33.
¶ John 14:15.
** John 15:10.
†† John 6:38.

accommodate their particular activities in accordance with these, so also, as there is one rule and standard prescribed for our works, to fulfil God's commandments in a manner pleasing to him (*eusebôs*), it is impossible for our work to be done carefully (*akribes*) unless it is performed in accordance with the will of him who has prescribed it. But in the careful (*akribês*) zeal (*spoudê*) to do our work as God wills we shall be joined to God in memory.

For just as a smith in making, say, an axe is mindful of the man who set the task and always has him in his thoughts. Just as he plans the right shape and size and directs the work according to the will of the one who ordered it – for if he forgets he will produce something other than or different from what he set out to make. So also the Christian, directing all his energies small and great to the fulfilment of God's will, at one and the same time accomplishes the work with care (*akribeia*) and preserves the intention of him who gave the order. He fulfils what was said, 'I shall keep the Lord always in my sight, because he is at my right hand I shall not be moved.'* And he performs what is commanded, 'Whether you eat or drink, or whatever you do, do all to the glory of God.'† But if anyone corrupts the exactness (*akribeia*) of the commandment in doing it, clearly his memory of God is weakened.

We ought therefore to perform every act as happening beneath the eyes of the Lord, and every thought as observed by him, remembering the voice of him who said, 'Do I not fill heaven and earth? says the Lord', and 'I am a God at hand, and not a God far off'‡ and, 'where two or three are gathered in my name, there I am in the midst of them';§ for thus enduring fear will really be present, hating iniquity, as it is written,‖ and also arrogance and pride; and love (*agapê*) will be perfected, fulfilling what was said by the Lord, 'I do not seek my own will but the will of the Father who sent me.'¶ The soul is thus convinced with certainty that good deeds are acceptable to the Judge and Umpire of our life, while their opposites receive condemnation from the same source.

I think, moreover, it must be added that the Lord's commandments

---

* Ps. 15:8.
† 1 Cor. 10:31.
‡ Jer. 23:24, 23.
§ Matt. 18:20.
‖ Ps. 118:163.
¶ John 5:30.

themselves cannot be performed with the intent of pleasing men. For no one turns to an inferior if he is convinced that a superior is present. On the contrary if it should happen that something is acceptable and pleasing to the more important person, but seems undesirable and less important to the less important, the one values the acceptance of the superior and disdains the criticism of the inferior. But if this is the case in human society, would any soul that is truly sober and sound, convinced of the presence of God, give up acting to please God and turn itself to the good opinion of men? Or will any such soul neglect God's commandments and be enslaved to human customs or ruled by common prejudice or be troubled by honours? Such was the disposition of the one who said, 'The lawless spoke idle words, but not according to your Law, O Lord.'* And again, 'And I spoke your testimonies before kings and was not ashamed.'†

Commentary

In the first Longer Rules Basil has established the importance of the command to love. He has shown that to love is both possible and natural. He now turns, after the brief interlude on fear, to the actual practice of the commandments. In particular he examines in this Rule the *internal* aspects of this praxis. This leads on to the discussion of separation and community in Longer Rules 6 and 7 and then to the concrete proposals of the second section on renunciation (Longer Rules 8–15).

Our text here raises some of the central concepts of Basil's distinctive ascetic theory: a single-minded and undistracted disposition in pursuit of the goal; an inner withdrawal from the world and from past habits; the memory of God and the thought of divine supervision. It is interesting to note that these themes are already present in Letter 2, from his first retreat in Pontus. In our text the various aspects develop naturally out of each other: we start with the observation that one can not keep the commandments if one's mind is distracted. Successfully to perform any task, one needs to know what one is aiming at and direct all efforts to that goal. In the case of the art of

---

* Ps. 118:85.
† Ps. 118:46.

being well-pleasing to God we need to withdraw from cares and disturbances and cultivate an undistracted disposition. Forgetting our former life we must cultivate the memory of God which inspires love and the practice of the commandments. The memory of God implies the recognition that he is always present and watching us, and this naturally leads us always to act in the way pleasing to him. We are here at the heart of Basil's spirituality and each of the concepts involved deserves further study.

Before doing so, however, it is worth comparing our text with its original in the second answer of the Small Asceticon, translated into Latin by Rufinus.[1] We find that, besides the addition of two Scripture quotations from John 6 and Psalm 15, two long passages have been inserted by Basil as part of his process of revision.[2] They develop themes in the original text but in doing so, as we will see, the original shape of the section is changed.

Anachôrêsis: an inner withdrawal

The first sentence looks back to the previous discussion of love and the commandments but it introduces a new perspective. We cannot keep the commandments if our minds are distracted. The rest of the Rule attempts an answer to this problem, the first element of which is ascetic effort expressed in the practice of retirement or withdrawal, in Greek *anachôrêsis*. This is an important word in monastic history. Its immediate secular roots are in the economic situation of third century Egypt. Here it meant a flight from one's public responsibilities, especially the burden of taxation, and in some cases it led to the depopulation of whole villages. It came to be applied also to a similar flight undertaken for religious reasons, when men and women went to live on the edge of inhabited areas or even in the desert proper.[3] St Antony is the classic example of a religious anchorite and even Basil himself withdrew from the world to his retreat at Annisa. In this sacred context the word came to have two aspects in the Christian vocabulary, firstly indicating a physical flight and secondly referring to an inner spiritual attitude which could exist on its own apart from the question of location.

In Letter 2, from his Pontic solitude, St Basil mentions both aspects. He writes, 'I have indeed left my life in the city' to come to 'this out of the way place', but he says that he has derived no great benefits from this physical retirement. The problem is that 'I have not yet been able to leave myself behind.' The only real escape is 'separation from the world altogether, but withdrawal (*anachôrêsis*) from the world does not mean bodily removal from it, but rather the severance of the soul from sympathy with the body.'[4] There is nothing explicitly Christian here and Rousseau speaks of the 'formal antiquity' of this letter, but we find exactly the same idea of spiritual *anachôrêsis* in this Rule. It is a retirement from the cares of the world and from former habits, although the text does also imply a physical withdrawal from 'relations according to the flesh and worldly society'. The only explicit way in which the word is used in the Rules, however, would seem to be interior withdrawal, for example in Longer Rule 7, '*anachôrêsis* from sin', and in Shorter Rule 128, 'perfect *anachôrêsis* from one's own will'. In our Rule this retirement is to be done explicitly in order to be 'well-pleasing to God according to Christ's Gospel', and this interior migration is linked with St Paul's words that, 'Our homeland is in heaven'. The practical result of this is shown by the use of the programmatic text Luke 14:33 to be not seclusion but renunciation, the subject of the second group of Longer Rules.

Undistracted exile of the mind

Basil's prime concern is thus an interior withdrawal from the world, which is understood in the Johannine sense as that which is hostile to God. The three quotations from St John in the second paragraph confirm this. This is a movement of the mind, a migration or exile. Exile from one's homeland for the sake of Christ, *xeniteia* in Greek or *peregrinatio* in Latin, was to be an important element in later Celtic and Greek spirituality, but here the exile is interior and its aim is the elimination of distractions. Here we meet the characteristic Basilian word *ameteôristos*, undistracted, which a later editor has used in the title. Most of the occurrences of this word and its associated adverb *ameteôristôs* are in sections not present in the Small Asceticon.[5]

This is true here where it occurs in the middle of the first inserted passage, which develops the theme of the danger of distraction and proposes a remedy in withdrawal from the world.

Avoidance of distraction is linked to the text from 1 Corinthians 7 on the disadvantages of the married life. It is important to notice that Basil expressly mentions that marriage is good and worthy of blessing. There was a tendency in some ascetic groups to denigrate it and this hostility could be used as an argument against the ascetic life, as in the case of the Council of Gangra. To speak of the disadvantages of marriage as opposed to the celibate life, though, does have a scriptural basis and also conforms to an ancient literary topos. Basil describes these disadvantages at length in Letter 2, ending with the words we have already quoted, 'there is but one escape from all this – separation from the world altogether'. The text of the Small Asceticon could be addressed to all Christians, married and single, but by the time that Basil added this inserted passage it looks as if he were thinking only of dedicated celibates. These would be separated from the 'world' by their celibacy, but probably also in other ways too. Between the Small Asceticon and the Great we are able to glimpse the development of separate ascetic communities and also Basil's acceptance of this development. Again, as in the case of Hellenistic language, we find a passage inserted in the later Great Asceticon which reconnects with ideas in Basil's earliest extant ascetic writing. These ideas are now more integrated with scriptural teaching, but it almost seems as if Basil had the letter in mind when adding this passage.

A clear goal (*skopos*)

The purpose of retirement from the world is an undistracted disposition (*diathesis*) which is orientated towards a clear goal (*skopos*), to live a life pleasing to God, the life of the commandments. These two Greek words are of central importance in Basil's spiritual teaching, referring as they do to internal attitude and external determinant.

Skopos is only found once in the New Testament, Philippians 3:14, but it is very common in the Asceticon, occurring more than 60 times. This is much more frequent than the usual biblical word for goal or end, *telos*. One could say that both terms describe the same reality but that *telos* describes it in itself, whereas *skopos* describes it from the perspective of the person aiming at it. Basil is here more interested in the person trying to live a Christian life than in the exploration of the theological reality at which he aims. With this concept we again find a link with John Cassian. He considered it so important that in his *Conferences*, written in the 420s, he places first the Conference on the goal or end of the monk. Here Abba Moses says, 'All the arts and disciplines have a certain *skopos* or goal and a *telos* which is the end proper to them, on which the lover of any art sets his gaze and for which he gladly endures every labour and danger and expense.'[6] From this Cassian distinguishes between the more immediate goal of purity of heart and the final end of the Kingdom of God. Again, as with fear, the Cassianic distinction is not present in Basil who uses the two terms interchangeably.

The content of this goal or aim is described by Basil in different ways, as we have seen, and later in the Rule it is identified with the will of God. Here he has inserted John 6:38 into the text, 'I have come . . . not to do my own will, but the will of him who sent me.' Apart from this positive use of this scriptural quotation, Basil elsewhere always uses it in the Asceticon to express opposition to ones's own will.[7] This is one of the two main monastic interpretations of this text,[8] the other, which he does not use, is its application to obedience to a Superior.[9] As Christ obeyed the Father, so the monk obeys his Abbot. Basil's use of this text reflects both his interest in spiritual psychology and the less exalted place of the Superior in his teaching compared with later writings. Our text, however, is not dealing with community order but with singleminded pursuit of a goal. This brings us to the second term, *diathesis*.

Dreams and *diathesis*

Disposition (*diathesis*), which is used in the first inserted passage to describe the undistracted attitude of mind of the Lord's disciples, also occurs over 60 times in the Asceticon. This shows its importance when compared with the frequency of more usual ascetic terms such as *kardia* (heart), 39 times; *pneuma* (spirit), 24 times; and *nous* (mind), 14 times. John Eudes Bamberger has done an important study of this term[10] which establishes its central place in Basil's ascetic psychology. It is a technical medical term, and Basil had an interest in medicine, possibly having studied it.[11] Longer Rule 55, the last of the series, on 'Whether the use of Medical Remedies is Consistent with the Ideal of Piety', states that the medical art is a type of the healing of the soul and medical imagery is not uncommon in Basil's answers.[12]

This does not, however, fully explain his use of this term, which is so important in his teaching. It had been used in Greek philosophy, but only in Basil does it hold this central position. It seems from the questions put to Basil that it was a word in common use among the Cappadocian and Pontine Ascetics. A whole section of the Shorter Rules, 157–186, is devoted to it and most of these are also found in the Small Asceticon. Examples of questions in this section are: 'With what kind of disposition must one serve God?', 'With what disposition ought one to receive a punishment?', 'With what disposition must one receive a garment or shoes, of any kind whatsoever?', and 'With what disposition and attention ought we to listen to what is read to us at meal times?'[13] This section and other similar Rules show a tremendous interest in interior attitudes and their development. Bamberger, himself a psychologist, defines *diathesis* as, 'a deep and stable emotional attitude',[14] but it also has a moral value, as shown in Shorter Rule 81 on evaluating sins: 'If we look at the *diathesis* of the sinner and the manner (*tropos*) of his sin, we shall know also the manner of rebuke . . .'

Basil recognises that our fundamental disposition is in part unconscious, as in Shorter Rule 301 where diseases of the soul are compared to physical diseases that the patient may not realise he has. It also affects one's dreams, as is illustrated by Shorter Rule 22 which teaches that 'disgraceful fantasies of the night' come from 'the wrong movements of the soul in the day'. If the soul is pure during the day and 'practices continually what is good and well-pleasing to God' then 'it will have dreams of a corresponding sort'. From this Bamberger concludes that, 'it follows that the dreams reflect the state of the *diathesis* ... Basil would have had very little difficulty about accepting Freud's dictum that "the dream is the royal road to the unconscious." '[15] The theme of erotic dreams and nocturnal emissions is taken up by Evagrius and, at length, by Cassian, who both accept Basil's link between dreams and experiences while awake. This idea is also found in earlier classical and Christian writers.[16] One example is found in the *de vita contemplativa* of Philo of Alexandria, where he is describing the Jewish contemplatives of Egypt called Therapeutae: 'They always retain an imperishable memory of God, so that not even in their dreams is any other object ever presented to their eyes except the beauty of the divine virtues and of the divine powers.'[17] This is especially relevant as it explicitly mentions the idea of memory of God which, as will be seen, is closely associated by Basil with *diathesis*. Gribomont notes that this passage quite probably influenced Basil in developing his spiritual doctrine.[18]

One important aspect of *diathesis* is not mentioned in our Rule, but it is developed in a number of places where Basil stresses the importance of the ascetic's appearance and behaviour. The end of Letter 2 is an example of this as is this famous passage from Longer Rule 17: 'For as firm flesh and a healthy colour characterise the athlete, so the Christian is marked out by emaciation of body and paleness, which is the bloom of self-control, showing that he is truly an athlete of Christ's commandments.' The inner *diathesis* is thus revealed by the body just as it is reflected in dreams.

A dispassionate disposition: *apatheia*

In Shorter Rule 157 Basil speaks of an unchangeable *diathesis* attained by contemplation and memory of God and which leads to love. This is very close to the concept of *apatheia* in other systems such as that of Evagrius of Pontus.[19] *Apatheia* can be understood as freedom from passion or sin, as tranquillity or integration – it is very hard to translate properly. In Longer Rule 8 Basil says that 'perfect renunciation consists in attaining freedom from desire (*aprospathês*).' Later in the Rule, however, he speaks of the necessity of freedom from all harmful passions of the soul. Basil therefore distinguishes between types of passion. There are also 'necessary passions of the flesh' shared in by Christ[20] and good passions such as that passionate desiring love we have met in Longer Rule 2. Basil's teaching gives a prominent place to these good passions whereas Evagrius stresses *apatheia*. One is reminded of the later teaching of St Maximus the Confessor: 'for the mind of the one who is continually with God, even his concupiscence abounds beyond measure into a divine desire and his entire irascible element is transformed into divine love.'[21] Basil's sister Macrina, speaking in their brother Gregory's *On the Soul and the Resurrection*,[22] also allows a positive role to the passion of desire in the spiritual life. She makes it clear, however, that there will be no passion in the perfect life after death.

Apatheia as something that humans can aspire after was taught by Clement of Alexandria. Among the Latins, on the other hand, the irascible St Jerome had a violent antipathy to the word, and Evagrius's disciple Cassian changed his terminology so that *apatheia* became 'purity of heart'.[23] Evagrius, the great teacher of *apatheia*, follows Clement, but Basil's use of the word is different. It only occurs three times in the Rules: in Longer Rule 55 and in the Prologue to the Longer Rules with the different meaning of freedom from disease,[24] and in Longer Rule 15 where the brother in charge of the boys is to punish sin and train them in *apatheia*. The last suggests the Clementine use, but in Basil's other works he follows Origen in having *apatheia* as a divine attribute.[25] The fact that the word is used by Basil less than ten times, and without a consistent meaning, suggests that, although the concept of freedom from the passions is present in Basil's thought, it is not a significant theme in his spirituality.

Returning to *diathesis*, one can note that Basil's understanding of this concept seems to have influenced Gregory of Nyssa, Diadochus of Photike, Dorotheus of Gaza and Maximus the Confessor, but Evagrius, although he knew Basil and had a fine grasp of psychology, does not take it up.[26] Our examination of the terms has hopefully shown that *diathesis* and *skopos*, unlike *apatheia*, play a central and distinctive role in Basil's spirituality. They express the essentially dynamic quality of his spiritual anthropology. The sole occurrence of *skopos* in the New Testament in Philippians 3:13–14, 'forgetting what lies behind and straining forward to what lies ahead, I press on towards the goal (*skopos*) for the prize of the upward call of God in Jesus Christ', perfectly illustrates the orientation to the future of Basil's use of *skopos* and *diathesis*. One might think that the second great theme of the Rule, the Memory of God, represents a corresponding orientation to the past, but for Basil this concept is far more powerful than mere mental archaeology.

'I remembered God and rejoiced': the memory of God

The word memory occurs four times in Longer Rule 5, each time referring to the remembrance of God. All of these are in the central section which is taken from the Small Asceticon.[27] If this had not been added to in the Great Asceticon, then a more apt title for this Rule would have been 'On the Memory of God'. As it is, the two inserted passages, on *anachôrêsis* to avoid distraction and on divine supervision, are just developments of themes tributary to that of memory of God. This concept is thus central to the Rule in more than just the spatial sense.

The purpose of avoiding distraction is that we may 'bear about the holy thought of God with continual and pure memory imprinted on our souls like an indelible seal'.[28] For Basil this memory is not a mere storehouse of recollection, nor is it concerned with a theory of knowledge as in Plato. More psychological than metaphysical, it is none the less a faculty of great power and is the means of gaining love towards God, the very apex of Basil's spirituality. Memory of God's wonders leads to love, which leads to the practice of the commandments, which in turn preserves the memory and love. The themes of the earlier Rules converge in the Christian's memory, indeed the second Longer Rule in speaking of love teaches that we should cling to the memory of God as a child does to its mother.

Memory can have a more normal meaning for Basil, as in in Shorter Rule 17 where the memory is said to recall the thought of food before hunger requires it. The specialised meaning that it has in our Rule is well expressed in Shorter Rule 157 (R 14):

With what kind of disposition must one serve God?

Basil answers by saying:

> I consider a good disposition to be a desire of pleasing God that is vehement, insatiable, firmly fixed and unchangeable. It is attained by wise and continuous contemplation of the majesty of the glories of God, by good thoughts, and by ceaseless remembrance of the blessings that have come to us from God.

Memory here builds up the *diathesis* and Bamberger's study of the relation between the two terms concludes that there is such an overlap between them that they are, in modern terms, 'the dynamic unconscious seen from different aspects'.[29] This identity would seem to be reflected in the section above where Basil speaks of a smith making an axe. His disposition is always towards the will of the man who ordered it and this is always held in his memory. If he forgets, then he fails. The same is true for the Christian seeking to do the will of God. Here another typically Basilian word comes into focus, *akribeia* – exactness or strictness. Twice he notes that careful and exact practice of the commandments is linked to the inner practice of the memory of God.

The memory of God in liturgy and contemplation

The expression 'memory of God' (*mnêmê tou theou*) is not in the Bible, although Psalm 76:4 is close, 'I remembered God and I rejoiced.'[30] It is however a very biblical activity, *anamnêsis* (an active calling to mind), which is also of the essence of Liturgy. The Liturgy of St Basil, as we have seen, is a great example of this recalling of salvation history, and Basil speaks here, as elsewhere, of the 'memory of his wonders', God's saving acts. We have already noticed that this memory is a powerful 'making present' of that which is recalled, causing an indwelling of God in the soul. After the Institution Narrative, Jesus' words at the Last Supper, in the Eucharistic Prayer there is a section called the Anamnesis. In the Anaphora of St Basil it is as follows:

> Therefore we also remember (*memnêmenoi*), O Master, his

saving sufferings, the life-giving cross, the three days burial, the resurrection from the dead, the ascension into heaven, the sitting at your right hand O God and Father, and his glorious and fearful second coming.

What is significant here is that we 'remember' the second coming.[31] If this expression was current in Basil's day, and this would seem to be so as it is in the Egyptian version of the Anaphora, it helps us see that his concept of memory is more than just a recalling of the past, even to make it active in the present. In addition to this recollection, and in Longer Rule 2 we have seen an impressive example of the remembrance of God's past benefits, there is a sense that memory is also a holding in mind, an indwelling, an active presence of God. Rousseau speaks of a 'pathway, an axis of discipline, which runs from the recollection of God's goodness... to the experience of God's presence'.[32] This experience purifies one's *diathesis* and thus the memory of God is so powerful that it overcomes sin and bad habits and changes one's character.

When Basil speaks of continual and pure memory one is reminded of the command to 'pray without ceasing' (1 Thess. 5:17, Eph. 6:18) which has always exercised such an appeal to Christian ascetics. In Shorter Rule 157 the memory of God's blessings is put in parallel with contemplation, and in Letter 2 Basil explicitly links memory of God and prayer:

> Prayer is to be commended, for it engenders in the soul a distinct conception of God. And the indwelling of God is this – to have God set firm within oneself through the process of memory. We thus become a temple of God whenever earthly cares cease to interrupt the continuity of our memory of him.

The memory of God thus involves a real presence of him in the soul. It is more than just a recollection of the past. In this we again find continuity between this early Letter and the Rules. For Basil, then, the memory of God is a form of prayer or contemplation.[33] In Letter 2 the memory of God, a concept which may have its own roots in Platonism, coexists with more explicitly Platonic terminology such as, 'the mind . . . withdraws within itself, and of its own accord ascends to the contemplation of God.' Rousseau rightly recognises that in the Letter Basil has not yet fully integrated classical philosophical aspirations with Christianity.[34] When the two are most closely integrated in the Rules, it is however a true integration, not a triumph of Christianity over Hellenism. It is interesting to note that Basil does not develop an intellectualist idea of prayer centred on the mind (*nous*) as his brother Gregory and his disciple Evagrius were to do. In developing the idea of memory of God, Basil is cutting a path close to Scripture and Christian tradition. Gribomont suggests that this may be a result of Basil's frequent fraternal contact with ascetics of limited culture, although the same was surely true of Evagrius in the Egyptian desert.[35] Perhaps Basil had more pastoral sympathy with the poor in Christ?

Good and bad forgetting

The other side of memory is forgetfulness (*lêthê*). As there is a bad memory of one's former life, mentioned in Shorter Rule 10, so also there is a bad forgetfulness of our Benefactor and his judgements which leads one away from 'the precious memory of God' and is described as the greatest and most deadly evil.[36] This is concisely expressed in Shorter Rule 294:

> For what reason does one lose the continuous memory of God?
> By becoming forgetful of God's benefits and insensitive towards one's Benefactor.

The memory of God necessarily involves also a positive forgetfulness of one's own past life. This process is linked to the theme of *anachôrêsis*, 'complete withdrawal from and forgetfulness of former habits'. This recalls the passage in Letter 2 on the ascent of the mind to God where the mind, illuminated by God's glory, is said to become forgetful even of its own nature. The Rules transpose this concept from the ontological to the moral plane, but the moral meaning is also present earlier in the Letter when Basil speaks of an unlearning (*apomathêsis*) of teachings derived from evil habits. In Longer Rule

13, 'That the practise of silence is beneficial for novices', silence is said to induce forgetfulness (*lêthê*) of the past and former habits so that one can learn the habits of piety. Sleep on the other hand, or at least 'untimely and immoderate sleep', is a sign of a weakness in the memory of God and the remedy is the resumption of such thoughts and desires.[37] The theme of memory of God/forgetfulness of past habits is thus very important in Basil's spiritual teaching and Longer Rule 5 is a privileged locus of its expression. Whence did Basil derive this idea and how exclusively Basilian is it?

Memory of God: an Egyptian inheritance?

We have already noted the biblical and liturgical roots of Basil's teaching on the memory of God. This fits well with what we know of his interests. Gribomont notes that while the term (*mnêmê tou theou*) occurs a few times in earlier writers such as Philo,[38] Clement of Alexandria and Origen, the developed concept, especially as linked with prayer, seems proper to Basil himself.[39] This would certainly appear to be true regarding what Bamberger calls 'this system of dynamic psychology' based on *mnêmê/diathesis*, but the idea of memory of God as an ascetic practice appears in accounts of the teaching of fourth-century Egyptian Monastic Fathers without any indication that it is at all unusual. The *Life of Pachomius* says that, 'He (Pachomius) taught them to repel (temptations) by the remembrance of God (*mnêmê tou theou*).'[40] There is also this saying of Abba Macarius the Great in the *Apophthegmata*, 'If we keep remembering the wrongs that men have done us, we destroy the power of the memory of God (*mnêmê tou theou*). But if we remember the evil deeds of the demons we shall be invulnerable.'[41] Together with the Alexandrian provenance of the pre-Basilian sources using the term, these quotations suggest that the theory and practice of 'memory of God' was a part of the general inheritance of Egyptian monastic wisdom. Modern scholarship repudiates the thought that Basil was dependant on the ascetics of Egypt, especially the Pachomians, an idea popular with earlier scholars such as W. K. L. Clarke.[42] This would argue against a direct dependence but, while we have seen the profundity of Basil's development of the concept, one should beware of attributing to him too unique a role in its genesis.

Divine supervision

The final major spiritual theme in this Rule occurs in the second and last inserted passage. The idea of divine observation follows on naturally from that of the memory of God, it is implied in the example of the smith making the axe which is in the text of the Small Asceticon. We hold the Lord in our mind, just as he is holding us in his. Basil uses three scriptural texts to reinforce this idea, which is not uncommon in the Rules.[43] As well as establishing the true environment for religious action, which is developed in the last paragraph, this awareness of observation also becomes a source of that action.[44] The thought of divine supervision is effective against wandering thoughts at prayer, against anger or the vice of men-pleasing, indeed everything should be done 'as if God were beholding'.[45] Shorter Rule 306 shows all the Persons of the Holy Trinity and also the angels observing us and it uses David the psalmist as a literary icon of the true attitude of the Christian in this regard. David also occurs at the end of our Rule when the words of Psalm 118 are used to illustrate the disposition of the one indifferent to human customs or common prejudice.

Basil's spirituality is eminently practical and most of the Rules are answers to practical problems. In Shorter Rule 196 (R 57) we see most of the spiritual themes discussed here brought to bear on a specific problem:

> How does one eat and drink to the glory of God?*

Basil answers:

> By the memory (*mnêmê*) of one's Benefactor, and by having such a disposition (*diathesis*) of the soul, attested by the appearance of the body, that one does not eat thoughtlessly but as one watched by God; and by the aim (*skopos*) of eating not as a slave of the

---

* cf. 1 Cor. 10:31.

belly through pleasure, but as God's workman, in order to persevere in the works demanded by the commandment of Christ.

NOTES

1. *Basili Regula* 2:74–93.
2. The passages not in Rufinus are from 'nor even to master one', line 5, to 'it is fitting for us', line 33, and the last two paragraphs beginning 'We ought therefore to perform . . .'
3. A good brief treatment of Egyptian *anachôrêsis* is found in Burton-Christie, *The Word in the Desert*, pp. 40–2, 54–6. Historians disagree over the sacred and profane motivations for religious *anachôrêsis*.
4. The same is taught by Evagrius in *Praktikos* 52, 'To separate the body from the soul is the privilege only of the One who has joined them together. But to separate the soul from the body lies as well in the power of the man who pursues virtue. For the fathers gave to the meditation of death and to the flight from the body a special name: *anachôrêsis*.'
5. LRs 5, 6, 13 and SRs 141, 230, 306 (twice). It is translated by *non vagari* and *intentus* in the Small Asceticon's equivalents to SRs 197 (R 58), 201 (R 108, thrice) and 202 (R 109).
6. *Conferences* 1:2:1.
7. SRs 1, 60, 74, 137. In *Moralia* 70:11, although he is speaking of those 'set over the Word', he would seem to be using it in the same sense.
8. This interpretation is also found in *Barsanuphius and John*, Answers 150, 239, 288, and in the *Rule of St Benedict* 7:32. It may be that Basil was the source of this use? According to Regnault's scriptural index this passage is not used in any of the *Apophthegmata Patrum*.
9. Found for example in the *Bohairic Life of St Pachomius* 64 (also in the *First Greek Life*), Cassian's *Conferences* 19:6:6, 24:20:14, *Barsanuphius and John* Answer 356, and the *Rule of St Benedict* 5:13.
10. 'MNÊMÊ-DIATHESIS: The Psychic Dynamisms in the Ascetical Theology of St Basil' (see Bibliography).
11. Rousseau, *Basil*, p. 220.
12. For example: LRs 28, 43, 46, 51, 52.
13. SR 157 (R 14), SR 158 (R 24), SR 168 (R 45), SR 180 (not in R).
14. op. cit. p. 241.
15. op. cit. p. 243.
16. For Evagrius see, for example, *Praktikos* 55. For Cassian and the background to the question see Stewart, *Cassian the Monk*, pp 81–3, especially n185, and also Kardong, *Cassian on Chastity*.
17. *De vita contemplativa* 26, tr C. D. Yonge.
18. 'La prière selon Saint Basile', p. 442 n37.
19. In *Praktikos* 64 Evagrius teaches that tranquillity in the face of dream-images is

a proof of *apatheia*. On *apatheia* see: Špidlik, *The Spirituality of the Christian East*, pp. 270–7; Pierre Miquel, *Lexique du Désert*, pp. 113–34; Stewart, *Cassian the Monk*, pp. 42–5; *Évagre le Pontique: Traité pratique ou le moine*, SC 170, Introduction pp. 98–112.

20. LR 17.

21. *Centuries on Charity* 2:48 (in Berthold [1985] *Maximus*). See also 3:67 which speaks of the need for the 'blessed passion of holy love'.

22. See especially Chs. 3 and 6.

23. Jerome, *Letter* 133:1, 3, cf. also Augustine, *City of God*, 9:5, 14:9.

24. cf. also Letter 265 where, attacking Apollinarius of Laodicea, he says 'he proclaims . . . cleansing of leprosy after we have had the *apatheia* of the resurrection'.

25. *On the Holy Spirit* 8:18; twice in *Against Eunomius* 2:23 (*PG* 29:621); and also in relation to the generation of the Divine Word in the Homily '*In the Beginning was the Word*' 3, 4 (*PG* 31:480). With Letter 265 and the three occurrences in the Asceticon this makes, as far as I can discover, eight uses of *apatheia* in the genuine works of St Basil. It is found 3 times in the *First Ascetic Discourse* (*CPG* 2891) where fallen man is said to regain the lost image of God by imitating the divine *apatheia*. This work is, however, probably not by Basil, see Clarke (1925) p. 11 and Gribomont, *Histoire du texte*, p. 313.

26. Bamberger, op. cit. pp. 250–1.

27. *Basili Regula* 2:74–93.

28. This is the exact opposite of the teaching of Evagrius in *Chapters on Prayer* 66: 'When you are praying do not fancy the Divinity like some image formed within yourself. Avoid also allowing your spirit to be impressed with the seal of some particular shape, but rather, free from all matter, draw near the immaterial Being and you will attain to understanding.'

29. op. cit. p. 246.

30. LXX, modern versions from the Hebrew have ' . . . and I groaned'.

31. The same idea is present in the Liturgy of St John Chrysostom, although the word 'fearful' is left out. In the modern Roman Catholic Eucharistic Prayer 4, inspired by the Anaphora of St Basil, this remembering of an event in the future is obviously seen as problematic, and we remember Christ's death but *wait for* (*expectantes*) his coming in glory.

32. Rousseau, *Basil*, p. 225.

33. cf. article 'Contemplation chez les orientaux chrétiens: le souvenir de Dieu', *DSp* 2:1858; and Gribomont, 'La prière selon saint Basile', pp. 434–7.

34. Rousseau, *Basil*, p. 79.

35. 'La prière . . .' p. 435. See also the seventh saying of Evagrius in the Alphabetical collection of Apophthegmata.

36. Longer Rule 6, cf. LR 2.

37. R 55 (SR 32). *Memoria dei* is only mentioned in Rufinus' text, the Great Asceticon has 'thoughts (*ennoias*) of God'.

38. 5 times, a significant passage has already been quoted.

39. Gribomont, 'La prière . . .' p. 48 n74.

40. *First Greek Life of Pachomius* 83.

41. *Alphabetical Collection*, tr. Ward; Macarius 36. *PG* 65:277D.
42. See for example Rousseau, *Basil*, p. 73 n53.
43. e.g. LR 41, SRs 21 (R 34), 29 (R 46), 34 (R 60), 127 (R 79), 201 (R 108), 306.
44. Rousseau, *Basil*, p. 226.
45. LR 41.

Chapter Ten

'Come out from among them and be separate'

LONGER RULE 6
THE NECESSITY OF RETIREMENT (idiazô)

A retired habitation (*to idiazein kata tên oikêsin*) is a help to the soul in avoiding distraction (*ameteôriston*). For to have one's life always mixed up with those who are fearlessly and scornfully disposed towards the exact (*akribês*) observance of the commandments is shown to be harmful by the words of Solomon who teaches us, 'Do not make friends with an angry man, nor be a companion of a wrathful man; lest you learn his ways and entangle yourself in a snare.'* And, 'Come out from among them and be separate, says the Lord'† points in the same direction.

Accordingly, that we may not through eyes or ears receive incitements to sin and imperceptively become accustomed to it; that the impression and forms of things seen or heard may not dwell in the soul causing destruction and loss; and in order that we may be able to continue in prayer, our first step is to seek to live apart (*aphidiazô*). For thus we should overcome previously formed habits, in which we lived alienated from the commandments of Christ – this means no small struggle, to overcome one's usual mode of life, for habit strengthened by lapse of time gains the strength of nature (*physis*). We shall be able to rub out the stains of sin by toiling in prayer and persistent meditation on the will of God. It is impossible to attain to this meditation and prayer in a crowd (*en pollois*) which distracts the soul and introduces worldly cares. Whoever in a crowd could fulfil this, 'If anyone would come

---

* Prov. 22:24–5.
† 2 Cor. 6:17, cf. Isa. 52:11.

after me, let him deny himself'?* For we must deny ourselves and take up the cross of Christ and thus follow him. But to deny oneself means complete forgetfulness (*lêthê*) of the past and retirement (*anachôrêsis*) from one's own will, in which it is very hard, almost impossible, to succeed if one is living with unrestricted communication. Indeed mixing in such a life impedes even the taking of one's cross and following Christ. For being ready to die on Christ's behalf, to put to death what is earthly in you,† and to stand in the battle-line meeting every danger that comes upon us for the name of Christ, and not to be moved by the passions (*aprospathôs*) of this present life – this is to take up one's cross. We see that the obstacles put in the way of this by the communications of the common life (*koinos bios*) are great.

In addition to all the many other things, the soul, looking at the crowd of offenders, in the first place has no opportunity to become aware of its own sins and to become contrite by repentance of its misdeeds, but by comparison with worse people acquires pretensions to virtue. Secondly, led away from the precious memory of God by the tumults and distractions which common life (*koinos bios*) produces, it is not only deprived of exultation and joy in God, and of delighting in the Lord, and tasting the sweetness of his words, so as to say, 'I remembered God and rejoiced'‡ and, 'How sweet are your words to my throat, sweeter than honey to my mouth.'§ It also grows accustomed to complete contempt and forgetfulness (*lêthê*) of his judgements, than which it could suffer no greater or more deadly evil.

Commentary

In this Rule we have reached the last section of Basil's second answer in the Small Asceticon.[1] In our text 'a retired habitation' is said to be useful in avoiding distraction, whereas the earlier version says that it helps 'to preserve the memory of God'. Both of these reasons connect closely with what has already been discussed in the previous Rule. This text could, however, be associated with Longer Rule 7, the third answer in the *Regula Basili*, because together they answer one question and thus conclude the first section of the Longer Rules. The

---

* Matt. 16:24, Luke 9:23.
† Col. 3:5.
‡ Ps. 76:4.
§ Ps. 118:103.

previous Rule has dealt with our interior response to the commandment of love and now we turn to the first stage of our exterior
action: we must separate ourselves from the ungodly and live apart
(*aphidiazô*). The purpose of this is to love God without distraction.
This is not explicitly stated but it is implied in all the reasons given.
Rule 7 follows this by asking if this withdrawal should be to solitude
or to a community of the godly. For many reasons but especially, as
we shall see, for love of neighbour, the latter option is chosen. The
question is, therefore: what practical way of life is appropriate for
those who wish to obey the double commandment of love introduced
in the first Rule? The answer is given in these two Rules, the unity
of which thus becomes clear: we go apart from the crowd to love
God, but live in community to love our neighbour.

Separation from the ungodly

The subject of this Rule is anticipated in the first inserted section of
Longer Rule 5. In dealing with the interior withdrawal (*anachôrêsis*)
from distractions and former habits and in advocating a mental
migration to heaven, it begs the question: would this not be greatly
helped by an exterior retirement? This is suggested there by the
mention of exile from relatives and worldly society, but only in our
text is it fully developed. The first thing to note is that it is a
separation from the ungodly, 'the crowd of offenders' and 'those who
are fearlessly and scornfully disposed towards the exact observance
of the commandments'. To modern Christians who are concerned to
be in the world and working alongside unbelievers, this call to 'come
out from among them and be separate' seems alien to the Gospel.
As we have already seen with regard to the motivation for charitable
work, those influenced by liberal and secularising trends in Christian
thought can have great trouble understanding Basil's teaching. Its
roots are in a different aspect of the Gospel, for example the Johannine texts we have already noted or this section of 2 Corinthians, just
before the verse quoted by St Basil: 'Do not be mismated with
unbelievers. For what partnership have righteousness and iniquity?
Or what fellowship has light and darkness? . . . Or what has a believer

in common with an unbeliever?'[2] One needs to read Basil in his own context and in relation to his own way of reading his sources. This may even help us gain a more balanced reading of these same scriptural sources.

Can you be a Christian in the crowd?

The distinction between the crowd and those for whom Basil is writing is based on the commandments. It is not founded on the observance of counsels such as chastity, poverty and obedience. The commandments are addressed to all Christians and this raises the question of whether he saw the ascetics as the only true Christians? If so then the crowd would include, as well as non-Christians, the majority of negligent Christians caught up in worldly activity. This would seem to be true from the Preface to the Longer Rules where he speaks of 'the multitude of Christians who do not keep all the commandments'. Shorter Rule 263 teaches that it is impossible to please God, 'under conditions which distract the soul', and in our Rule Basil says that it is impossible to attain undistracted prayer in the crowd. The multitude of Christians therefore do not please God. One could answer that interior *anachôrêsis* is enough, but the thrust of our Rule is that this practice demands physical retirement. On the other hand, despite the later title of our Rule speaking of necessity, the first sentence states that physical retirement is only *helpful*[3] in avoiding distraction. Basil also says that following the command to deny oneself while in 'undistracted communication' is *almost* impossible. The standard set is high, undistractedly keeping all the commandments, and he is concerned with the best conditions for its observance. But in his carefully constructed opening sentence he does allow for a true Christian life apart from communities separated from the world.[4] This is illustrated at the end of a public sermon 'Against Drunkards' where he advocates interior withdrawal and uses the same quotation from 2 Corinthians 6:17.[5] Gregory Nazianzen in his *Oration 40* 'On Holy Baptism' invites his Constantinopolitan congregation to withdraw physically from city life, 'flee . . . even from the forum'[6] but he also allows the possibility of interiorising the practice of flight by those who are tied to public life. For Basil it is also not clear what degree of separation is envisaged. The Great Asceticon presumes separate communities of ascetics, and these certainly existed in Anatolia throughout Basil's active life. On the other hand, he could be recommending the life of devout households 'in the world but not of it', similar to the lifestyle of modern Orthodox Jews.

The separation advocated here forms yet another link with the teaching of Letter 2. Although he says there that the withdrawal is primarily internal, he was writing from his retreat by the River Iris and presupposes physical separation. He says that solitude (*erêmia*) calms the passions and gives reason leisure to sever them completely from the soul, 'therefore let the place of withdrawal be such as ours, so separated from human society that the continuity of our ascesis may not be interrupted by any external distraction'.

Basil's constant advocacy of physical separation from the early Letter 2 through the Small Asceticon to the Great, although in fact he always seems to have had companions, warns us to be cautious in stating baldly that he moved from dealing with all Christians to legislating for separate ascetic communities. Ascetic communities were in existence in Asia Minor before Basil came on the scene, and in Part One we have noted the variety of forms of ascetic life in the region. The original context of the Small Asceticon is almost certainly groups of the disciples of Eustathius.[7] There is certainly a greater interest in institutions and the mechanics of community in the later Rules, but the impulse to separation is not absent from the Small Asceticon. Although the text of this Rule has been modified in a number of ways, the Great Asceticon has significantly left its content substantially unaltered. There are only three short inserted passages,[8] in one of which, on not being moved by the passions of this life, we seem again to be returning to the language of Letter 2.

Why go apart?

Most of this Rule is taken up with motivations for separation from the crowd. Two main groups of reasons emerge: the fostering of that inner activity recommended in Longer Rule 5, and the avoidance and defeat of sin. The latter also raises the question of our sharing in the effects of Adam's original sin. Separation from the ungodly enables one to be undistracted and practise the memory of God, which is again associated with prayer. Prayer is here seen as a work, 'toiling in prayer and persistent meditation on the will of God' and, as we noted when discussing *diathesis*, it should be a constant state: 'to continue in prayer'. To live in the crowd is bad because 'the impressions and forms of things seen and heard' can cause destruction and loss by entering into the mind that should be concerned with God.

Basil, as noted above, draws a defining line along the edge of the commandments: the crowd are those who scorn them and such people are described as offenders. One can not positively attain the state of prayer among the many, but on the contrary one is kept down in their state of sin and forgets the judgements of God. A black picture is painted of becoming accustomed to sin and not being aware of one's transgressions, and even of believing oneself virtuous in comparison with the prevalent iniquity. It is not, however, the fact of separation from this environment that overcomes sin and previously formed habits, but rather the space that it gives for spiritual struggle, prayer and ascesis. This is the other side of Basil's positive view of nature. In the current human condition the habit of sin and distraction 'gain the strength of nature' and so our natural desire for God is trapped under this other, anti-nature.

Excursus: Basil and original sin

We seem to pass here into the territory of what is usually called original or ancestral sin, how the original fault of Adam and Eve affects and is transmitted to their descendants. Basil shows that sin is the result of living among the many, the ungodly crowd. If we put this together with his positive anthropology, it could suggest that the human tendency to sin is a result of one's environment and not of an inherited inner corruption in human nature.

It is worth looking at his other writings to see how he deals with this question elsewhere. This is an area where there are major differences between the Latin West and the Greek East. The dominant Augustinian tradition in the West is based on writings of the great doctor of Hippo which were produced in the heat of the Pelagian controversy, especially his interpretation of certain texts of St Paul. Augustine teaches that we each inherit from our first parents a wounded nature deprived of original holiness and justice, and an inherited guilt which excludes us from the Kingdom of Heaven. In this tradition the Council of Trent in 1546 defined that original sin was transmitted 'by propagation, not by imitation', and, following Augustine, used the fact that babies are baptised as a proof that we are in this state of sin from the beginning.[9]

The two Gregories on the other hand, Basil's friend and his brother, teach that the natural state of newly born babies is without sin. The Cappadocian Fathers in general seem not to have held that our soul is in the strict sense polluted by Adam's sin, although we will qualify this opinion later.[10] They almost always use the word 'sin' solely for what Western theologians call actual sin,[11] which fits well with Basil's strong emphasis on the human will as the cause of sinful thoughts and actions. Basil says in his second Homily on the Hexameron, 'Do not then look round for evil beyond yourself, neither imagine that there is an original nature of wickedness, but let each acknowledge himself as the author of his own evil.'[12]

Basil certainly believed in an original Fall which had disastrous effects on humanity, as described in the Book of Genesis. Does this Rule and the Homily just quoted mean that he thought its effect was solely external and environmental? It would appear not. Ascetic effort is required, not just withdrawal, in order to 'rub out the stains of sin'. This is, however, not decisive for our question as it could refer just to the removal of the effects of living in the crowd, where evil habits gain the strength of nature, and not to an inherent interior contamination. In his *Homily preached in a time of drought and famine*, though, Basil suggests a certain participation of all human beings in the sin of Adam:

Give a little and you will gain a lot. Undo the first (*prôtotupos*) sin by sharing food. Just as Adam by evil eating passed on (*parapempô*) sin, so we can wipe out this harmful eating if we relieve the hunger and need of our brother.[13]

This is confirmed by his Letter 261 to the people at Sozopolis who were troubled by Docetists, those who denied that Christ had come in the flesh and taught that he had assumed a phantom or ethereal body. To counter their doctrine Basil insisted that Christ shared the same human nature as Adam, and while teaching this he states that we inherit the effects of Adam's sin:

> If the flesh which was ruled over by death was not that which was assumed by the Lord ... we who had died in Adam would not have been made alive in Christ (1 Cor. 15:22); that which had fallen in pieces would not have been put together again, that which had been shattered would not have been set up again, that which by the serpent's deceit had been estranged from God would never have been made once more his own.

And,

> Just as death which is in the flesh, transmitted (*parapempô*) to us through Adam, was swallowed up by the divine nature, so was the sin taken away by the righteousness which is in Jesus Christ, so that in the resurrection we receive back the flesh neither liable to death nor subject to sin (cf. Rom. 5:12, 17).[14]

It is clear that death, as the effect of Adam's sin, was passed on to us (*parapempô*). In this passage from his *On the Holy Spirit* we find the same idea but with a stress on our solidarity in Adam. Basil is discussing Old Testament typology:

> Adam was a type of him who was to come (Rom. 5:14) ... The blood of the lamb is a type of the blood of Christ, and the firstborn is a type of the first-formed man (cf. Exod. 12). Since the first-formed man necessarily exists in each of us and will continue to be transmitted (*parapempô*) among us until the end, it is said that in Adam we all die (1 Cor. 15:22) and that death reigned ... until the coming of Christ.[15]

This time it is Adam himself who is transmitted in us, but the extract from the Homily above uses the same verb for the passing on of sin. The word there could mean that Adam 'let in' sin, but its use in the other two documents suggests that Basil did use it in the sense of 'pass on' or 'transmit'. We are thus all united in Adam and inherit physical consequences of the Fall, primarily death,[16] and also moral consequences indicated when he says we have 'fallen in pieces . . . been shattered'. These latter could include distraction, an inner dividedness and a weakness of the will which hinder the development of a right *diathesis* and the memory of God. This causes a tendency to sin, what the West calls concupiscence, but the Homily also suggests that Adam's *sin* itself is transmitted to us, and the Letter, with its dependence on Romans, speaks of us being alienated from God.

There is a suggestion here of an inherited 'original sin' similar to that which Augustine develops at such great length. This is often thought to be absent from the Greek Fathers[17] but Kallistos Ware has shown that 'the notion of an inherited sinfulness can be found, at any rate in a rudimentary form' in Greek Fathers such as Gregory of Nyssa and Mark the Monk.[18] It may be that when Basil speaks of sin being transmitted he is using the word sin in a different way to when he speaks of actual sin, here referring solely to the effects of the sin of our first parents and without invoking any guilt, blame or punishment for us.[19] To say this, however, would be to go beyond the evidence just as much as if we followed the eighteenth century Benedictine Editors of Basil in saying that his doctrine on this subject is the same as that of Augustine.[20] There is no evidence that Basil could conceive of a sin to which no blame was attached, although one can not categorically reject this possibility. The extracts do, however, show that he saw the effects of ancestral sin to be more than either environmental influence, situated in the ungodly crowd which we imitate in sin, or mere human mortality. There is a rudimentary notion that we inherit within ourselves the effects of Adam's sin and also in some way the sin itself,[21] although to speak of this as an inherited guilt in the Augustinian sense is to go too far. The inheritance of ancestral sin is, however, not as central to Basil's anthropology as it is to that of Augustine. Basil places the emphasis far more on the solidarity of Christians in Christ, as is shown by his use of the Pauline image of the body and in his advocacy of godly community, than on the solidarity of all humanity in Adam, although we have seen that he does allude to this.[22] We have inherited from Adam's sin moral imperfections in our, naturally good, nature, which impede us in our attempt to please God by obeying the commandments. We therefore need to toil in prayer and asceticism, and we need a suitable environment in which to do so.

The whole picture of Basil's spirituality is not, however, contained in sin, toil and ascesis. At the end of our Rule he notes how the tumult of the common life draws one away from the memory of God which is described in terms of sweetness, joy and exaltation. In the Great Asceticon he adds the quotation from Psalm 76 to emphasise this. We are left with the image of a withdrawal which leads to joy and happiness in the Lord.

Following Christ

We have looked at the two clusters of reasons for withdrawal, and the second of these has led us to examine in some detail Basil's views on the effects of Adam's original sin. There is also a third reason for retirement: the following of Christ. This may again seem strange to modern Christians as Jesus spent most of his life in the crowd living the common life. The key to understanding Basil's teaching here is the text, 'If any one would come after me, let him deny himself and take up his cross and follow me',[23] which is alluded to in the Small Asceticon and quoted in part in the Great Asceticon. This is the defining text of Longer Rule 8 where it is explored at length, but here the stress is on denying oneself which is interpreted as 'forgetfulness of the past and *anachôrêsis* from one's own will'. Following Christ is described in terms of a spiritual combat which is to take up one's cross. Again Basil notes that this is impeded by the 'common life', which in our text replaces this more descriptive phrase in the Small Asceticon: 'those who are unlike us either in life or in character'. The separation which Basil advocates is thus not in the cause of un-distracted Platonic contemplation but is a response to a basic commandment of Christ. Whether or not this is a valid interpretation of the Gospel – and the facts of Christian tradition would seem to say that it is – it is clear that this call to physical separation is rooted by Basil in the scriptural commandments.

In the next Rule we see that this flight from the common life (*koinos bios*) is not a rejection of community life (*koinônia*).

NOTES

1. *Basili Regula* 2:94–112.
2. 2 Cor. 6:14–15. Many scholars believe that 6:14–7:1 is a later insertion into the text of 2 Cor., but it is still regarded by Christians as inspired Scripture.
3. *Sunteleô* with the dative; *prodest* in Rufinus.
4. cf. Gribomont, *É&É*, p. 37.
5. Homily 324, *PG* 31:443–64.
6. *Oration 40* 19.
7. Gribomont, *É&É*, p. 334.
8. a) From 'We shall be able to rub out . . .' to the quotation from Luke 9: b) 'And not to be moved by the passions of this life': c) the quotation from Ps. 76.
9. The Nicene–Constantinopolitan creed states, 'We acknowledge one baptism for the forgiveness of sins.' On Augustine see: Gerald Bonner *St Augustine of Hippo: Life and Controversies*, pp. 370–82. The Tridentine Decree on Original Sin is in *Decrees of the Ecumenical Councils*, ed. Tanner, vol. 2, pp. 665–7. The question of the development of the doctrine of original sin by Catholics and Protestants is interesting but not relevant here.
10. Gregory of Nyssa, *On Infants who Die Prematurely*, and Gregory Nazianzen, *Oration 40* 23. Both quoted in 'Péché Originel: Les Cappadociens', *DTC* XIIA:348.
11. The free decision of the human person against the will of God.
12. *PG* 29:37D–40A.
13. Homily 325, *PG* 31:324C.
14. Letter 261, tr. Jackson.
15. *On the Holy Spirit* 14:32 (tr. Anderson), *PG* 32:121C–124A.
16. In LR 55 he mentions agriculture and disease as effects of the Fall and then refers to death saying that we are 'condemned to destruction because of sin'.
17. 'There is indeed a consensus in Greek Patristic and Byzantine traditions in identifying the inheritance of the Fall as an inheritance essentially of mortality rather than of sinfulness, sinfulness being merely a consequence of mortality.' John Meyendorff, *Byzantine Theology*, p. 145.
18. Kallistos Ware, *How are we Saved: The Understanding of Salvation in the Orthodox Tradition* (1996), pp. 14–28. He quotes Gregory's fifth Homily *On the Lord's Prayer* where, in commenting on 'forgive us our debts' he says, 'we share in Adam's nature and therefore share also in his Fall', and we also share in his penitence.

He comments, 'the fact that we are called also to share in his penitence must signify that we share likewise in his sinfulness and guilt', p. 21.

19. This use of the Greek Fathers is noted by Jean-Claude Larchet when discussing the same subject in St Maximus the Confessor. 'This use of the word "sin" to designate the effects of ancestral sin, without any connotation of responsibility and guilt, takes place in other Greek Fathers too, and is obviously a source of confusion when its meaning is not precisely given', *Sobornost* 20:1, p. 47 n84.

20. Basil's view on original sin is briefly discussed in a Preface to the Benedictine edition of his works, reprinted in *PG* 32:60–61, which seeks to show his conformity to the Augustinian view.

21. It is worth noting here that while the Catholic Church teaches that original sin is 'proper to each individual' through the transmission of human *nature*, it 'does not have the character of a *personal* fault in any of Adam's descendants'. It is thus 'called sin only in an analogical sense'. *Catechism of the Catholic Church*, 404, 405.

22. The two scriptural passages which teach a solidarity in Adam put right through solidarity in Christ the new Adam, 1 Cor. 15:22 and Rom. 5:12–21, are not quoted in the Asceticon. In the Letters, apart from Letter 261, we find an allusion to Rom. 5:14 in the *Letter of Consolation to the Widow of Arinthaeus*, 269. The same text is quoted in *Homily 354 on Psalm 48* (*PG* 29:452C). The only other relevant texts that I could find among the genuine works were *Homily 342 on the Trinity* which states that the Incarnation happened on account of the fallen man (*ekpeson anthrôpon*) Adam (*PG* 31:1493C) and *Homily 321 On the Holy Generation of Christ*, preached on the feast of the Theophany, which declares that 'today the judgement against Adam is set aside' (*PG* 31:1473A).

23. Matt. 16:24, Luke 9:23 adds 'take up his cross *daily*'.

Chapter Eleven

'Whose feet will you wash?': Solitude or Community?

LONGER RULE 7

THAT IT IS NECESSARY, FOR THE END (*skopos*) OF PLEASING GOD, TO
LIVE WITH LIKE-MINDED PERSONS, AND THAT SOLITUDE (*monazô*) IS
DIFFICULT AND DANGEROUS.

*Since your words have convinced us that a life lived with those who are con-
temptuous of the commandments of the Lord is dangerous, we want to learn
next whether the one who has withdrawn* (anachôreô) *from these should live
privately* (idiazô) *by himself, or live together with like-minded brothers who have
chosen the same aim* (skopos) *of piety* (eusebeia).

I recognise that life lived in common (*epi to auto*) with others is more useful
in many ways. To begin with none of us has self-sufficiency (*autarkê*) even
regarding bodily needs, but we need one another's help in getting necessities.
For just as the foot has certain powers and lacks others, and without the help
of the other limbs neither finds its own strength sufficient for endurance nor
has the support of what is lacking, so in the solitary life (*monerês bios*) both
what we have becomes useless and what we lack becomes unobtainable, since
God the Creator ordained that we need one another, as it is written,* in order
that we may be linked with one another. But apart from this the manner of
the love of Christ does not allow us each to be concerned solely with his own
interests. For 'love', we read, 'does not seek its own'.† Now the solitary life
(*aphidiastikos bios*) has one aim (*skopos*), the service of the needs of the
individual. But this is plainly in conflict with the law of love, which the Apostle

---

* cf. Sirach 13:15–16 and 1 Cor. 12.
† 1 Cor. 13:5.

fulfilled when he sought not his own advantage but that of the many, that they might be saved.*

Secondly, a person living in such seclusion (*katachôrismos*) will not even readily recognise his own defects, not having anyone to reprove him and to set him right with kindness and compassion. For it often happens that rebuke even from an enemy causes a good person to desire to be cured. But a cure of sin with understanding is carried out by a man who has loved sincerely, as it says, 'the one who loves corrects with care'.† Such a person is difficult to find in solitude (*monôsis*) unless one has already formed a link with him in one's previous life. The solitary, consequently, experiences the truth of the saying, 'Woe to the one who lives alone, for if he falls there will be none to raise him up.'‡ And many commandments are easily performed by a number living together, but not by one living on his own; for when he does one commandment he is hindered from doing another. For example when we visit the sick we cannot welcome a stranger; when we give out and share (*koinônia*) the necessities of life – especially when these services have to be done at a distance – we are kept from zeal (*spoudê*) at work; so that the greatest commandment of all and the one that leads to salvation is neglected and neither are the hungry fed nor the naked clothed. Who then would chose the idle and fruitless life in preference to the fruitful life which is led in accordance with the Lord's commandments?

Now all of us who have been received in the one hope of our vocation§ are one body having Christ as head, and we are also members one of another.‖ If we are not joined together harmoniously in the close links of one body in the Holy Spirit, but each of us chooses solitude (*monôsis*), not serving the common welfare in a way well-pleasing to God but fulfilling our own passion for self-pleasing (*to idion tês autareskeias pathos*), how, when we are thus separated and divided, can we preserve the mutual relations and service of the limbs to each other, or their subjection to our head, who is Christ? For it is impossible to rejoice with the one who is honoured, or to suffer with the

---

* 1 Cor. 10:33.
† Prov. 13:24.
‡ Eccles. 4:10.
§ Eph. 4:4.
‖ 1 Cor. 12:12, cf. Rom. 12:5.

sufferer when our life is thus divided,* as each one cannot know the affairs of his neighbour.

In addition, no one is sufficient to receive all spiritual gifts (*charismata*), but the gifts of the Spirit are given in accordance to the faith of each;† thus when one is living in Communion of life (*koinônia tês zoês*) with others the private gift of each becomes the common property of his fellows. 'For to one is given the word of wisdom, to another the word of knowledge, to another faith, to another gifts of healing etc.'‡ The one who receives these gifts has them as much for others as for himself. So that of necessity in the community life (*koinônikos bios*) the working of the Holy Spirit in one person passes over to all the rest together. Now all you who have read the gospels know the great danger brought on himself by the man living alone, who has perhaps one gift, and makes it useless by idleness, digging a hole for it in himself.§ Whereas when a number live together a person enjoys his own gift, multiplying it by sharing it with others, and reaps the fruits of other's gifts as if they were his own.

Life together (*hê epi to auto zôê*) also has other benefits, all of which are not easily enumerated. For it is more useful than solitude (*monôsis*) both for keeping the good things given us by God and for warding off the external attacks of the enemy. If any should happen to fall into that sleep which leads to death, which we have been taught by David to pray may not be our fate when he said 'enlighten my eyes lest I sleep in death',‖ then being woken by those already on watch is safer. For the sinner, moreover, withdrawal (*anachôrêsis*) from sin is easier when he fears the condemnation of the majority who are in agreement, so that the words apply to him, 'for such a one this punishment by the majority is enough'.¶ The righteous person on the other hand is greatly reassured when the many approve and assent to his work. For if by the mouth of two or three witnesses every word shall be confirmed,** how much more will he who does a good work be sustained by the testimony of the many. But the solitary life (*monastikê zoê*) has other dangers besides

---

* cf. Rom. 12:15.
† Rom. 12:6.
‡ cf. 1 Cor. 12:8–9.
§ cf. Matt. 25:14–30.
‖ Ps. 12:3
¶ 2 Cor. 2:6
** Matt. 18:16.

those we have mentioned. The first and greatest is that of self-pleasing (*autareskeia*); for having no one to test his work, he will think he has reached the perfection of the commandment. Secondly, because he never tests his state of soul by exercise, he neither recognises his defects nor knows his progress in good works, since he has taken away all the material for doing the commandments.

How shall someone show humility, if he has no one in comparison with whom to show himself humble? How shall he show compassion, when he is cut off from the fellowship (*koinônia*) of the many? How can he exercise himself (*gymnazô*) in patience, if no one contradicts his wishes? If someone says he finds the teaching of the Holy Scriptures sufficient to correct his character, he makes himself like a person who learns the theory of carpentry but never makes anything, or one who is taught metalworking but prefers not to put this teaching into practice. To such a person the Apostle would say, 'It is not the hearers of the Law who are righteous before God, but the doers of the Law who will be justified.'* For, behold, the Lord, because of his great love of mankind, was not content only with teaching the word, but, so that he might accurately (*akribôs*) and clearly give us an example of humility in the perfection of love, he girded himself and washed the feet of the disciples in person.† Whose feet then will you wash? Who will you care for? In comparison to whom will you be last if you live by yourself? That good and pleasant thing, brothers living in unity, which the Holy Spirit likens to oil flowing down the High Priest's head,‡ how will this be accomplished by living alone (*katamonas*)? So, when brothers live in unity it is a stadium for athletics, a method for travelling forward, a continual exercise (*gymnasia*) and a practice of the Lord's commandments. It has as its object (*skopos*) the glory of God according to the commandments of our Lord Jesus Christ who said, 'Let your light so shine before men, that they may see your good works and give glory to your Father who is in heaven.'§ And it keeps the exact likeness (*charaktêr*) of those Saints mentioned in Acts, of whom it is written, 'And all who believed were together and had all things in common.'|| And again, 'now the multitude

* Rom. 2:13.
† John 13:5.
‡ Ps. 132:2.
§ Matt. 5:16.
|| Acts 2:44.

of those who believed were of one heart and soul, and no one said that any of the things which he possessed was his own, but they had all things in common.'*

Commentary

This is a powerful and well-constructed argument, rooted in Scripture, against the solitary life. Basil is attacking a fundamental area of Christian experience which came to prominence in his century when the fame of the Egyptian hermits spread over the whole Christian world. Having established in the previous Rule the importance of separation from the ungodly for a serious Christian life, he now establishes the necessity of 'living together with like-minded brothers who have chosen the same aim of piety'. In rejecting a devout solitude and advocating Christian community, this controversial text is one of the more important documents in the history of spirituality.

Solitude in Christian tradition

Before examining Basil's vocabulary and arguments, it is worth asking how his rejection of solitude fits within the broader stream of Christian tradition. Although dedicated celibacy has been present from the beginnings of Christianity,[1] solitude, apart from Christ's temptation in the wilderness and periodic withdrawals to pray, was not at first a distinguishing feature. Tertullian (*c.* 155–220) wrote, 'We are no Brahmins or Indian gymnosophists living in woods and exiles from life . . . we live with you in the world not avoiding the forum.'[2] Although Eusebius records that a late second-century bishop of Jerusalem, Narcissius, spent time in philosophical seclusion in the Judaean desert,[3] it was not until the end of the third century that the solitary life for Christians began to develop. This flowered in the next century with the fame of St Antony.

Community life was important for the Egyptian Desert Fathers,[4] but it is clear that for them solitude had pride of place. Abba Moses said, 'The man who flees and lives in solitude is like a bunch of

---

* Acts 4:32.

grapes ripened by the sun, but he who remains amongst men is an unripe grape.'[5] It was to this tradition that Basil's disciple Evagrius attached himself. Even leaders of Egyptian cenobitic communities such as Shenoute (*c.* 355–466) allowed their disciples to retire into solitude,[6] but in the case of the most famous cenobitic founder, Pachomius, we find a teaching on solitude similar to that of Basil. In the *Bohairic Life of Pachomius* he is recorded as teaching that, 'the honour and glory of the men of the Koinonia (community) who have a good way of life together . . . is superior to those who live the anchoritic life.'[7] The *Life* even has the great Antony saying, in a piece of cenobitic propaganda, that Pachomius was superior to him because he took 'the path of the Apostles, that is, the Koinonia'.[8]

The 'path of the Apostles', as described in the opening chapters of Acts, also motivated another cenobitic founder, Augustine in the Latin West. He had been inspired by the story of the anchorite Antony,[9] but his own teaching was firmly cenobitic and one commentator notes of him that 'Augustine was rarely alone'.[10] There are many similarities between the monastic teaching of Pachomius, Basil and Augustine, but no evidence of direct influence. They all formulated their doctrine within the same Christian and scriptural tradition.

Basil's place in this tradition

There are therefore two strands of opinion over the relative merits of solitude and community and in reading Longer Rule 7 we find ourselves drawn into a passionate controversy at the heart of the Christian monastic tradition. The earlier version of our Rule in the Small Asceticon, translated by Rufinus, is found in the early sixth-century composite Latin *Rule of Eugippius*,[11] where it may have been selected for polemic purposes. Basil is an uncompromising upholder of community but it is interesting to see how one of his heirs as a cenobitic legislator, Benedict, deals with the problem.

The *Rule of St Benedict* is firmly cenobitic and uses Rufinus' translation of the Small Asceticon, which means that he knew Basil's case against solitaries. In his first chapter, however, 'On the Types of Monks', Benedict does allow the hermit life for monks who have lived in the community for a long time. These are capable of going 'from the battle line of their brothers to the single combat of the desert. They are able now to live without the support of others, and by their own strength and God's help to fight against the vices of mind and body.'[12] This chapter, taken from the *Rule of the Master*, is based on a text of St John Cassian and thus reflects Cassian's Egyptian tradition. In Conference 18 Cassian teaches the superiority of the anchoritic life to that of the cenobium.[13]

There has been a vigorous controversy between the Benedictine scholars Jean Gribomont and Adalbert de Vogüé on Benedict's attitude to the solitary life, and, indeed, on the whole question of Basil's influence on Benedict.[14] De Vogüé lists the traditional witnesses to this movement from the cenobitic to the eremitic life and implies that Basil was out of step with Tradition. Gribomont, on the other hand, says that the *Rule of St Benedict* has a very strong bias to the cenobitic life, and that de Vogüé's emphasis on Cassian in interpreting Benedict effectively eliminates Pachomius, Basil, Augustine and Eugippius from Benedict's 'Great Tradition'. The two also come to blows over the weight to be given to Benedict's words 'our holy father Basil' in the final chapter of his *Rule*, with de Vogüé tending to minimise their importance. In allowing the possibility of monks retiring to solitude and in hinting that it is a higher form of life, Benedict is clearly departing from the teaching of Basil in this Rule.

Upholders of monastic community life such as St Benedict in the West and St Theodore the Studite in the Byzantine East generally follow Basil in his positive teaching on the cenobitic life, but his hostility to hermits seems to have had fewer followers in later centuries. A desire for the solitary life constantly recurs, as was the case with innumerable individual monastic hermits, the eleventh century Camaldolese Benedictines and the later Byzantine Hesychasts. One also frequently finds hermitages developing into fully fledged cenobia. It would appear that wise cenobiarchs need to leave an opening to solitude as it responds to a natural need in some devout Christians. Benedict's qualification that aspiring hermits need first to spend years in community shows an awareness of the real dangers of solitude and reflects what became the mainstream tradition in East and West. We will investigate later whether this answers Basil's objections.

Basil himself, like Augustine,[15] seems at first to have been drawn by solitude when he withdrew to his *monê* in Pontus. The life of Pachomius provides an interesting comparison. He began the ascetic life in a loose, semi-anchoritic group in the desert tradition around a spiritual father called Apa Palamon. A vision instructed him to move to Tabennesi, but it was an encounter with an angel who said three times, 'the will of God is to serve the human race and to reconcile them to himself',[16] which caused him to found a truly cenobitic community. Although Basil, who probably did not know the Pachomians, seems naturally inclined to community life, one wonders if an unknown but similarly decisive experience made him such a defender of cenobitism and enemy of hermits. The Small Asceticon contains our Rule with substantially the same argument[17] and so the ideas expressed here must have come together at the start of Basil's ascetic life around the year 360. Perhaps he had been adversely influenced by the eccentricities of the Syrian ascetics. Did he encounter this type of asceticism on his journey in 356/7?

Basil's vocabulary of solitude

On reading Longer Rules 6 and 7, one is struck by the variety of terms Basil uses to describe the types of life he is discussing. It is clear from this, and from a certain confusion in the use of the words, that the descriptive vocabulary of forms of ascetic life was not yet fixed. The vocabulary of solitude is particularly broad.

We have already noted that Basil avoids the positive use of 'monastic' language and that the word *anachôrêsis* is only used in the Asceticon of an interior withdrawal. The question at the head of Longer Rule 7 confuses matters when the related verb *anachôreô* is used of the physical withdrawal from the ungodly advocated in the previous Rule. When someone has performed such a retirement, he is faced with a choice of two types of life. One is to live together with others and its opposite is defined by the verb *idiazô*. This way of life is then described by a veritable litany of terms: *monêrês bios*, *aphidiastikos bios, monôsis, monastikê zôê, katachôrismos,* and *kata-monas* (the title, probably not by Basil, adds *monazô*). To Basil, all these here describe a bad state of life. There is more confusion as *idiazô,* and the verb related to *aphidiastikos – aphidiazô –* are strongly recommended in the different context of Longer Rule 6. In our Rule their negative connotations call to mind Basil's hostility to private (*idios*) possessions and self-will (*idion thelêma*). Almost two centuries later St John Climacus, Abbot of Mount Sinai, used *aphidiazô* in a similar way to Basil here. Climacus was a hermit for most of his life and valued the solitary life but he was aware of its dangers. In Step 8 of *The Ladder of Divine Ascent* he describes hearing angry solitaries fighting imaginary offenders in their cells 'like caged partridges' and he advised them not to remain in solitude (*apidiazô*). It is significant that, no doubt following Basil, he uses this verb of a bad solitude.

Returning to Basil, it seems that we find him doing something new here with the other terms. He is giving a negative meaning to words which Christians usually used in a positive sense. *Katamonas* is used in the *Life of Antony*[18] of those ascetics living alone not far from a village, whose life Antony was to surpass by seeking greater solitude. In Longer Rule 3 we saw the adjective *monastikos,* used of solitary wild animals, employed by Basil in a negative sense. His friend Gregory Nazianzen, however, in his poem 'Concerning his own Life', uses it to describe a highly desired state, 'I was possessed by a greater love for the solitary life (*tôn monastikôn pothos*).'[19] *Monêrês bios* is used by Clement of Alexandria of Christian celibates, and *monôsis,* apart from its classical meaning of 'separation from',[20] seems to be generally used by Christians of a beneficial solitude. Basil's use of these words is thrown into relief by their use in a positive sense by non-authentic works in the Basilian corpus. The spurious Letter 42 advocates the 'life of monks' which it calls '*monêrês bios*', and the pseudo-Basilian *Ascetic Constitutions* legislate for those living in the cenobium or *katamonas.*[21] The occurrence of *katachôr-ismos* in this Rule is the only example of its use in Basil's works, and it would seem that it was coined by him.[22]

Basil has thus formed a distinctive vocabulary of solitude by giving negative connotations to words generally used positively and appropriating language such as *aphidiazô* and *idiazô* otherwise used by the Cappadocians in their theological writings. He probably even created a new word. He is defining a vocabulary and so does not use only one or two generally accepted words for each type of ascetic life. We can here see a stage in the formation of a distinctive ascetic vocabulary but it is probable that further study would show that, with the general acceptance of at least some opening to the solitary life, these negative terms and definitions will only be found in a few later writers.

The vocabulary of community

The words Basil uses to describe community are similarly imprecise but are fewer, as the main thrust of Basil's argument is against the solitary life. He speaks of living *epi to auto* (together), of the *koinônikos bios* and of *koinônia tês zôês* (Communion of life) or just plain *koinônia*. We have already met the word *koinônikos* in Basil's definition of man in Longer Rule 3 where it is, as here, used in opposition to the adjective *monastikos*. The other two terms have strong scriptural associations with the Apostolic Church described in the first chapters of Acts, especially in the two quotations with which this Rule ends.

The first, Acts 2:44, describes the believers as being together, *epi to auto*, while two verses previously they are said to have devoted themselves to the *koinônia* or fellowship. Letter 295 refers to this text of Acts and confirms the importance of the first of these terms for Basil. He exhorts the ascetics to whom it is addressed to accept the community life (*hê epi to auto zôê*) in imitation of the apostolic way of life (*politeia*). The second quotation, Acts 4:32, reinforces this picture stressing that no one said that any of his possessions was his own (*idion*) but all was held in common (*koinos*).

Koinônia is the key term. Basil, however, does not employ a word that was frequently used later for the monastic community, *koinobion* (cenobium).[23] *Koinobion* is from the Greek expression for common life *koinos bios*, a phrase which Basil uses in a negative sense in Longer Rule 6 to describe the ungodly crowd. *Koinônia*, for its part, is used by Basil with a variety of meanings and connotations. In Shorter Rule 309 it is used of the Eucharist, Holy Communion (*koinônia tôn hagiôn*), and in Longer Rule 44 it is used in a neutral sense of keeping company on a journey. There is also a bad *koinônia* at the fairs at Martyrs' tombs (Longer Rule 40) or with heretics and sinners (Shorter Rule 20), as well as a good fellowship in co-operation between communities (Longer Rule 35). This last is similar to the first use in our Rule. The word is only once used unambiguously to mean the community, and this is in the later answer of Longer Rule 36. *Koinônia* is also a concept fundamental to classical Greek discourse on friendship, which Carolinne White has shown influenced Basil's teaching both on the Church and on ascetic community.[24] The proverb attributed to Pythagoras, 'friends have all things in common', could be applied to Basil's communities. From all this we can conclude that the vocabulary of community is more scriptural than that of solitude, that it also has its roots in the Hellenic world, but that it is similarly undeveloped.

The case against the solitary life

If the terminology is undeveloped, Basil's argument is not. This text stands in the Christian tradition as the classic expression of hostility to the solitary life, being copied for this purpose by Eugippius in the sixth century and still being quoted as such by twentieth-century theologians such as Edmund Hill op in his book on Christian anthropology.[25] The case is put, as one would expect from reading the earlier Rules, in terms partly scriptural and partly practical. Community life is natural, useful and the way to fulfil the commandments. All of the parts of his case are integrated and interlinked with each other. He does not argue first in terms of pure philosophy and then in terms of revelation. This connects with what we have already suggested concerning the relation between nature and grace. In analysing his argument, however, it is helpful to separate as far as one can the practical and the scriptural.

The case from Scripture: the Body of Christ

The answer starts with allusions to St Paul's teaching on the Church
as the Body of Christ in 1 Corinthians 12:12–27 and Romans 12:4–5,
and it ends with the depiction of the apostolic community at Jerusalem in the early chapters of Acts. These Pauline and Lucan images
give the fundamental scriptural foundation for Basil's teaching on
community, and it is notable that they are both in origin models of
the Church. Basil's ascetic teaching is profoundly ecclesial and one
of his greatest achievements was to integrate the spiritual energies of
the enthusiasts into the Church.

It is perhaps the image of the Body, with its different parts in
harmonious unity, which is most important here. In using this Paul
took an analogy which was common in antiquity, as in this example
from Seneca: 'All this which you see in which divine and human
things are undivided is one thing. We are members of a large body . . .
This justifies for us mutual love and makes us sociable.'[26] While Basil's
source was Scripture, it is worth noting that the concept was by no
means alien to the secular and philosophical thought-world in which
he moved with ease if not with comfort. Basil starts in the Rule with
the idea of mutual support between members and, in the third
paragraph, follows Paul in elevating the image to the theological
plane. Christ is the head of the body but Basil does not say, as
Benedict did later, that the Superior holds the place of Christ in the
community.[27] This suggests that although he uses ecclesial imagery
of the ascetic community, he does not yet see it as itself a 'little
church'. His emphasis is on the communities as part of the local
Church around the bishop.[28]

The Holy Spirit is the power that holds the community together
in harmony. As the aim of the life is to be pleasing to God (the
Father), we thus find the community situated in a trinitarian framework. The Spirit is mentioned four times in this Rule and it is clear
that Basil regards the ascetic community as the place of the Holy
Spirit,[29] where his gifts (*charismata*) can be used most fruitfully. The
section on the Body in 1 Corinthians 12 follows a discussion of the
gifts of the Spirit. This stress on the Holy Spirit is characteristic of

Basil and connects with his theological work. It also reveals him as one of the charismatic enthusiasts. The order of the Body is held together by the Spirit under Christ the head, but solitude breaks this solidarity and divides the Body of Christ. The allusion to Romans 12:15, 'rejoice with those who rejoice; weep with those who weep', reinforces the theme of solidarity and connects it with love of neighbour. One could also note that the body is characterised by an ordered harmony of different functions and not by an egalitarian uniformity. The Holy Spirit brings order and hierarchy, not anarchy. The analogy thus allows Basil to develop community structures in an ordered and more hierarchical manner, as we see in the later Rules.

This model is thus a fruitful one and is used elsewhere in the Asceticon. In Longer Rule 24, for example, where Basil starts the section of answers on 'the manner of our life together', he states that 'the principle of the members of the body must be preserved'.[30]

The Apostolic Church in Acts

We have already noted the importance of the image of the Church in the early chapters of Acts. Basil recommends it to the ascetics in Letter 295. It is again an ecclesial model for the community, but it is also, in Cassian's theory of the origin of monasticism, a monastic model of the Church. The first part of our text is based on the First Letter to the Corinthians, but at the end of the Rule all Basil's teaching on the importance of living together leads us to this Lucan 'icon' of the ideal Christian community. The mention of *koinônia* in other parts of the Rule also suggest this model, and Basil reinforces its importance in the Great Asceticon by adding the second classical text, Acts 4:32. He often introduces biblical texts by allusion and in his reworking of the Asceticon sometimes reinforces this by a direct quotation.[31] Like the image of the body, that of the Apostolic community recurs throughout the Rules,[32] and in Longer Rule 35 we find both models being deployed to argue against having more than one brotherhood in the same place.

'Woe to the one who lives alone': other Scriptural reasons

Basil's case is supported by other scriptural texts. Perhaps the most effective is Ecclesiastes 4:10 which is part of a small dossier of texts, 4:9–12, on the theme 'two are better than one'. It is surprising that Basil does not use Genesis 2:18, 'it is not good for man to be alone.' The lone talent, however, buried by the worthless and lazy servant in Matthew 25, provides another stick with which he may beat the solitary. When he considers the benefits of community life, Psalm 132 on 'brothers living in unity' is an obvious text. St Augustine even claims that this psalm 'produced the monasteries' and he links it with the apostolic community in Acts. From it, he says, comes the name 'monk' which he associates with a united community.[33] Basil on the other hand opposes this psalm to 'monastic' solitude (*katamonas*), which he sees as being in conflict with the 'law of love'. Here we return to the commandment of love in the first Rule, on which the whole first section of the Longer Rules is a commentary. This commandment provides the bedrock for the two foundational images from Paul and Luke.

In our Rule Basil speaks of 'the greatest commandment of all' being neglected by the solitary. In the Gospel this is the command to love God, but the context here, where it is said to 'lead to salvation', is associated with love of neighbour shown by feeding the hungry and clothing the naked. This recalls Jesus' teaching on the Last Judgement where people are separated like sheep and goats.[34] There Jesus says that these acts of love are done to him and so we return to the idea of the coinherence of the two commandments of love. Love is here given its own icon in the Lord washing the feet of his disciples, 'humility in the perfection of love', which leads to the powerful question, 'whose feet will you wash?'

The case from the Bible against solitude is thus well developed and constructed. Basil, however, also says that learning from the Scriptures is not enough. Using the example of crafts practised among the brotherhoods he stresses the importance of deeds. Likewise the scriptural case is united with arguments which are practical or philosophical, which themselves are often closely connected to the Bible.

Self-sufficiency: pleasing God or pleasing self

Community life is natural, as man is a sociable animal, and it is part of God's plan in creation revealed in the Book of Genesis: 'God the Creator ordained that we need each other.' As such it is useful for obtaining necessities and for mutual support. This is linked with the Body of Christ and the law of love, and again we see the seamless connection between nature and the supernatural. On this basis Basil constructs his attack against things private and selfish, by which he defines solitude. Shorter Rule 74 asks, 'whether those who go out from the brotherhood and desire to live a solitary life (*monêrês bios*), or to follow the same ideal of piety in company with a few others, should be cut off?' In his answer he situates even the desire for solitude at the level of self-will. This desire is based on a lie, the concept of self-sufficiency or autarky, which is both false, as we need others, and conflicts with the law of love. Shorter Rule 86 takes up the same theme and in it he advocates expulsion for the person who says, 'I neither take anything from the brotherhood nor do I give them anything, but I am content with my own things.' Such a one rejects the law of love.

The adjective *autarkês* (self-sufficient, satisfied) and the noun *autarkeia* (which in an objective sense means 'what is necessary'; in a subjective, self-sufficiency or satisfaction) both occur in the New Testament. The first is in Philippians 4:11 and the second in 2 Corinthians 9:8 and 1 Timothy 6:6, 'There is much gain in godliness (*eusebeia*) with *autarkeia*.' The sense in all of these verses is positive, meaning 'having enough' and 'contentment with what one has'. A similar meaning, relating to things both physical and spiritual, is found among the ancient philosophers, especially the Stoics.[35] It is used in the latter sense to indicate detachment from the world and worldly values. The use in 1 Timothy is closest to that of the Stoics. Basil's own use of the concept is distinctive in that he denies it any value. Self-sufficiency is not only not possible but not even to be aimed at. The austere, imperturbable and self-sufficient Stoic sage is *not* the ideal. In departing from this Christian/Stoic tradition in order to uphold the value of community he shows how his thought is permeated by the New Testament value of communion (*koinônia*). Here again we see that Christianity determines his use of philosophical language and that his Christian teaching has not been deformed by Greek philosophy.

Autarky is the opposite of community 'which has as its *skopos* the glory of God'. The centre of gravity of the community-person is outside himself, with God, and his aim is to live a life pleasing to God, whereas the solitary is centred on himself, indulging 'his own passion for self-pleasing'. This dichotomy, self-pleasing (*autareskeia*)/ well-pleasing to God (*euareston tô theô*), is fundamental to Basil's thought. In Shorter Rule 117 it is applied to obedience and here *autareskeia* produces division and frustrates the work of the Holy Spirit. The opposite of self-pleasing is described as servitude in Letter 22 where he says that the Christian should not consider himself as his own master, but as having been delivered by God into servitude to his brethren of like spirit. Rousseau notes that this whole Letter is 'filled with a sense of mutual obligation and dependence'.[36]

Community as the middle way

The community offers essential advantages to one's spiritual life and helps growth in self-knowledge. Brethren can offer friendly rebuke and thus help one avoid that self-delusion about one's faults mentioned in the previous Rule as a result of living among the ungodly. Community thus offers a middle way – conforming to the commandment of love – between the parallel disadvantages of solitude and life in the crowd. Gregory Nazianzen, in his poem 'Concerning his own life', speaks of a similar middle way in his own life. This poem was written after Basil's death but we can see the influence of his ideas:

> I realised that those who enjoy a practical life
> are useful to others who are in the thick of things
> but do not benefit themselves:
>   they are distracted by the wicked, too,
> who disrupt their calm disposition. On the other hand,
> those who have withdrawn are in some way more stable

and with a tranquil mind can keep their gaze
    directed towards God,
but they only benefit themselves,
    for their love is a narrow one
and strange and hard is the life they lead.
So I chose a middle path between solitude and involvement,
adopting the meditative ways of the one,
    the usefulness of the other.[37]

Gregory's argument here is clearly similar to that in our Rule. Solitaries 'only benefit themselves, for their love is a narrow one', whereas those living the practical life, like the common life rejected in Longer Rule 6, 'are distracted by the crowd'.

In Longer Rule 7, we find that peer-pressure from the community, far from distracting the ascetic, acts as an incentive to withdraw from sin and as a reassurance in good works. These advantages are not available in solitude where there is no means of testing one's soul and the absence of neighbours means lack of 'material for doing the commandments'. Basil's spiritual teaching puts great stress on 'doing', on performing good works or on simply doing work. For Basil the life pleasing to God is a life of the commandments and life in the Holy Spirit. In the Preface to the Longer Rules, Basil insists that one must obey *all* the commandments:

> . . . for if the man of God must be perfect (2 Tim. 3:17) . . . it is before all things necessary that he be made perfect in *every* commandment . . . for by the divine law a beast with a blemish, even if he was clean, was not accepted as a sacrifice to God.

Our text shows that, 'many commandments are easily performed by a number living together, and not by one living on his own'. It is the same with the gifts of the Spirit which are given 'as much for others as for oneself'. Christian community is thus the place both of divine action through the Spirit and of human effort in the performance of the commandments.

In reading Basil's arguments here one could be forgiven for thinking of a more psychological reason for his championing of community against solitude and isolation. It is very difficult to imagine Basil being alone. One thinks of him with his large family surrounded by servants, with Gregory and their mutual friends at Athens, with his ascetic brethren in his early retreat in Pontus where he was still close to his family and received visits from Eustathius. Later, when he became a central figure in the crises facing the Church, his letters show him in constant touch with clergy and laity in Asia Minor and beyond, and the Asceticon leaves a picture of him surrounded by ascetics enjoying his position as a teacher. In this he is similar to Augustine and it reveals a very different type of person from his less robust friend Gregory, whom one can easily imagine writing his poems in seclusion at Arianzus.

Was Basil consistent?

Basil's case against the solitary life is thorough, but one may wonder if he always followed these principles in his life as a bishop and leader of ascetics. Clarke's study of all the relevant texts in Basil and Gregory Nazianzen[38] shows that he was indeed consistent in his opposition to the solitary life. He may, though, have reluctantly accepted it especially when as a bishop he had dealings with many different types of ascetic. The section of our text which says that a spiritual father 'is difficult to find in solitude unless one has already formed a link with him in one's previous life', suggests that he recognised the possibility of a solitary avoiding some of the pitfalls of the life. In Letter 295 we see Basil's principles in action when he exhorts what is presumably a loosely organised group of hermits to accept life together 'in imitation of the apostolic manner of living' and sends a brother to bring them together. He hopes to hear that they do not favour 'the life that lacks witnesses', but rather help each other. There is obviously a connection here with the themes of Longer Rule 7. An *Ascetic Discourse*, possibly by Basil, has a similar message: 'Those who have separated themselves from the common life (*koinos bios*) and are training themselves for the divine life must not do so by themselves or without help. For such a life should have witnesses, so as to be free from evil suspicion.'[39]

The text that caused Clarke most trouble in showing that Basil consistently opposed the solitary life is in section 62 of Gregory of Nazianzen's *Funeral Oration*:

> The solitary life (*erêmikos bios*) and community life (*migas*) were then in conflict and dissension in many ways, and neither completely possessed advantages or disadvantages that were unmixed. The one is more tranquil (*hêsychios*) and stable and leads to union with God, but it is not free from pride, because its virtue escapes testing and comparison. The other is more practical and useful, but does not escape turbulence. Basil reconciled and united the two in the most excellent way. He caused hermitages and monasteries (*askêtêria* and *monastêria*) to be built not far from cenobites and communities of ascetics (*koinônikôi* and *migades*). He did not divide and separate them from each other by any intervening wall, as it were. He brought them close together, yet kept them distinct, that the life of contemplation (*philosophon*) might not be divorced from community life or the active life (*praktikon*) from contemplation.[40]

This would seem to contradict the idea that Basil was hostile to the solitary life. Clarke[41] makes sense of it by understanding it as saying that Basil founded a third type of life by the side of two existing forms of asceticism, the solitary life and the *migades* -- those living the 'mixed life' i.e. the ascetic life lived in the world. He founded *asketêria* and *monastêria* -- two names for the same thing, a common technique in this type of literature -- not far in spirit from the communities of *migades*. For Clark the last section just means that he combined in his own communities the advantages of both, identified by Gregory with the philosophical concepts of the practical life on the one hand and the contemplative life on the other.

In the extract already quoted from his poem 'Concerning his own life', Gregory Nazianzen speaks in similar terms, 'I chose a middle path between solitude (*erêmikôi*) and involvement (*migades*).'[42] This Rule teaches a middle path between the solitary life and involvement in the ungodly crowd. Elm takes this explanation further.[43] The solitary life of the hermit was that lived by such as Naucratius, the young Basil and the more radical Eustathians; the *migas bios* was that of the homoiousian ascetics who lived in communities, were active in practical charity, and were involved in conflicts over doctrine and church politics. This seems to fit the evidence well as city dwelling ascetics were certainly involved in 'turbulence'. Elm quotes the example of the 'Nazarites'[44] (ascetics) of Caesarea who tried to cause a schism in the Church there in 363 between Basil and his bishop, Eusebius.[45]

Basil therefore created a new form of ascetic life in common, drawing on features of two more traditional ways of life. These new communities were generally situated in the countryside, like Annisa. They were thus both separated from the centres of controversy and so integrated into the normal life of the Church as not to be centres of turbulence. Basil's hospices for the poor staffed by ascetics, such as the famous Basileiados at Caesarea, seem to have been situated just outside the City. One could speak of a suburban asceticism. They were also often double communities with men and women living together, as in previous models, but separated by very human precautions into two groups. Elm suggests tentatively that it was the indiscriminate mixing of the earlier model which gave rise to the name '*migas bios*'.[46]

Thus, despite this seemingly contradictory evidence from his friend, it would seem that Basil held to the teaching of Longer Rules 6 and 7 and that his communities combined the benefits of separation and community without encouraging the truly solitary life.

A defence of solitude

Basil's case for community against solitude is well argued but it is not the only view in Christian tradition and his points can be effectively answered. The allusion in the Rule to a spiritual father suggests one response. Hermits invariably do have a spiritual guide who helps them avoid the dangers of solitude. Solitude itself is thus not absolute; it is only a means not the end. Those most solitary of men, the Egyptian Desert Fathers, did actually have a developed sense of the importance of community.[47] The dangers of the 'single combat of the desert' do not mean that it should not be attempted; they even support Cassian's belief that it was a higher form of life. The greater the risks the higher the prize. Christian history shows that hermits have often played an important role in society, serving their fellow men precisely because of their separation, as Peter Brown has demonstrated.[48]

This, however, still does not address the heart of Basil's critique, which is that a life of solitude is less human and less Christian. An answer to this is given by his ex-disciple who went to join the solitaries of Egypt, Evagrius of Pontus. He teaches that, 'A monk is one who is separated from all and who is united to all.'[49] The Christian hermit separates himself from the world in order to meet God, and in doing so he meets the world at the deepest level of its own being, that is in Christ. The selfish isolation which Basil attacks is a caricature of the life of the true solitary. His mystical union has meaning in the context of the Body of Christ, which has a deeper significance than just assisting others with bodily needs. Edmund Hill, in his discussion of this Rule, also suggests another answer to Basil's objections.[50] St Paul writes that 'the form of this world is passing away' (1 Cor. 7:31). In this sense God does not intend to salvage the world, our human society, but abolish it and replace it with the Kingdom of God. By his withdrawal the solitary protests against the corruption of our world and shows that we are 'strangers and exiles on the earth' (Heb. 11:13). In looking forward to the perfect society that will come with the Last Judgement, the hermit teaches the provisional nature of our world and is a profound expression of Christian eschatology. Basil's strong stress on what is natural, and perhaps even a lingering attachment to the values of the *polis*, would not incline him to accept this case for the solitary life. It is however implied in his case for separation in Longer Rule 6. One could even argue on the other hand that the cenobitic life, in its separation from the profane world, is a more perfect prefiguration of the heavenly society than is that of the solitary.

Many of Basil's concerns about the solitary life could be answered by the monasteries known as lavras or sketes, mentioned in the Introduction, which originated in Egypt and Palestine. These, like

the Carthusians of the West, combined the advantages of a devout
solitude with elements of community in a life which can be called
either semi-eremitical or semi-cenobitic. The newcomer would be
formed in the monastic life by a spiritual father. This could be in a
small community at the centre of the lavra or, as in the case of St
Sabas in fifth-century Palestine, he might be sent for training in a
cenobium. When the brother was ready he could be allowed to move
out to one of the outlying cells. While there, the hermits usually
returned each week to the Church and the common buildings at the
centre of the community.[51]

Basil may have heard of the monks of Nitria and Scetis during his
visit to Egypt but he did not imitate their way of life. His own
teaching is closer to that of the Pachomians, with whom he probably
had no contact. In the following century a number of the Fathers of
the Judaean desert were Cappadocians and knew Basilian cenobitism.
One suspects though that the lavra, as a response to the twofold
dynamic of solitude and community, would not have been fully
satisfactory for Basil, even though the monks played an important
role in the Palestinian Church. His emphasis on the positive value of
community life is too central to his ascetic spirituality.

Our attempts to counter Basil's case against solitude, and thus
defend an important strand of Christian tradition, should not obscure
the power of his argument. Many Christians, and especially bishops
and cenobitic monks, have rejected the hermit life on grounds similar
to those of Basil. This has particularly been so in the post-Refor-
mation Western Church where it is only in the last half-century that
there has been a revival of the solitary life.

Conclusion

Commenting on this first section of the Longer Rules has led to the
investigation of many profound theological and spiritual questions.
One hopes that this has allowed the distinctive lines of Basilian
spirituality to emerge. Among its most important characteristics is
the stress on community life and this whole section builds up to the
teaching on the necessity of community in Longer Rule 7. Most of

the rest of the Longer Rules consider aspects of community life and it is to these that we turn in the final part of this book.

NOTES

1. For example: Matt. 19:10–12; Mark 14:26–7, 33; Luke 20:34–6; 1 Cor. 7; Rev. 14:4; cf. also Old Testament texts such as Jer. 16:1–2; Isa. 54:1; Isa. 56:3–5.
2. *Apology* 42.
3. *History of the Church* 6:9.
4. See Gould, *The Desert Fathers on Monastic Community* (1993).
5. *Alphabetical Collection* Moses 7; cf. also Antony 11, Arsenius 44, and Theodore of Pherme 5. Even Abba Matoes' saying, ' . . . it is not through virtue that I live in solitude, but through weakness, those who live in the midst of men are the strong ones', when read in context is a witness to the importance of solitude.
6. Elm, *Virgins of God*, pp. 303–4. Shenoute's Uncle and predecessor as Superior of the White Monastery, Pgol, started as an anchorite and preserved many features of this life when he founded the community in the mid fourth century, *Virgins of God*, pp. 297–8.
7. *Bohairic Life* 105, cf. *Bohairic Life* 35 which speaks of the dangers of solitude.
8. *Bohairic Life* 126–7. The same story in the *First Greek Life* 120 has Antony praising Pachomius but he does not say that his style of life is superior. Both of these Lives depend on a common source, see *Pachomian Koinonia* vol. 1, pp. 1–21.
9. *Confessions* 8:6:15, 8:12:29.
10. George Lawless OSA, *Augustine of Hippo and his Monastic Rule*, p. 3.
11. *Eugippii Regula*, CSEL 87 (1976) ed. Villegas and de Vogüé. The Rule of Eugippius, a contemporary of St Benedict and Benedict's source the anonymous Master, was hostile to the eremitic life. After this section from Basil it gives an extract from St Jerome's Letter 125 on the same theme.
12. *Regula Benedicti* 1:5.
13. See the note on interpreting this teaching in Boniface Ramsey's translation of the *Conferences*, p. 631. Book 5 of the *Institutes* contains similar doctrine. Conference 19 continues the discussion of Conference 18 on the difference between hermits and cenobites and, while allowing an important place for the monastic community, still holds to the anchoritic life as the ideal.
14. See the section *St Basil and St Benedict* in the bibliography.
15. *Confessions* 10:43:70. Augustine significantly rejected solitude because the Lord 'forbade me . . . saying "that is why Christ died for all, so that those who live should not live for themselves, but for him who died for them"? (2 Cor. 5:15)'.
16. *First Greek Life of Pachomius* 23, *Bohairic Life* 22. Translations given in *Pachomian Koinonia*.
17. There are four main inserted sections in the first part of the answer in the Great Asceticon and two passages from Scripture added in the rest of the text – Rom. 2:13 and Acts 4:32.

18. *Life of Antony* 3:2. But note that it is not used in a positive sense in Ps. 140:10 (LXX) where the psalmist is *kata monas* until he escapes the sinners' net.
19. 'Concerning his own life', line 327, tr. Carolinne White.
20. For example used of separation from a husband by Gregory of Nyssa in *On Virginity* 3.
21. In the title *PG* 31:1521. The work is printed in Migne at the end of the Asceticon.
22. Lampe's *Patristic Greek Lexicon* only cites this occurrence and a computer search of Greek literature before AD 400 has failed to find any other instance of its use.
23. It is only found in the Migne edition of Basil's works in two title headings of the pseudo-Basilian *Ascetic Constitutions*.
24. White, *Christian Friendship*, pp. 19, 75–82.
25. Edmund Hill, *Being Human* (1984).
26. Letter 95:52.
27. *Regula Benedicti* 2:2. The Abbot 'is believed to hold the place of Christ in the monastery'. Cf. RB 63:13.
28. This is implicit rather than explicit as there are only two places in the Rules where bishops are mentioned as being involved with the communities. In these they are only referred to as 'Leaders (*Proestôtas*) of the Church' (LR 15, this could also refer to lower ranking clergy) and 'He who is entrusted (*pepisteumenos*) with the care of the Churches of the neighbourhood' (SR 187). The most important episcopal presence in the Rules is Basil himself.
29. cf. *On the Holy Spirit* 26:62, 'Although paradoxical, it is nevertheless true that Scripture frequently speaks of the Spirit in terms of a place – a place in which people are made holy.' It is a short journey from the Spirit as a place to the community as the place of the Spirit.
30. cf. also LRs 28, 35, 41, and SRs 175, 182.
31. An example is Matt. 16:24 in the previous Rule.
32. e.g. LRs 34, 35; SRs 85, 252; R 89 (the equivalent SR 129 does not reproduce the quote from Acts 4:32).
33. Exposition of Psalm 132.
34. Matt. 25:31–46.
35. References in C. Spicq OP, *Les Épitres Pastorales* Tome I (1969), pp. 560–1, quoting among others Aristotle, Philo, and the Stoics Diogenes, Zeno, Seneca and Epictetus.
36. *Basil of Caesarea*, p. 207.
37. 'Concerning his own life', lines 302–12, tr. Carolinne White.
38. Clarke (1913), pp. 109–13.
39. *Sermo Asceticus*, Clarke (1925), pp. 133–9, *CPG* 2891.
40. Translation from McCauley (1953), compared with the Greek in Clarke (1913), p. 111.
41. Clarke (1913), pp. 112–13.
42. White uses Jungck's 1974 edition of the Greek which has *mesên tin'êlthon erêmikôn kai migadôn*. Clarke (1913) uses the Migne text which has *azugôn* (unmarried/single) instead of *erêmikôn*. In each case the text seems to refer to two types of ascetic life.

43. *Virgins of God*, pp. 203–11. She does not do justice to Clarke's explanation, only recording his questions about the text.

44. Named after the Nazirites of the Old Testament who were consecrated to God, e.g. Samson in Judg. 13:4–7, Num. 6 and Amos 2:11–12.

45. Gregory of Nazianzen, *Oration 43* (On Basil) 28.

46. *Virgins of God*, p. 210.

47. See the conclusion to Gould's, *The Desert Fathers on Monastic Community*.

48. See for example his seminal article, 'The Rise and Function of the Holy Man in Late Antiquity' (1971).

49. *Chapters on Prayer* 124. 'United to' is a better translation of *sunarmozô* than Bamberger's 'in harmony with'.

50. *Being Human*, pp. 141–2.

51. For Nitria and the Cells see Derwas Chitty, *The Desert a City*, pp. 29–35 and Palladius, *The Lausiac History* 7. For Palestinian monasticism see *Cyril of Scythopolis: The Lives of The Monks of Palestine*, tr. Price; *Ascetics and Ambassadors of Christ* (1994), Binns; *The Desert a City* esp. chs. 5 and 6; *Sabas, Leader of Palestinian Monasticism* (1995), Patrich. A brief overview of Eastern Monasticism is given in Kallistos Ware ' "Separated from All and United to All", The Hermit Life in the Christian East' in *Solitude and Communion: Papers on the Hermit Life*, ed. A. M. Allchin (Oxford 1977), pp. 30–47.

PART THREE

'Let All Be Done Decently and in Order'

A COMMENTARY ON ELEVEN RULES DEALING
WITH CHRISTIAN COMMUNITY

Introduction to Part Three

I once saw a swarm of bees flying in military formation according to the law of their nature and following their king in good order.
Preface to the *Moralia*, 'On the Judgement of God'

Basil was a keen observer of nature and did not disdain to draw lessons from God's creation. In this case he deduces the necessity of harmony (*symphônia*) in the Church of God. In the Asceticon much of his teaching is concerned with 'the manner of our life together'[1] and it recalls these bees in emphasising the naturally social nature of man and the necessity of obedience in community. His guiding principle in all this is expressed in the words of Paul from 1 Corinthians 14:40: 'Let all be done decently (*euschêmôs*) and in order (*kata taxin*).' This text heads the second section of the Longer Rules, but the concern for order and harmony is present throughout the Asceticon.

In the eleven Rules of this final section we shall examine aspects of Basil's teaching on community. To gain a balanced picture of his ascetic spirituality, it is essential not to stop at its interior aspects; he regarded equally seriously questions of external behaviour and mutual relations. We shall not only look at the structure and dynamics of community, but also at the external aspects of the life of the individual brothers or sisters: what they wore, what they ate and how they spoke. Although, as we shall see, there is a development in Basil's teaching as the communities develop, the central concerns are constant.

Chapter Twelve

The Anatomy of Community

For Basil man is a sociable animal. We have seen that he believed that the way of life best suited to following the commandments was that lived in a community to some extent separated from the world. As a consequence of this we find throughout the Rules an interest in obedience, an enthusiasm for fraternal correction and a concern with how to ensure genuine union among men and women. These are paralleled by his own involvement in the life of the wider Church. One thinks of his vigorous opposition to heresy, his fearless confrontation with the Prefect Modestus, and his concern for unity between and within the Churches as shown by his intervention in Antioch. Basil's interest in the dynamics of the ascetic community is thus worthy of explanation, against the background of the gradual development of ascetic institutions revealed by the Rules.

Gribomont's suggestion of three stages in the evolution of Basil's teaching on obedience helps us here by giving a model for the development of the community itself:[2]

a) Basil was often present and played a role like that of Paul with the Corinthians. Among the ascetics obedience to Scripture was interpreted as 'everyone is my Superior, without any juridical precedence'.

b) Out of this there developed in the community, itself emerging out of the mass of Christians, a group of charismatic leaders who were recognised as having special gifts. These performed the function of the eye in the body and were able to discern what is the will of God.

c) This function became concentrated in one individual, who was assisted by other officials.

While recognising that Basil was dealing with a number of communities which grew in different ways, this model does explain the difference between the earlier texts in the Small Asceticon and those that were added later. In examining Basil's teaching on obedience and the community we will begin with Shorter Rule 114, the thirteenth Answer of the Small Asceticon, and then turn to the later Longer Rule 24, which deals with the Superior. In the next chapter we shall look at Longer Rule 28 which responds to the practical case of a brother who fails to obey.

SHORTER RULE 114 (R 13)

The Lord commands, if anyone forces you to go one mile, go with him two miles,* and the Apostle teaches us to be subject to one another in the fear of Christ.† Must we then obey any and every one who gives us orders?

A difference in those who give orders ought not to hinder the obedience of those who receive them. For Moses did not fail to obey Jethro when he gave good advice. But there is no small difference in the orders given: for some are contrary to the commandment of the Lord, or perhaps destroy and corrupt it by mixing in what is forbidden; others help to fulfil the commandments; others again, if not obviously fulfilling it, still contribute towards this end and help keep the commandment. It is necessary therefore to remember the Apostle's words, 'Do not despise prophesying, but test every thing; hold fast what is good, abstain from every form of evil';‡ and again, 'We destroy arguments and every proud obstacle to the knowledge of God, and take every thought captive to obey Christ.'§

If we are given an order which fulfils the commandment of the Lord, or contributes to its fulfilment, we must thus receive it eagerly and carefully as the will of God, fulfilling the saying, 'being patient with one another in the love of Christ'.‖ But when we receive an order from anyone which is contrary to the commandment of the Lord, or destroys or corrupts it, then it is

---

* Matt. 5:41.
† Eph. 5:21.
‡ 1 Thess. 5:20–22.
§ 2 Cor. 10:5.
‖ Eph. 4:2.

time to say, 'We must obey God rather than men',* remembering the Lord's words, 'A stranger they will not follow, but they will flee from him, for they do not know the voice of strangers';† and those of the Apostle, who for our safety dared to attack even angels, when he said, 'But if even we, or an angel from heaven, should preach to you a gospel contrary to that which we preached to you, let him be anathema.'‡

We are taught by this that even if the one who hinders us from doing the Lord's command, or persuades us to do what is forbidden by him, is well-born or exceedingly illustrious, he ought to be shunned and abominated by every one of those who love the Lord.

Commentary

In this Rule there is no mention of a Superior, or even of an ascetic community. If one reads it in the context of such a community, though, it does make sense and, apart from the addition of the two commands in the question, the Great Asceticon leaves the original text intact. Basil teaches that it is not the person who gives the order which is important but rather the content of the command. We are far from the teaching of St Benedict who states that the Abbot takes the place of Christ in the monastery and is to be obeyed as such.

Obedience and Scripture

In our text the contents of the Rule are to be judged by the typically Basilian criterion of the commandments. These are scriptural and this fact led Sr Margaret Gertrude Murphy to make an important point about the principle on which Basil bases his teaching on obedience:[3] the Scriptures contain, either explicitly or implicitly, the totality of ascetic theory and practice and thus they furnish the true Rule. This is clearly shown by the *Moralia*, and the Rules are simply an epitome of the teachings of Scripture with directions for practical matters not covered by, yet not contrary to, the sacred text. This fits perfectly with the two types of commands to be obeyed mentioned

---

* Acts 5:29.
† John 10:5.
‡ Gal. 1:8.

in our Rule. Murphy contrasts this with Pachomius. In the Pachomian literature, however, we find a similar emphasis on observing the commandments and on Scripture as the source of rules and traditions.[4] The contrast is more with Benedict whose Rule, while clearly based on Scripture, has itself a central role. The Benedictine monk lives 'under a Rule and an Abbot', a phrase alien to Basil's thought on the subject.[5]

Our Rule is part of a group of answers in the Small Asceticon which deal with obedience and they show us an early stratum of Basil's teaching.[6] The twelfth Answer has the same category of things not commanded or forbidden in the commandments and it teaches that 'it is absolutely necessary either to be subject to God according to his commandments or to others because of his commandments.' It also situates obedience in a trinitarian framework, relating it to the obedience of the Son and Spirit to the Father.[7] In Answer 15 we see the first appearance of the Superior as a settled office rather than just one who happens to give a command. His disposition should be that he is afraid of regulating anything contrary to the will of God as revealed in the Scriptures. Using the words of Paul in 1 Thessalonians 2:7 the Superior is to be like a nurse (*trophos*) to the brethren, and his ministry is a way of practising love of neighbour. We here see the emergence of the Superior, but it is clear that he is firmly subject to the Scriptures. In our Rule there is the same concern about the supremacy of the scriptural commandments and anyone – one could add even a Superior – who obstructs them is to be abominated.

In Longer Rules 24 and 28, which are later in date, we have a much more positive appreciation of the Superior and we also see him in action, confidently dealing with a difficult situation. These lead us on in this and the following chapters to a broader consideration of the structure and images of both community and obedience.

LONGER RULE 24

As these things have been adequately explained to us, next we would like to learn about how we should live together.

Since the Apostle says, 'Let all things be done decently and in order',* we reckon that a decent and well-ordered (*eutakton*) way of life among the community (*sunapheia*) of believers is one where the due relationship of the members of the body is preserved: so that one has the powers of the eye, being entrusted with the general oversight both in evaluating what has been done and in anticipating and arranging what is to be done; and another the powers of the ear or hand with respect to hearing or doing what is necessary – and so on.

Know then that just as with our members it is dangerous for any one part to neglect its functions, or not to use another for the purpose for which it was made by God the Creator – (for if the hand or foot do not obey the guidance of the eye, the one will inevitably touch dangerous things and destroy the whole body, and the other will knock against them or fall over a cliff; or if the eye is closed so that it can not see, it will necessarily be destroyed with the other members, all sharing the same fate) – So also negligence by the Superior (*ephestôs*) is not without danger since he has to answer for all, and disobedience by a subordinate is harmful and wrong, and especially dangerous if it causes others to offend. Each one therefore in his own place showing willing zeal (*spoudê*) and fulfilling the Apostle's command, 'Not lazy in zeal',† receives praise for his eagerness: but if he is negligent the contrary is true, he receives misery and woe. For 'cursed' it says 'is everyone who does the work of the Lord carelessly.'‡

Commentary

The question shows clearly that we are beginning a new section in the Rules. Together with the next text to be considered it was originally part of one long answer, which in the Vulgate recension was divided up into Longer Rules 24–32. This group and the subsequent four Rules, which were formerly two answers, form a clear section on relations within and between communities.[8]

---

* 1 Cor. 14:40.
† Rom. 12:11.
† Jer. 48:10.

The superior as Eye

The main subject of these late texts is the Superior. We are thus clearly in Gribomont's third stage of community development. The scriptural text at the head of our Rule is the starting point of Basil's reflections, performing a similar role in the second half of the Longer Rules as the double commandment of love did in the first. 1 Corinthians 14:40 is one of the most quoted texts in the Rules,[9] which shows the importance of good order in Basil's thought. Similar words are used by Gregory of Nyssa to characterise the ascetic teaching of Macrina. He is addressing her community at her deathbed: 'Look at her and be mindful of the instructions she gave you for order (*tetagmenon*) and graciousness (*euschêmon*) in everything.'[10]

In our Rule the text is immediately related to another characteristic Basilian theme: the unity of the body. In this context he calls the community by the interesting word *sunapheia*. This term, meaning union, is used by Basil in relation to the Holy Trinity in other works and it later became a controversial term in christology during the Nestorian controversy. Like *koinônia* it is used of spiritual and eucharistic union, of man's union with God and of sexual union. Its use here shows that Basil's concept of community order is organic and spiritual, and that for him *eutaxia* does not mean a rigid regimentation.

Although Basil mentions ear, hand and eye, the emphasis here is firmly on the eye. This designates the Superior, on whom falls responsibility for the community. He is not the Head, that is Christ, and so he is just one organ among many. But we have moved away here from mutual and general obedience to a situation where the dynamics of obedience are centred on one person. The analogy of the body is developed so as to look at the question from two points of view, that of the other member who does not obey and that of the eye which does not perform its role. Both situations are disastrous. This concern with the Superior performing his proper role, especially as regards correction, is important for Basil who was himself a 'Superior of Superiors'. The possibility of one member leading another astray is looked at with horror here as in Longer Rule 28.

The sound functioning of the body is in accordance with the plan of God the Creator and we can safely say that the *eutaxia* of the community comes from the same source.

Good order and keeping one's place: a hierarchy of fiery zeal

The Rule ends with the vision of the well-ordered community as a fiery hierarchy[11] where each has his own place in which he shows an eager zeal. The idea of remaining in one's place was a favourite one for Basil, as shown by his frequent use of 1 Corinthians 7:24, 'Let each one, brothers, remain in the state in which he was called.'[12] Shorter Rule 259 asks what 'not lazy in zeal' (Rom. 12:1) means, and Basil answers with a cascade of his favourite terms:

> He who with fiery eagerness (*prothumia*), insatiable desire (*epithumia*) and tireless zeal (*spoudê*) does the will of God in the love (*agapê*) of Christ Jesus our Lord, according to the scripture saying, 'He will greatly delight in his commandments' (Ps 111.1).

Whereas remaining in one's place in a hierarchical secular society could be oppressive, this short answer shows that, for Basil, when one is living in the community of the godly it can be a source of passionate delight. Negligence, whether by the Superior or subordinate, is on the other hand the cause of misery, a belief supported by Basil's favourite Old Testament text, Jeremiah 48:10.[13]

The same New Testament principles of charity and good order which regulate the mutual relations of brothers in the same community also guide the relations between communities. Basil regrets trading between brotherhoods in Shorter Rule 285, discusses the situation of poor and rich brotherhoods in the same area in Shorter Rule 181, encourages cooperation in Longer Rule 54 to minimise contact with the outside world, and in Longer Rule 35 advocates the amalgamation of brotherhoods in the same parish (*kômê*).

The position and title of the Superior

Basil's Superior is not as clearly defined as Benedict's Abbot. His titles are suitably vague,[14] just as Basil uses diverse words for each form of ascetic life. Here he is the Eye, the one who is entrusted with general oversight, and he is given the title *Ephestôs*. Basil seems to prefer participles to describe the leader: *Proestôs* is the most common (47 times and twice in the feminine), *pepisteumenos* (he who is entrusted) as used here is also found elsewhere as is *epitetagmenos* (he who is appointed). Other terms are also used such as *Presbyteros* (elder, five times and four times in the feminine), *prokathistôn* (LR 44), and *proechôn* (LR 49). Some of these are used of subordinate officials and sometimes they are in the plural, suggesting Gribomont's second stage or, especially in the case of the *presbyteroi*, the group of seniors in the community. This vagueness in terminology clearly represents an early stage in the development of cenobitic leadership.

Although at first Superiors probably arose naturally from among the brothers when their charism was recognised, Longer Rule 43 speaks of a Superior being appointed by the Superiors of other brotherhoods. This Rule is also important as it is a supplement to the section of the Longer Rules dealing with community structure and it outlines the qualities expected of a Superior. These qualities are seen as important because the ruled tend to become like the ruler. He should thus make his life a clear example of every commandment. His virtues should include humility, compassion and the ability to deal prudently with different types of person and to cure different types of fault. The late Shorter Rule 303 implies that the testing of Superiors along these lines may involve a period of probation. This testing and the firm subordination of the Superior to Scripture, shows that his was a very different position to that of the Egyptian Abba whose words had an oracular character for his disciples. Once appointed the Superior is exhorted to 'do everything with counsel',[15] which may imply that there was sometimes a Council of Seniors.[16] There is however no evidence in the Rules of a council of all the brethren as is found in the *Rule of the Master* and in Chapter 3 of the *Rule of St Benedict*.

It would seem that whereas Basil did not accept a rigid boundary between ascetics and the less committed, pressure of circumstance and his emphasis on charisms led to his accepting two classes of brothers in the community. In the late Shorter Rule 235, not in the Small Asceticon, on whether one should learn much Scripture by heart, we are told that, 'the brethren fall into two general divisions (*tagmata*), those who are entrusted with leadership (*prostasia pepisteumenoi*) and those whose duty is to defer and obey.' One could see how such a situation could easily evolve from the establishment of a Council of gifted elders. The distinction is here based on teaching the ministry of the Word, as those entrusted 'with the care of the larger body' should memorise what they have to teach. Basil is very concerned about speech and the ministry of the Word among the ascetics. A typical example of this is in Longer Rule 49: 'If no one would entrust the use of tools to inexperienced persons, much more is it necessary to put the management of speech in the hands of competent men.' It would seem that de Vogüé is right when he says that Basil is concerned 'to bring out an élite, upon whom would devolve an important part of the direction of the brotherhoods'.[17]

Mutual responsibility and sharing of authority

The Superior thus came to be the central guarantee of good order in the community, though always in the cause of the spiritual development of the brothers. Although the communities became more institutional over time, their fundamental structure remained based on mutual responsibility. This involved the basic Christian values of surrender to the other and the stronger giving help to the weak.[18] This structure was expressed in spiritual dialogue, which gives the Asceticon its very form and context in question and answer, but which also operated within the communities in the absence of Basil. This is an extension of the interest in the Superior–subject relationship which is so important in these later Rules. One can see this in the practice of confession, which was not the modern sacrament but the monastic manifestation of thoughts, as found in the Pachomian literature, Cassian and the *Rule of St Benedict*.[19] Confession was made 'to those brethren who are entrusted with the task of caring for weak souls tenderly and sympathetically'.[20] The frequent questions on what one's attitude should be towards sinners shows a more general concern for mutual responsibility.

We have already noticed that the responsibilities of the Superior were shared and that there developed within the communities bodies of elders. There was also a more specific sharing of authority with brothers responsible for certain areas: the Cellarer, responsible for provisions etc.,[21] who has an assistant (SR 156) and the Oeconomus or Steward, if he be another person (LR 34, SR 149).[22] Other officials include the Overseer of work (SR 141, 142), the Superintendent of the common discipline (LR 53), and the brother in charge of the boys (LR 15).

Connected to this last position, Shorter Rule 292 mentions a school (*didaskaleion*) or teacher (*didaskalon*) – the word depends on the manuscript recension – for children not destined for the brotherhood. Basil gives this a qualified welcome *if* it serves the right end of education in piety. Longer Rule 15 shows that boys and girls were to be part of the community in obedience to the commandment, 'let the children come to me' (Mark 10:14). Their lives, though, were to be subject to a special order in separate houses. This was for a number of reasons; they might see their elders punished, they might be encouraged to inappropriate zeal, and their lessons would disturb the brothers. One of the Egyptian Desert Fathers took a different view of the disturbance caused by children:

> Abba Poemen's brethren said to him, 'Let us leave this place, for the monasteries here worry us and we are losing our souls; even the little children who cry do not let us have interior peace.' Abba Poemen said to them, 'Is it because of voices of angels that you wish to go away from here?'[23]

Democracy and the deputy-Superior

Another important officer in the community was the Superior's deputy. Basil doesn't give him a title, just referring to him as 'another' in Longer Rule 45. He was chosen by the Superior with 'others able to decide' and the reason for his appointment was the maintenance of good order (not to be interpreted in a 'police' sense) in the absence or indisposition of the Superior. It is interesting to note that the Superior is often absent. The deputy is to serve the ministry of the Word both to the brothers and to visitors. This is because if all rush to speak one gets that disorder (*ataxia*) which Paul had to rebuke amongst the Corinthians. Longer Rule 45 states that his presence avoids the disorder of democracy (*dêmokratikon ti schêma*). One could compare this to Shorter Rule 123 which seems to advocate democracy:

> If anyone is sad that he is not allowed to do what he cannot do well should we bear with him?

> Concerning this we have said in many places that in general to use one's own will (*idion thelêma*) or to allow this is contrary to sound reason; and not to submit to the decision of the majority is as dangerous as disobedience and arguing.[24]

This answer may perhaps best be interpreted as a warning against 'singularity', as in the eighth step of humility in the *Rule of St Benedict*,[25] rather than as an isolated example of 'community democracy' in the Asceticon.

We can thus see in the Asceticon the development of a practical way of governing communities which were themselves evolving into distinct institutions. It is a mistake to project a developed structure onto early texts, but it is also wrong to concentrate so much on the original looser lifestyle of the ascetics that one forgets that the structures, officials and regulations were a response in the spirit of the Scriptures to real problems and needs. The spirit of the 1960s should not colour our reading of these fourth-century texts.

NOTES FOR INTRODUCTION TO PART THREE AND CHAPTER TWELVE

1. From the question at the head of LR 24.
2. 'Commandments du Seigneur', *É&É*, pp. 304–5.
3. *St Basil and Monasticism*, pp. 35–41.
4. Rousseau, *Pachomius*, pp. 100–101 shows that the commands of the Superiors and the rules of the monastery were both seen as 'established by God's precept', and Pachomius is reported in his Rules as teaching his monks to obey each of the scriptural commandments. The same elements are present in Basil but the Scriptures have an even more prominent place.
5. *Rule of St Benedict* 1:2, but see RB 2:4 when it is said the Abbot must never teach anything contrary to Scripture.
6. R 12 (SR 1), R 13 (SR 114), R 14 (SR 157) and R 15 (SR 98 – Clarke is surely wrong in saying SR 184).
7. Answer 64 (SR 115) also deals with mutual obedience, does not mention a Superior, and it again relates this to the Son and the Spirit.
8. The titles of some of these Rules are: LR 25, 'That a Superior who does not rebuke sinners will undergo a fearful condemnation'; LR 26, 'That all things, even the secrets of the heart, are to be revealed to the Superior'; LR 26, 'That even the Superior himself, should he stumble, must be admonished by the pre-eminent among the brethren'; LR 29, 'Concerning him who works with pride or murmuring'; LR 32, 'How we should behave towards relatives according to the flesh'; LR 35, 'The character of those who administer the necessities of life in the brotherhoods'.
9. Seven times: LR 21, SR 72 on behaviour at mealtimes; LR 33, SR 108 on relations with the sisters; LR 24, SRs 238, 276. In the editions of Clarke and Frank only Matt. 18:15, Acts 4:35 (both dealing with community) and 1 Cor. 10:31 (do all to the glory of God) are quoted more frequently. The Italian version of Neri includes allusions as well as direct quotations and adds another six texts.
10. *Life of Macrina* 27:6–7.
11. The term hierarchy was not coined until later, by Pseudo-Dionysius the Areopagite, but the concept is perennial.
12. Quoted in SRs 100, 125, 136, 141 and 147. In Letter 22 he writes that 'each one should remain where he has been placed'.
13. This text is also quoted in LRs 9, 34 and SRs 150, 169. It connects with Basil's concern for *akribeia*, strictness or exactness, in obeying the commandments.
14. For lists of the titles see Clarke (1913), p. 92, Clarke (1925) pp. 39–40, Murphy, p. 46.
15. Prov. 31:4, quoted in LR 48, SR 104 and also used in Chapter 3 of the *Rule of St Benedict*.
16. e.g. LRs 29, 33, 35 and SRs 96, 105, 106, 119.
17. 'The Greater Rules', *Word and Spirit* 1, p. 63.
18. e.g. SRs 117, 178.
19. Pachomius: 'It is a great evil not to confess one's temptations quickly to someone

who has knowledge, before evil has matured', *First Greek Life of Pachomius*, 96.

Cassian: 'They are next taught not to conceal by a false shame any itching thoughts in their hearts, but as soon as such arrive, to lay them bare to the Senior, and, in forming a judgement about them, not to trust anything to their own discretion, but to take it on trust that it is good or bad which is considered and pronounced so by the examination of the Senior' *Inst.* 4:9; cf. *Conf.* 2:10, 11.

Rule of St Benedict 4:50, 7:44–8, 46:5–6.

Clarke (1925) reviews the evidence on pp. 45–52. Murphy, pp. 93, 95–6, criticises him but on the anachronistic grounds that there was individual sacramental confession at that time.

20. LR 26, the title is misleading as it only mentions the Superior, see also LRs 10, 15, SRs 15, 110, 229, 288, 301 and, concerning the sisters, 227.

21. e.g. SR 148 (*ho pisteutheis tēn phrontida tou kellariou*) and SR 156. SR 147 does not have the noun *kellarios* for cellarer, as Lampe's *Patristic Greek Lexicon* states, but rather *kellarion*, storeroom, thus: 'he who is engaged in the storeroom'. Such official titles belong to a later stage of cenobitic organisation as in the pseudo-Basilian *Poenae* 51 (*PG* 31:1313A).

22. Murphy, p. 50, lists other titles for the Oeconomus.

23. *Sayings of the Desert Fathers*, tr. Ward, Poemen 155.

24. The version in R 176 has 'the decision of the majority *or the Superiors*' (*vel multorum vel eorum qui praesunt*), but this may be an addition by Rufinus.

25. *Rule of St Benedict* 7:55. 'The eighth step of humility is that a monk does only what is endorsed by the common Rule of the monastery and the example set by his superiors.'

Chapter Thirteen

'Obedience unto death': The Case of the Disobedient Brother

In examining Basil's teaching on community structure in the previous chapter, we have noted the importance of obedience. Mixed with love, this could be characterised as the mortar holding together the house of the community. Disobedience is thus a most serious fault. As we see how Basil deals with this problem in Longer Rule 28 we are given a good opportunity to attempt a broader examination of his views on this important Christian virtue.

LONGER RULE 28

How all should behave towards a disobedient brother.

As for one who is hesitant in obeying the commandments of the Lord, first of all everyone should sympathise with him as a sick member of the body and the Superior (*proestôs*) should try to cure his infirmity with private admonitions. If however he perseveres in disobedience and will not amend, then the Superior must correct him sharply before all the brotherhood and, with every type of exhortation, apply medicinal remedies (*iatreia*). But if after much warning he is still not ashamed and shows no improvement in his conduct, he becomes, as the saying goes, his own destroyer. With many tears and lamentations, but nevertheless firmly, we must imitate the doctors and cut him away from the body as a corrupted and totally useless member. For they, whenever they find one member affected by an incurable disease, remove it by surgery and cauterisation so that the harm may not spread further and corrupt the neighbouring parts. We too must necessarily adopt this practice in the case of those who hate or oppose the commandments of the Lord, following the instruction of the Lord himself who said, 'if your right eye causes you to stumble, pluck it out and throw it away.'* For kindness in such cases is like the uninstructed generosity of Eli which he showed to his sons in a manner displeasing to God. He was suitably punished.† Such spurious kindness towards the wicked is a betrayal of the truth and a plot against the common good. It accustoms one to indifference towards evil, since on the one hand what is written is no longer observed: 'Why did you not rather mourn, that he who had done this deed might be taken away from your midst?'‡ – and on the other what is added inevitably comes to pass, 'a little leaven leavens the whole lump'.§ 'Rebuke sinners', says the Apostle, 'in the presence of all', and he immediately gives the reason, 'that the rest may also fear.'‖

To sum up, he who does not accept the treatment applied by his brother¶ is inconsistent. For if he does not accept subordination, and asserts his own will, why does he remain with him? Why does he choose him as the ruler of his life? When someone has once accepted enrolment in the body of the brotherhood and has been judged a vessel fit for service, even if a command seems beyond his strength, let him cast the responsibility on the one who gave the excessive order, and show submission and obedience even unto death, remembering the Lord who 'became obedient unto death, even death on a cross'.** Rebellion and contradiction, however, reveal many evils – a diseased faith, a doubtful hope, a proud and arrogant character. For no one disobeys a command unless he has first condemned the giver of the command; nor will one who trusts in God's promises and has his hope firmly fixed on them ever shrink from performing orders, however laborious. For he knows, 'that the sufferings of this present time are not worth comparing with the glory that is to be revealed.'†† The one who is persuaded that 'whoever humbles himself will be exalted'‡‡ will show greater eagerness than his teacher expects,

---

* Matt. 5:29, cf. Mark 9:47.
† 1 Sam. 2:11–4:18.
‡ 1 Cor. 5:2.
§ 1 Cor. 5:6.
‖ 1 Tim. 5:20.
¶ Thus most mss, the Benedictine text in *PG* 31 has 'the Superior (*proestôs*)'.
** Phil. 2:8.
†† Rom. 8:18.
‡‡ Matt. 23:12.

being aware that 'the temporary light burden of our hardship is preparing for us an utterly incomparable eternal fullness of glory.'*

Commentary

This Rule is in two parts. The first shows how the community should deal with a disobedient brother and ends with proof from Scripture that it is essential to take action against offenders. The second looks at the issues involved in the question of obedience from the point of view of the subordinate, teaching a high view of obedience unto death and relating it to the free choice of the subject. It also situates obedience in the context of eschatology, the reward which awaits the virtuous in heaven. It is clear that this is a very important issue for Basil. It is significant that the only saying of Basil in the Alphabetical Collection of Apophthegmata is on this very subject:

> One of the old men said, 'When Saint Basil came to the monastery one day, he said to the Abbot, after the customary exhortation, "Have you a brother here who is obedient?" The other replied, "They are all your servants, master, and strive for their salvation." But he repeated, "Have you a brother who is really obedient?" The Abbot then led a brother to him and Saint Basil used him to serve during the meal. When the meal was ended, the brother brought him some water for rinsing his hands and Saint Basil said to him, "Come here so that I also may offer you water." The brother allowed the Bishop to pour the water. Then Saint Basil said to him, "When I enter the sanctuary, come, that I may ordain you deacon." When this was done, he ordained him priest and took him with him to the bishop's palace because of his obedience.'

Models from medicine and Scripture

In our Rule we again we find the image of the body, but this time it is a sick body, or rather a body with a sick member. Basil uses the language of treatment and amputation. We have already seen that he

---

* 2 Cor. 4:17.

favours medical imagery, possibly because of his own medical studies or from his own frequent experience of ill health.[2] Gregory Nazianzen writes, in an admittedly rhetorical list, of Basil's prowess in various forms of learning:

> Medicine, the result of philosophy and laboriousness, was also rendered necessary for him by his physical delicacy and his care of the sick. From these beginnings he attained to a mastery of the art, not only in its empirical and practical branches but also in its theory and principles.[3]

Even as early as Letter 2, Basil compares the scriptural 'icons' of various virtues to remedies in the shop of a public physician. Although this is commonplace in Christian literature, one can perhaps see Basil's influence in his brother's use of medical imagery concerning the ascetic Superior in *On the Christian Mode of Life*.[4]

The mutual responsibility we have noticed above is seen in action in our Rule where, although the Superior has the leading role, the whole community is involved in the care of the disobedient brother. The procedure is firmly based on Scripture because in the life of the commandments good order is scriptural order. The model here, as it is in at least six other places in the Rules,[5] is Matthew 18:15–17: 'If your brother sins against you, go and show him his fault, just between the two of you. If he listens to you, you have won your brother over. But if he will not listen, take one or two others along, so that every matter may be established by the testimony of two or three witnesses. If he refuses to listen to them, tell it to the Church; and if he refuses to listen even to the Church, treat him as you would a pagan or a tax collector.' Basil speaks of the slightly different situation of a *public* fault and has three stages: a) a private warning by the Superior, significantly in the context of the sympathy of all and the idea of the community as a body; b) a public and sharp rebuke before all the brothers, who are thus parallel to 'the Church' in the Gospel; c) if this does not work, then there should be, to continue the bodily and medical imagery, an amputation.

'Cut him away from the body': excommunication

One may be surprised that a freely constituted community based on repentance should need recourse to excommunication. In Shorter Rule 3, also based on Matthew 18:15–17, the use of 2 Thessalonians 3:14, 'have nothing to do with him, that he may be ashamed', is significant. This excommunication is not a definitive expulsion, but rather a remedial 'sending to Coventry' aiming to induce repentance. On the basis of the importance he gives to free will, however, and the seriousness with which he views sin and judgement, one should not be surprised that Basil believed in a definitive expulsion as a last resort. This is also shown in Shorter Rule 7, 'What is the judgement against those who defend sinners?', where he quotes Matthew 5:29: 'better that you lose one of your members than that your whole body be thrown into hell.' The medical image of amputation and the Pauline notion of the community as body unite here. One could view this as parallel to his rejection of Origenist speculation on the end of eternal punishment.

The use of excommunication is also significant in another area. Basil was both a bishop and an ascetic. Even before he was elected to the see of Caesarea he had taken an active role in Church life and politics in close association with bishops such as Eustathius of Sebaste and Dianius of Caesarea. Excommunication is *par excellence* something episcopal and his Canonical Letters show it to have been something of prime concern to Basil as a Shepherd of the Church. It is also a means of drawing and defining boundaries. Such boundaries defined by excommunication and admission came to be more important as Basil's communities grew and became more structured. In this question of excommunication from and within the communities, we thus see a typical conflation of concerns on the part of Basil the ascetic and bishop. While ascetic interests could both determine and support his episcopal policies, so his ascetic teaching is also influenced by his experience in the wider Church. It has already been noted more than once that one of his great achievements was the integration of this potentially divisive movement of enthusiasts into the normal life of the Church. This could not be done without influencing in its turn the style and structure of the ascetic life itself.

'False kindness to the wicked': the duty of correction

The second part of the first paragraph of this Rule stresses the duty of correction. Basil emphasises this so much that he must have had bitter experience of the results of laxity and false kindness in ascetic communities. Necessary correction is mentioned in Letter 2 where he emphasises that it needs to be done humbly and wisely so as to touch 'the heart of him who needs your ministrations'. Similar concerns are found in Letter 22 but here we find the additional consideration that the Christian, 'should not be indifferent to sinners or silent before them', a teaching also found in the *Moralia*.[6] Basil's interest moves from the individual level to that of the one responsible for others, and his teaching on this subject grows progressively more insistent. The theme is frequent in the Asceticon.[7] The classical scriptural example of the duty to correct is the punishment of Eli, priest of Shiloh, who did not restrain the wickedness of his sons. This is developed at length in the first prologue to the *Moralia*, 'On the Judgement of God', and in Shorter Rule 47, 'Should we keep silence when men sin?', where it is pointed out that Eli did rebuke them but did not take appropriate action or show a fitting zeal. The same example is used by Cassian and Benedict.[8] Basil completes his case with St Paul's instructions on this topic.

The freely obeying subject

The second half of this Rule looks at the problem of disobedience from the point of view of the brother who should obey. In examining Basil's teaching on *diathesis* we noted his interest in interior attitude. Here the stress is on freedom of will in the subject: having freely chosen subordination, he is inconsistent if he then asserts his own will (*to heautou thelēma*). It is significant that the emphasis is on the moral responsibility of the person obeying rather than on the authority of the one giving the command. This is close to what we noticed in Shorter Rule 114 where it is the content of the order and not the one who gives it which is important. There one has a duty to disobey for 'we must obey God rather than men' (Acts 5:29), and thus one's own judgement, or rather one's use of Scripture, takes priority.

Here it is the disobedient brother who is rhetorically invited to leave. The shift in emphasis is important although the stress on free judgement remains. In our later text one freely chooses enrolment and then obeys those who are judged worthy. The language Basil uses is significant, 'Why does he choose him as the ruler of his life (*prostatên auton . . . epigraphetai*)?' *Prostatên epigraphô* in ancient Athens meant to choose a man as a patron and protector (*prostatês*), and in Basil's time society was held together by a web of patronage in which he too played his part.[9] Here we have another example of the continuity between Basil's social and ascetic contexts. There is thus a free choice of Superior, or better of community (the word for Superior is absent here from most manuscripts). There is also a choice of the brother by the community, as he 'has been judged a vessel fit for service'. We will return to the theme of enrolment later.

Even after entry into the community, however, the brother is not bound by unbreakable chains. Apart from the possibility of the community expelling him, Longer Rule 36 allows a positive reason for departure, 'harm received from living together', as well as the negative one of instability. It recommends, using Matthew 18, an attempt to reform the community, but if this fails one will 'be departing no longer from brethren but strangers'. The only valid reason for departure is thus to 'keep the commandment of the Lord', and this action should be done publicly in front of witnesses. This is the positive counterpart of the self-willed departure mentioned here. That one retains moral responsibility after enrolment is confirmed by Shorter Rule 230 on 'reasonable service' (Rom. 12:1) where the 'irrational one' goes as he is *led* and is 'carried away by the authority of the leader', whereas the man with sound reason does what is pleasing to God with much thought.

A more common ancient doctrine, as in the *Rule of the Master*, is that the disciple abdicates responsibility and does not assess the Master's orders.[10] This is based on the Master's spiritual authority and a distrust of self-will. The latter is very Basilian, but in *his* teaching on obedience he has a more positive view of human responsibility and brings higher principles into play. In his brotherhoods the central part played by the spiritual father in the Egyptian desert tradition is partly taken on by the community itself.

Obedience unto death

In our Rule we find a different situation from Shorter Rule 230 and Longer Rule 36. This is a command which is presumably sound but which seems to the brother to be impossible. The response is to put responsibility on the person giving the order and 'show obedience and submission even unto death'. This refers to the death of self-will rather than physical death,[11] but it does imply that the ascetic is a successor to the martyrs in this martyrdom of obedience. The theme of the ascetic as successor to the martyr is a common one in monastic literature and also involves a continuity of terminology. In the *Life of Theodotus of Ancyra*, written during Basil's lifetime in 360–63 and describing events of fifty years before, this shopkeeper and martyr is described as having *eusebeia*, zeal for *askêsis* and *enkrateia*, as well as being an 'athlete'.[12] Basil's teaching on obedience even unto death is also Christological, based as it is on one of his favourite texts, Philippians 2:8.[13] This verse is given in the Small Asceticon as the answer to question 65, 'To what length of obedience must we go in order to keep the rule of being well-pleasing to God?'

Obedience is thus absolute when it is according to the commandments. Basil, though, is concerned that the Superiors should, as well as conforming their commands to the Scriptures, adapt them to the 'suitability and strength of the worker'.[14] He also makes allowance for dealing with Superiors who do wrong, although *eutaxia* demands that the rebuke is administered by the Seniors. Answer 69 in Rufinus, 'is someone allowed to refuse the work assigned to him and seek another?', allows dialogue with the Superiors but states that 'the limit of obedience is death'. It is significant that even in this early text he says that 'since the individual cannot decide for himself what is expedient, he often chooses for himself a work that is harmful.' One can see why structures of obedience had to emerge and why Basil spoke of two types of brother in the community. This answer is, together with certain texts of Cassian[15] and the pseudo-Basilian 'Admonition to a Spiritual Son', the source of Benedict's Chapter 68, 'The assignment of impossible tasks to a brother'. In it Benedict also allows a humble discussion of the problem with the Superior and follows Basil in making obedience the final solution. With his higher view of the office of Superior, however, Benedict does not allow for the rebuke of the Abbot by the community, only for the intervention of those outside, 'the Bishop of the diocese or the Abbots or Christians of the area'.[16]

Basil's doctrine of obedience is thus both high and qualified. It is based more on the scriptural commandments and the needs of the community than on the special position of the Superior. We have seen how obedience is seen in a Christological context, but the three texts at the end of our Rule also situate it eschatologically. The difficulties we encounter in obedience are as nothing compared to the glory that awaits us in heaven. Hope for this future glory is thus an essential motivation for the ascetic.

Obedience as characteristic of the Basilian movement

As a final thought, given the profound doctrine outlined above, it is not surprising that Basil is associated with obedience, as in the Saying from the Apophthegmata. This virtue came to be a characteristic of the Basilian movement in asceticism and a key means to reform and moderate the extremism of the enthusiasts. Gregory of Nyssa writes of the importance of having a Superior and teacher in his treatise 'On Virginity', which was inspired by his brother Basil. In mentioning the dangers of not having one he touches on some characteristically Basilian themes:

> Therefore, since the majority of persons who desire to live a life of virginity are still young and immature, they must concern

themselves with this above all, the finding of a good guide (*kathêgoumenon*) and teacher on this path, lest, on account of their ignorance, they enter upon trackless places and wander away from the straight road. For as Ecclesiastes says, 'two are better than one' (Eccles. 4:9) . . . and 'woe to the one who lives alone, for if he falls there will be none to raise him up' (Eccles. 4:10).

Gregory then criticises those who deviate from this norm of obedience: those who deceive themselves by thinking their own desires good, who do not work for their daily bread, who follow private revelations rather than the Gospel, who live a solitary life in their own houses, 'and still others who consider being unsociable and brutish a virtue without recognising the command to love and without knowing the fruit of longsuffering and humility'.[17]

The Basilian notion of obedience in community as set forth in the Rules was thus seen as the only safeguard against the dangers inherent in other forms of ascetic life lived at the time.

NOTES

1. *The Sayings of the Desert Fathers* tr. Ward, Basil 1. This story recalls Longer Rule 31: 'That it is necessary to accept the services rendered by the Superior.'
2. cf. LRs 51, 52, 53 and SR 301 with Gribomont's SR 314. It is significant that LR 55, the last of the series, shows that the use of medicine is consistent with the life of piety.
3. Gregory Nazianzen, *Oration 43* 23.
4. In *St Gregory of Nyssa: Ascetic Works*, tr. Woods Callahan, pp. 146–7.
5. LR 36, SRs 3, 47, 178, 232, 293. Cf. also LR 9, SRs 9, 41. A similar use of Matt. 18 is found in Chapter 23 of the *Rule of St Benedict*.
6. *Moralia* 52:1–4.
7. Examples include: in the Small Asceticon R 16 (SR 3), R 17 (SR 4), R 72 (SR 40), R 121 (SR 47). In the Great Asceticon there are also LRs 25, 28, 43, 47, 50–53, SRs 19, 7, 239. This confirms that Basil's concern with correction grows greater over time.
8. Cassian, *Conferences* 16:6:4, 16:20. *Rule of St Benedict* 2:26.
9. One example among many is Letter 316 where he asks a dignitary to act as *Prostatês* for an unnamed individual. The word was also used of divine and heavenly protection and, as in our Rule, in an ascetic context. See Lampe, *Patristic Greek Lexicon*.

10. de Vogüé, *Community and Abbot* 1:197–8. In the context of the elder/disciple relationship, a more nuanced view of spiritual authority is given in a study of another sixth-century text, the Letters of Barsanuphius and John, in 'Aspects of Spiritual Direction: The Palestinian Tradition' by John Chryssavgis.

11. Murphy, p. 43.

12. Elm, *Virgins of God*, pp. 52–6.

13. Quoted here and in SRs 116 (R 65), 119 (R 69), 152 (R 131), 172 (R 134), 176 (R 156), 206 (R 126), 317.

14. SR 153 (R 131).

15. *Institutes* 4:9–10, 12:32:2 and *Conferences* 2:10.

16. cf. *Rule of St Benedict* 64:3–6.

17. 'On Virginity' 23, tr. Woods Callahan (1967), pp. 70–71.

Chapter Fourteen

'Those who profess great things': Admission to the Community and the Clothing of the Christian

All Christians did not accept Basil's teaching on the demands of the life of piety. It was thus inevitable that boundaries should emerge between the committed and the rest, as we have already noticed in a number of contexts. The formation of a frontier is particularly notice-able when one is looking at entry into the life of piety. The relevant Rules again reveal different stages of institutionalisation. In this area we see Basil, as both ascetic and bishop, responding to situations in ways which led to the development of what was to become the standard method of monastic initiation and profession. In a different way, his teaching in Longer Rule 22 on the appropriate clothing for a Christian inevitably led to a visible boundary between those who followed it and those who did not. One is reminded of the scandal caused by the young Eustathius' outlandish attire. Basil's teaching here contributed to the development of the monastic habit. This same theme of boundaries will be continued in the next section when we consider the boundary of gender and how Basil dealt with relations between male and female ascetics.

LONGER RULE 10

Should all who come be received or, if not, who? And should they be admitted at once or after testing? What form should this testing take?

Since our loving Lord and Saviour Jesus Christ proclaims, 'Come to me all who labour and are heavy laden, and I will give you rest',* it is dangerous to reject those who come to the Lord through us and wish to take up his easy yoke and the burden of his commandments that raises us to heaven. Yet we must not allow any to tread the hallowed ground of these teachings with unwashed feet. But as our Lord Jesus Christ asked the young man who came to him about his former life, and, having learned that it was good, commanded him to fulfil what was still lacking to perfection and then allowed him to follow, so obviously we should find out about the former life of applicants. If they have already led a good life, we should pass on to them the more perfect teachings; but when they are only beginning to turn from an evil life or have set out from a state of indifference towards the strict life of the knowledge of God, then we must examine their characters to see whether they are unstable and prone to sudden decisions.

For we must suspect the instability of such men as these, who, in addition to their failing to benefit themselves, actually cause harm to others by causing reproaches and lies and slanders about our work. But since all things are put right by care and the fear of God masters every defect of the soul, we must not despair right away even of these, but encourage them to submit to an appropriate course of training, testing their decision by time and hard work. Thus we may safely accept them if we find them steadfast, but otherwise send them away while they are still outside; the test will then involve no risk to the brotherhood. We must find out whether one who has been involved in sins freely confesses the things of shame and becomes his own accuser. By this he both puts to shame and renounces his companions in evil doing, according to the words of the psalmist, 'depart from me all you workers of evil',† and makes his future life free from a future fall into similar sins.

One method of testing may be applied to all: to see if they are so completely humble and devoid of false shame that they accept the lowliest tasks, providing that it be reasonably decided that their work at these tasks be useful. When each one, after full testing by those who are competent to make a skilful examination, has been accepted as a vessel useful to the Master and ready for every good work,‡ then let him be numbered with those who have dedicated themselves to the Lord. When a man from the higher ranks of society aspires

---

* Matt. 11:28.
† Ps 6:8.
‡ cf. 2 Tim. 2:21.

to humility after the likeness of our Lord Jesus Christ, it is especially necessary to impose some task which is distasteful to the worldly (*hoi exôthen*),
and to see whether he presents himself with full conviction to God as an
unashamed workman.

Commentary

This Rule is part of the section on renunciation begun by Longer
Rule 8. That text gives a theoretical exposition of the subject while
subsequent Rules examine aspects of the practice of renunciation.
This latter essentially means joining the ascetics. Hence these Rules
deal with the disposal of property (LR 9), who to receive and how
they are to be tested (LR 10), whether slaves or the married should
be received (LRs 11, 12), the place of silence in formation (LR 13) and
questions related to the making of profession (LRs 14, 15). The texts
in the Small Asceticon which lie behind these[1] have been much
expanded by Basil but even they speak of a definite boundary crossed
when joining the ascetics.

The references here to 'joining the servants of God', 'coming to the
service of God' and 'making a profession of virginity' do not necessarily mean a community living apart. John Chrysostom, when living
at home, began the ascetic life in a non-resident community in
Antioch.[2] The reception of children does, however, imply a separate
community and such a brotherhood is clearly present in Longer Rule
15. Rousseau says that at the time of the Small Asceticon these texts
were 'not yet capable of presenting the picture of a separate institution' but still used 'metaphors of threshold and frontier'.[3] It may
be that this presupposes too narrow and consistent a context for the
Rules. Basil could have dealt with a variety of situations at the same
time even while a presbyter. The ascetic landscape of Pontus and
Cappadocia in the 360s, under the influence of Eustathius and others,
would surely have included some distinct communities as well as
some groups almost indistinguishable from the local congregation.

What is clear, however, is that becoming a 'Servant of God' did
involve crossing a real frontier. Our concern here is with Longer Rule
10 in the Great Asceticon and so we will not involve ourselves in
institutional archaeology but rather see what this text has to say.

Starting from this we shall then move on to examine some of the broader issues it raises concerning admission.

'We must examine their characters': the testing of vocation

Our text starts with the call of Christ. The initiative in calling people to this form of life lies with him, and so those who come are not to be rejected out of hand. They are to be tested to see if the call is genuine. One notices that those who do the testing are not mentioned. Is it the Superior, the elders, or someone specially entrusted with the task? This, like the similar situation in Shorter Rule 114 on obedience, reflects the early date of the original text. Shorter Rule 112, however, says that one who 'comes to the life according to God' should not be received by the Superior alone without the consent of the brethren. The reception of candidates is thus a matter for the whole community, again showing the importance of mutual responsibility. In Longer Rule 13 those being formed in the ascetic life are called *eisagomenoi*, the word for catechumens we have already met in Longer Rule 4. This is another link between the ascetic life and baptism. The structure and development of monastic formation and initiation can be compared to the development of the catechumenate.[4] Among the Pachomians pagans were accepted into the community and spent time as genuine catechumens before being baptised,[5] but there is no evidence that this was the case in Asia Minor.

God's initiative is to call, but the community has the duty to test those who come to the life of the commandments. This means investigating their past lives, as Christ did with the rich young man. It also means observing how they react to performing humble tasks over a period of time. It is notable that Basil speaks in this context of different types of candidates. The first division is into those who were already living a good life and those converting from evil or indifference. Each type is to be dealt with in a different way, with the former being given 'the more perfect teachings' and the latter being helped by the fear of God. Here we have two more connections with Longer Rule 4 and two groups revealing people at different stages in the spiritual life. One method of testing is to be applied to all, however: performing humble tasks. This is a perennial feature of monastic formation which is still practised today. It is noteworthy, though, that Basil states that such work must be useful. There are examples in the sayings of the Desert Fathers of Elders giving useless tasks to their disciples to teach them obedience. John the Dwarf's Abba told him to water every day a dry stick.[6] One sees here Basil's moderation in comparison with the Egyptians; his maximalism took different forms.

The second division among candidates occurs when Basil mentions those who come 'from the higher ranks of society'. The distinction here is only in the intensity of testing, as for Basil all, whatever their origin, aspire to follow the same commandments. This special attention suggests that such men were not in the majority and that we are far from the classical aristocratic ideal of 'philosophical seclusion'.

Our Rule deals with the external crossing of a boundary but we find in addition a characteristically Basilian concern for inner attitude. The horror of instability connects with the stress elsewhere on a fixed *diathesis* and being *monotropos*. There is also the desire to help candidates break with sin which recalls the summons to repentance at the start of the *Moralia*. Even if the Rules themselves do not start with this turning from sin, it is clear that for certain brothers the life of piety must begin with confession and repentance.

Probation and formation

The dominant theme of this Rule is testing the one who comes. God calls him, he freely responds, but then the community must see if the call is genuine. It seems that at first those who desired an ascetic life either just adopted it or were given the monastic habit by an experienced elder who taught them its principles. A need to test the candidate also came to be important, as we see in the example of Pachomius being tested by Palamon.[7] The structure of testing and formation varied greatly, but in general the habit was sufficient to show that one professed the monastic life.

With the development of cenobitic monasteries we find a

systematisation of admission procedures, but in the case of Basil this is still in its early stages. In Pachomian houses the candidate was kept outside the monastery door for a few days while enquiries were made about him. He was taught some psalms and given other instruction and then he was brought in and clothed in the habit.[8] This period of probation was short, but it would seem that it grew longer. By the end of the fourth century the 'Rule of the Angel'[9] speaks of a three year period before reception into the community. This three year period is also found in Syrian Rules and in the legislation of Justinian,[10] but in the Latin West a year's noviciate gradually became the norm.[11]

Basil does not specify the length of the period of testing, which probably varied according to the needs of the individual. Distinctive clothing is important for him, but it is not clear when it was put on. It was possibly at first assumed from the time of one's decision to adopt an ascetic life, as Longer Rule 22 is an early text and does not refer to settled communities. The distinctive Basilian sign of entering the community was the public profession, to which we shall return later.

In Letter 23 Basil gives a vignette of a man who has decided to adopt the ascetic life. The ascetic to whom he writes is to see if this man has a true desire (*epithumia, erôs*) and love. If so he is to warn him of the difficulties of the 'narrow path' and to encourage him to hope for the unseen rewards. Then he is to mould him and instruct him in the written teachings of the Fathers so that he freely renounces the world and submits himself to Christ's yoke, imitating the Lord's own example. This is an informal initiation into the ascetic life by an experienced brother, chosen by the recipient of the letter and possibly at the request of the brother himself. It seems to be more like that practised among the hermits than that later found among cenobites.

Both the Letter and our text show a period of probation. Longer Rule 13 mentions novices learning in *hesycheia* (quiet) the mode of behaviour of 'religious' (*tois eusebesin*) and unlearning one's past. The children in the community were, in addition, to have studies appropriate to their '*skopos*'. This meant using Scripture and telling the stories of wonderful deeds, no doubt those of scriptural Saints. This recalls Basil's use of 'icons' of virtue in the Rules. This curriculum, with an emphasis on the Book of Proverbs, was almost identical to that described in the *Life of Macrina*,[12] which she was said to have followed. In reality, however, considering the position of her Father, her education was probably more classical and closer to that of her brothers. Certainly Gregory, in his Dialogue *On the Soul and Resurrection*[13] portrays her as well versed in philosophy, but it is difficult to tell how much this is just him putting words into her mouth and how much it reflects the real Macrina. The distrust of the classical Greek tradition shown by Basil and Gregory in the Rules and the *Life* here contrasts with Basil's pamphlet *ad Adulescentes*[14] on the Christian use of pagan literature in education. Even there, however, is found the same emphasis on the Christian and moral '*skopos*', but the contradiction is no doubt just a question of a different audience, the allowance for circumstances so frequent in the Rules. His use of scriptural saints is also probably modelled on the educational use of classical heroes.

Making profession

All this training leads up to the definitive step of entering the community. Connected to the defining of boundaries between ascetics and the rest of the Church, Basil's teaching on profession marks a definitive step in the development of monastic profession.[15] In early Christian literature the word 'profession' (*homologia*) was used of Martyrs and it was first used in the context of celibacy by Clement of Alexandria.[16] Basil speaks of the new ascetic being *numbered* among the brothers (*sunarithmeô*, LRs 10, 15, *enarithmon*, LR 15). What is particularly significant, though, is that he makes more explicit the *public* promise involved in this act, probably as a result of unfortunate experiences. It also reflects his involvement in the affairs of the wider Church as shown in the Canonical Letters 188, 199 and 217. Canon 19 of Letter 199 is often seen as at the origin of a public profession for men:

We do not recognise the profession of men except in the case of those who have enrolled (*enkatarithmeomai*) themselves in the order of monks (*tagmatôn tôn monazontôn*), and seem to have secretly adopted the celibate life. Yet in their case I think it becoming that there should be a previous examination, and that a distinct profession (*homologia*) should be received from them, so that whenever they revert to the life of the pleasures of the flesh they may be subjected to the punishment of fornicators.[17]

This context of failure for the definition of boundaries is prominent in the Asceticon. In Longer Rules 14 and 15 such failure is said to be sacrilege, robbing God of his votive-offering (*anathêma*). Basil's mother Emmelia is reported as saying on her deathbed concerning Macrina and their brother Peter, who were both living the ascetic life: 'both have been dedicated to you (God) by law and are your votive offerings (*anathêmata*)'.[18] It is probably partly to avoid potential failure in this area that Basil delays profession until the age of reason. He says that profession should be made, 'after careful examination and consideration – which he ought to be allowed to do by himself for a few days'[19] – what we today would call a pre-profession retreat. In Canon 18 of Letter 199, writing about virgins, Basil is more specific about the age. He says that, as children's words can not be taken as definitive, only the girl who is over 16 or 17 should be enrolled among the virgins. Even then she must be tested beforehand. He also brings in the local Church-leaders (*proestotas tôn ekklesiôn*) as witnesses. Here we again see Basil integrating the movement of ascetics into the life of the Church. The lack of this integration was one of the main complaints of the Synod of Gangra.

Longer Rule 10 has led us to a broader study of Basil's teaching on the important step of adopting the ascetic life. The texts concerned come from different periods in his life and different situations and, although certain elements such as the public profession were later to become normal, one should avoid trying to construct out of them a systematic structure of initiation. The important themes are testing, formation and profession. The distinctive dress of a religious person, the giving of which is so important in other Christian ascetic traditions, is the subject of the final text in this section. In examining it we shall again find ourselves at the boundary between the ascetic and the world.

LONGER RULE 22 (R 11)

What is the appropriate clothing for a Christian?

We have already shown the necessity of humility and simplicity, of cheapness and economy in all things, so that there may be few occasions of distraction on account of bodily needs. Our discussion of clothing must therefore keep the same principles (*skopoi*) in mind. For if we should zealously seek (*spoudazô*) to be last of all, it is quite clear that in this matter too the last place is to be chosen. For just as vain people (*philodoxoi*) seek glory for themselves even in the clothes they wear, striving to attract attention and arouse envy by reason of the splendour of their dress, so it is obvious that whoever has totally abased his life through humility should choose in this matter too the lowest possible. For just as the Corinthians are blamed because by their extravagance in the public feasts they put to shame those who have nothing,* so it is clear that in the ordinary and obvious style of dress, whoever is adorned above the common standard puts the poor person to shame. Since the Apostle says, 'do not be haughty, but associate with the lowly',† let each one examine himself who the Christian should more appropriately resemble; those who live in royal palaces and are clothed in soft garments, or the messenger and herald of the Lord's advent, than whom none greater born of women has arisen.‡ I mean John, the son of Zechariah, whose clothing was of camel's hair. The saints of old also went about in sheepskins (*mêlotai*) and even in goatskins.§

The Apostle has taught us the end (*skopos*) to be aimed at in a single phrase, saying, 'if we have food and clothing, with these we shall be content',‖ as if to say that we need covering only. Let us no longer fall into the forbidden vanity of ornamentation and the ostentation that comes from it – to say nothing worse. For these were introduced late into human society (*bios*),

---

* cf. 1 Cor. 11:22.
† Rom. 12:16.
‡ Matt. 11:8–11.
§ Heb. 11:37.
‖ 1 Tim. 6:8.

caused by needless and empty technology. But the original use of coverings is clear, for God himself gave them to those in need, as it says, 'God made for them garments of animal-skin'.* Such a use of clothes was quite sufficient for the covering of our private parts.

But as there is also another end (*skopos*), that of being warmed by coverings, both must have been aimed at, to cover our private parts and to be protected against bad weather. Since however there are some clothes that are very useful for this and others less so, we should prefer whatever sort serves several needs, in order to preserve the principle of poverty. To avoid having some things for show and others for use at home, one set of clothes for the day and another for the night, we should decide to acquire one garment which is sufficient for all our needs, a decent covering by day and necessary warmth by night. The result of this is that we all wear similar clothing (*schêma*) and the Christian is indicated by a distinctive mark even in his clothing. This is because things that have the same end (*skopos*) as far as possible agree with each other.

It is also useful to have distinctive clothing since it lets everyone know in advance that we have made profession (*epangelia*) of a godly life, so that those who meet us can demand appropriate behaviour. For unseemly and shameful behaviour is not equally noticeable in ordinary people and in those who profess great things. For one would not pay much attention to one of the lower classes or any one of the common crowd whom one found giving or receiving a beating in public, or shouting obscenities, or sitting in public houses, or doing any other unseemly thing of this kind, since one would take such conduct as being consistent with his whole way of life (*proairesis*). But when one has professed strictness, if he neglects his duty in the least respect, all people reproach him just as it is written, 'they will turn and attack you'.†

Therefore this profession (*epangelia*) by means of clothing forms a kind of discipline (*paidagôgia*) for the weaker brethren, so that even against their will they are kept from evil deeds. Just as the soldier has one type of distinctive clothing, and the senator another, and someone else another, from which their position may usually be guessed, so it is appropriate that a Christian be distinguished by his clothing which preserves the respectable sobriety commended by the Apostle; who now prescribes that the bishop should be

---

* Gen 3:21.

† Matt. 7:6. Pearls before swine, the same interpretation is given in SR 250.

respectable (*kosmios*), now bids the women dress respectably.* Respectability being of course understood in relation to the special aim (*skopos*) of Christianity.

I give the same directions about shoes: whatever is simple, easily obtained, and sufficient for the purpose (*skopos*) of necessity, should always be chosen.

Commentary

This Rule, corresponding to the greater part of Answer 11 in the Small Asceticon, follows a discussion of one's place at table which is alluded to in its first words. It has been called the 'first and most important' text on the monastic habit.[20] In its original context, however, it discusses appropriate clothing for the Christian.

From the first Basil was interested in the outward manifestation of one's inner disposition.[21] In Letter 2 he writes that,

> ... the humble and abject spirit is attended by a gloomy and downcast eye, neglected appearance, unkempt hair and dirty clothes; consequently the characteristics which mourners affect designedly are found in us as a matter of course. The tunic (*chitôn*) should be drawn close to the body by a belt (*zônê*); but let the belt not be above the flank, for that is effeminate, nor loose, so as to let the tunic slip through, for that is slovenly ... As for dress, its sole object is to be a covering for the flesh adequate for winter and summer. And let neither brilliancy of colour be sought, nor delicacy and softness of material ... however the tunic ought to be of such thickness that it will require no auxiliary garment to keep the wearer warm. The sandals should be inexpensive, yet completely adequate to one's needs. And in general, just as one should consider practical utility in the matter of clothing, so too should one in the matter of food.[22]

In the Great Asceticon the last part of Answer 11 has been detached to form Longer Rule 23 on the belt (*zônê*). Here our Rule is found in the section of the Longer Rules on self-control (*enkrateia*) after

---

* cf. 1 Tim. 3:2 and 1 Tim 2:9.

Answers dealing with food. At the start of the Rule it is made clear that with both food and clothing the same principles are followed: cheapness, simplicity and lack of ostentation. To choose cheap garments out of self-will and a desire to impress is, however, condemned in Shorter Rule 50. The concern with humility connects with Basil's sermon on this subject, which says that humility should be manifested in clothing and garments (*schêma* and *himation*) as well as posture and food.[23] The same concerns are thus taught to both ascetics in our Rule and the congregation in general in the sermon. The criteria given for the clothing of a Christian are here said to lead to uniformity, which would cause those who adopt them to become a clearly defined group. It is thus just a small step from this emerging boundary to a separate community.

The purpose of clothing

Basil cites John the Baptist and examples from St Paul to prove that clothing must manifest humility. The Apostle gives us one aim (*skopos*), covering, which is again connected to food, and Basil adds another, warmth. It can be very cold in Anatolia. A third principle (*logos*) is poverty which means that the Christian should have only one garment that fulfils all needs. This, also taught in Shorter Rule 90, recalls Matthew 10:10 and the command to the Twelve on their mission, and also John the Baptist's words in Luke 3:11 where giving away the second garment is connected with sharing food.[24] The result of all these aims is unity. Unity in clothing – Basil uses the word *schêma* which became a technical term for the monastic habit – shows that all have the same *skopos*. This unity is interior as well as communal and the Christian, 'as Basil says, aims at being the same everywhere and always, he has neither several faces nor several costumes'.[25] These principles were generally accepted by ascetics and Gregory of Nyssa records that Macrina, and presumably her female companions, wore a cloak (*himation*), a veil and worn sandals.[26] In this we see what became the basic elements of the monastic habit for men and women in East and West.

Distinctive dress also means that one has to live up to the profession that the clothing denotes. There are weaker brethren who are helped against their will to live the life of piety. Basil's little depiction of the life of the lower classes is an interesting glimpse of ordinary life in fourth century Asia Minor seen through the eyes of a devout member of the ruling class. The reference to casting pearls before swine in Matthew 7, quoted here, is used in a similar context in Shorter Rule 250 (R 171). Before finally referring to shoes, Basil refers to Paul's teaching in 1 Timothy and makes sober respectability (*kosmiotês*) the distinguishing mark of the clothing of a Christian. This eschews all ornamentation, which is itself a result of the fall from man's original state.

We find here the main themes we have already noted: separation from the world and community, which are the result of the double commandment of love, and also good order and the importance of one's aim (*skopos*). This external sign is thus the essential manifestation of interior values.

The importance of what is worn: Basil in tradition

The series of texts from 1 Timothy are very important in this Rule and they situate Basil in a tradition of Christian asceticism regarding clothing going back to the New Testament. This is noted by de Vogüé: 'What Peter and Paul, Clement and Cyprian had said of woman's clothing, Basil radicalised, applying it to men's clothing.'[27] Basil is thus part of a tradition stretching back into the past as well as standing at the origin of the monastic habit. This tradition is not only Christian but includes the distinctive dress of the ancient philosopher, which could be added to Basil's examples of soldier and senator. Eustathius was condemned for wearing the *schêma* of a philosopher.[28] When he broke with Eustathius, Basil wrote, 'I held that humility in dress was sufficient evidence of humility in spirit; and there was enough to convince me in the thick cloak (*himation*) and the belt and the sandals of untanned hide.'[29] In this as elsewhere, Basil's teaching is indebted to both Scripture and classical tradition.

In the monastic tradition proper, Basil's teaching here is distinguished from other early texts on the same subject by its practical nature and attention to the real purposes of the habit. Starting with Evagrius, in the Prologue to his *Praktikos*, other ascetic writers such as Cassian and Dorotheus of Gaza give a symbolic interpretation to the ascetic's items of clothing.[30] Basil only did this for the belt, in Longer Rule 23. He connects it with John, Elijah, Peter, Paul and Job and says that it is 'a token of manliness and preparedness for action'. Even here he gives the practical reasons that it draws the tunic to the body, keeping one warm and giving freedom of movement for work. For Evagrius the belt symbolised chastity, and all the other aspects of the monk's dress receive similar interpretations in line with the Alexandrian tradition of exegesis and Paul's imagery of clothing.[31] Evagrius only has few points of contact with Basil: the scapular allows free activity like Basil's belt, the clothing is different from that of seculars, and they both mention the sheepskin (*mêlotê*).[32]

Cassian is heavily influenced by his master Evagrius when he discusses the monastic habit in Book 1 of his *Institutes*. He also shows possible Basilian influence in a number of areas: the list of saints who wore the belt, the use of 1 Timothy 6:8 with the insistence on warmth and covering, and a mention of work and poverty. He also mentions uniformity of clothing but values it in itself whereas for Basil it is a valuable result of other criteria. As Cassian knew the Small Asceticon, it is likely that there is a direct dependence here[33] although such points of contact could have arisen solely through the use of common scriptural sources. On balance he seems to have been more influenced by Evagrian symbolism than by Basilian practicality. Descriptions of the items worn by Pachomian monks omit this symbolic element and the only discussion of garments is concerned with common ownership.[34] Such an absence of symbolism is also found in the Master and Benedict, whose texts on this subject are also largely descriptive and administrative. Benedict quotes from Answer 9 in Rufinus that clothing should be made from what can be got cheaply in the locality.[35] Like Pachomius, however, Benedict allows more than one garment.

This is just an outline of Basil's distinctive place in the early history of the monastic habit. One later reference to Basil's teaching is interesting. The earliest mention of the distinction in Byzantine

monasticism between the Small Schema and the Great Schema[36] is a
protest by St Theodore the Studite at the beginning of the ninth
century. He says: 'For there is one habit as there is one baptism, and
this is the practice of the holy Fathers. Depart not from the rules
and canons of the Fathers, especially our holy Father Basil.'

The clothes of the ascetic signify separation from the world, but
they are also a sign to the same world. As in the case of admission
to the communities, the life pleasing to God is seen to throw up
spontaneous boundaries between itself and the world of the less
committed. The next section, however, considers a boundary fixed
within human nature itself.

NOTES

1. LR 8 is from R 4, LR 9 from R 5, LR 10 from R 6, and LRs 14 and 15 much
   expanded from R 7.
2. Kelly, *Golden Mouth*, p. 19.
3. Rousseau, *Basil*, p. 201.
4. *RB 80* Appendix 5: 'Monastic formation and profession', p. 441.
5. A. Veilleux, 'La liturgie dans le cénobitisme pachomien au quatrième siècle', *Studia
   Anselmiana* 57 (1968), pp. 198–206.
6. This story is also found in Cassian and discussed in Chadwick's *Cassian*, p. 21.
7. *Bohairic Life* 10.
8. *Precepts* 49, cf. Cassian, *Institutes* 4:1–7, 30, and *Lausiac History* 18:12–13.
9. Said to have been given to Pachomius by an angel, *Lausiac History* 32, Cassian,
   Institutes 2:4–6, but the story probably was originally not from a Pachomian
   environment.
10. Patrich, *St Sabas*, pp. 28, 259–60. A later law of 546 restricted the three-year period
    to slaves and civil servants.
11. cf. Caesarius of Arles, *Rule for Virgins* 4, *Rule of the Master* 90:79–80, *Rule of St
    Benedict* 58:5–6.
12. *The Life of St Macrina* 3, tr. Woods Callahan (1967), p. 165. See Elm, *Virgins of
    God*, p. 71.
13. Woods Callahan (1967), pp. 198–272.
14. 'Letter to Young Men on Reading the Books of the Gentiles' – text in Deferrari,
    Letters, vol. 4, pp. 378–435. The date of composition is unknown.
15. *DIP* 7:886–7: 'Professione: ii – la professione tacita nei primi secoli'.
16. *Stromateis* 3:1, 4:1.
17. Letter 199, tr. Jackson.
18. *Vie de S. Macrine* (*SC* 178) 13:14–15, p. 186.
19. Longer Rule 15.
20. de Vogüé, *Doctrinal and Spiritual Commentary*, p. 269.

21. SRs 91, 93 and 168 show a concern with inward disposition related to clothing. The misuse of clothing is condemned in SR 70.
22. See also the later Letter 22: 'The Christian should not be ostentatious in clothing or sandals, . . . he should wear cheap clothes according to the needs of the body.'
23. Sermon *De Humilitate, CPG* 2865, *PG* 31:537A-B.
24. This probably in practice meant one set of clothes. Gregory of Nazianzen's *Oration 43* 61 speaks of Basil having two garments, a tunic (*chitonion*) and a well-worn cloak (*tribônion*). The latter is the characteristic garb of philosophers and monks. Basil's Letter 150 presents him teaching that one should only have one tunic (*chitôn*) using the same words of Jesus and John as here.
25. de Vogüé, *Reading St Benedict*, p. 264.
26. Gregory Nazianzen, *Oration 43* 61; Gregory of Nyssa *Life of Macrina* 29.
27. *Doctrinal and Spiritual Commentary*, p. 274.
28. Sozomen, *Ecclesiastical History* 2:43, cf. Elm, *Virgins of God*, p. 110. This recalls the idea of Christian ascetic life as the true philosophy.
29. Letter 223.
30. The Guillaumonts in *Traité Pratique* (*SC* 171, p. 484) say that Evagrius was probably the first to do so.
31. For Philo and Origen, see references in *Traité Pratique*, pp. 484–91. For St Paul – Rom. 13:14, Eph. 4:24, Eph. 6:13–17 etc.
32. *Traité Pratique*, p. 491.
33. cf. Gribomont, *Histoire de Texte*, p. 263.
34. *Precepts* 81, Jerome's *Preface to the Rules* 4, *Lausiac History* 31:3, Cassian, *Institutes* 4:13.
35. R 9 (LR 20). *Rule of St Benedict* 55:7, cf. also Cassian, *Institutes* 1:2.
36. The Great Schema is received later in one's monastic life and, especially in the Russian tradition, involves greater ascetic and spiritual duties.

Chapter Fifteen

'Are we not their equals in everything?': Gender and Asceticism

One notable feature of the Asceticon is the presence of thirteen Rules that mention sisters or female ascetics. The research of Susanna Elm and Daniel Stramara[1] has clarified the context of these, and, using their work, we can begin to understand Basil's role in forming a distinctive type of community life for both men and women. In comparison with the previous practice of uncontrolled mixing of the sexes, Basil established double communities and regulated the frontier between male and female in ascetic life. Longer Rule 33 gives us a good example of this. From a consideration of this text we can attempt a broader analysis of his approach to the question of relations between male and female ascetics. Behind questions of practice in this area, though, there lie certain theological issues and we shall briefly examine these before moving on to look at our text.

What is a double monastery?

It is first worth clarifying some terms:[2]
- A mixed monastery is one in which there is indiscriminate mixing of the sexes, even in the sleeping quarters.
- A double monastery is still a single monastic unit of men and women following the same Rule, under the same Superior and living in the same locality but the two sexes live in separate quarters. The term *diploun monastêrion* is first found in a law of the Emperor Justinian from AD 546,[3] but the reality is found in our Rules.
- A third model is that of twin monasteries, where communities of

monks and nuns are sited in close proximity but are each independent of the other.

The historical background: mixed monasticism

Mixed groups of ascetics were, as we have seen, a common feature of the movements of enthusiasts flourishing in Asia Minor in the mid fourth century. Male and female ascetics living together was characteristic of the 'Eustathians' condemned at Gangra, the urban 'Homoiousian' ascetics identified by Elm, and also of the wilder groups such as that around the renegade Deacon Glycerius. This practice was later found among the Messalians and it may have been observed in the early days of Macrina's community before a separate male community emerged under Peter.

Another pertinent but different case, also mentioned above, is that of the *syneisaktoi*, virgins living with ascetic men such as celibate clergy. This practice was condemned by many Councils, and by bishops including Basil, Gregory of Nyssa and Gregory Nazianzen.[4] In Letter 55 on this subject Basil says that 'the honour of celibacy (*agamia*) is this – that one is cut off from the society of women'. Such a practice was probably so widespread partly for practical reasons: when a female virgin was not living in her family or did not have sufficient wealth and influence to support herself, an alliance with a sympathetic man or with a community would be essential in the social climate of Late Antiquity.

Such indiscriminate mixing of the sexes in the ascetic life was frowned upon and censured for its danger to chastity. Even the foundation of double monasteries was forbidden by ecclesiastical legislation such as Canon 20 of the Second Ecumenical Council of Nicaea (787). Under this influence and reflecting later practice, all Rules concerning women were left out or changed in one family of manuscripts of the Great Asceticon, the 'Misogynous Recension'.

Transcending the sexes

Apart from practicalities, there was also a deeper theological reason for mixing the sexes in the ascetic life. Galatians 3:28, 'There is neither Jew nor Greek, there is neither slave nor free, there is neither male nor female; for you are all one in Jesus Christ', provides a theological foundation for this practice. Another relevant text is Luke 20:34–6,[5] where it is said that the sons of the resurrection do not marry and are equal to the angels. Such texts were interpreted to mean that through celibacy and ascetic struggle the lost likeness to God is restored, sexual differences are transcended and the life of the resurrection is lived on earth. This view was a common one in ascetic circles and is expressed in the following passage from the treatise 'On Virginity' by Basil of Ancyra, one of the leaders of the Homoiousian party. After saying that virgins live the angelic life mentioned in Matthew 22:30, he justifies a close mixing of the sexes in these words:

> They have a female body, but they repress the appearance of their body through ascesis, and become, through their virtue, like men, to whom they are already created equal in their soul. And while men through ascesis become angels instead of men, so do women, through exercise of the same virtues, gain the same value as men ... those who practice asceticism in this life have already succeeded in being just like angels: they have castrated the female and male desires to cohabit through virtue and live among men on earth with naked souls.[6]

Our Basil and his brother Gregory certainly seem to have had connections with Messalian circles. It also seems true that one aspect of the theology of Gregory of Nyssa is pertinent to this practice. He taught that humankind was first created in a state without sexual distinction and only then divided into the two sexes.[7] This teaching can be deduced from Genesis 1:27: 'God created man in his own image, in the image of God he created him [first creation]; male and female he created them [second creation].' According to Gregory the division of the sexes was not evil, a result of the Fall, but it was done in view of the Fall as a means of continuing the species in the face of death. In our fallen state this division is a source of conflict and Gregory argues that it is possible another way of propagating the species could have been devised without this division. One can see that from this view the Christian ascetic who 'transcended the sexes' is thus returning to God's primal design for humanity. This is the return to Paradise, when man was in harmony with all creation, which is so prominent in monastic literature.

This teaching is not the normal Christian view, but, through Gregory, it did enter into Orthodox thought and was taken up by St Maximus the Confessor. He related it to the transcending of divisions by the incarnate Christ, in this case by his virginal conception:

> The God-made-man has done away with the difference and division of nature into male and female, which human nature in no way needed for generation, as some hold, and without which it would have perhaps have been possible. There was no necessity for these things to have lasted forever. 'For in Christ Jesus,' says the divine Apostle, 'there is neither male nor female' (Gal. 3:28).[8]

There is an obvious connection between this theory and the practice of mixed communities. It means that transcending the sexes, when ascetic men and women dress alike and live together in chastity, is the highest form of Christian life. Given the early contact between Basil's family and the Homoiousians, it is quite possible that the source for his brother's teaching here came from that context.

Basil, equality and Galatians 3:28

Basil of Caesarea's reform of the ascetic life did not leave this cohabitation untouched, but neither did it enforce total separation. This reform is probably behind a letter of Gregory of Nyssa where he advocates a certain separation of the sexes in the ascetic life.[9] We have already seen the probable influence of Macrina on Basil's religious development and, possibly because of this influence, he stands out among the Fathers for his positive views of women. He puts into the mouth of the martyr Julitta these words:

We are made of the same dough as men. Just like them we were created in the image of God. Woman, just like a man, was made by the Creator capable of virtue. Are we not their equals in everything?[10]

It is however significant that Basil does not quote Galatians 3:28 anywhere in the Rules.[11] Stramara uses its citation by Basil of Ancyra and Gregory of Nyssa as a basis for saying that it 'functioned as the theological ideology for the equality of men and women pursuing the same goals in Basil's double monasteries', and 'one may safely propose that [Gal. 3:28] formed a theological foundation on which double monasticism arose.'[12] This is a strange conclusion given the absence of the text in the Rules; one would suggest that the contrary is true. The text was widely used in Basil's time as a justification for mixed monasticism but Basil deliberately moved away from this towards the practice of double monasteries with a well-regulated boundary between the sexes. The absence of this text in the Rules would more likely reflect this development.

Given this background we can now go on to read the text of our Rule which clearly does not refer to a community of the mixed type.

LONGER RULE 33

How should we associate with the Sisters?

He who has once renounced marriage will, needless to say, renounce even more those cares which the Apostle says distract the married man, that is how to please his wife.* He will totally cleanse himself from every care (*merimnê*) to please women, fearing the condemnation of Scripture, 'God has scattered the bones of the men-pleasers (*anthrôpareskoi*)'.† Thus he will not even consent to meet a man (*anêr*) in order to please him; but if necessity demands he will arrange a meeting for the sake of the service which, according to God's command, everyone has a right to expect from his neighbour.

Such meetings are however not to be allowed to anyone who wishes, nor is every time and place appropriate for them. But if we intend, according to

---

* 1 Cor. 7:33.
† Ps. 53:5 LXX.

the command of the Apostle, to be without offence both to Jews and Greeks and to the Church of God* and to do all things decently and in order† and with a view to edification, then it is necessary that person, time, occasion and place be carefully and fittingly chosen. By such precautions every shadow of evil suspicion will be banished. Seriousness and modesty will need to be shown in every respect by those who are chosen to see each other and consult about what is pleasing to God both regarding bodily needs and the care of souls. Let there be not less than two on each side; for one person is easily exposed to suspicion, to put it no stronger, and is unable to confirm a conversation, as indeed Scripture says that every word should be confirmed by two or three witnesses.‡ There should not be more than three lest this should impair the zeal for work (spoudê tês philergias) undertaken because of the commandment of our Lord Jesus Christ.

If there should be any need for some of the others in the brotherhood to give or receive a private message, they must not go to the meeting in person. But let selected senior brothers (presbyteroi) deliver their message to selected senior sisters (presbyterai), and so let the need for speech be met through their mediation.§ In such cases, besides observing piety and proper conduct in all things, let them be discreet both in questions and answers, and trustworthy and prudent in managing conversation, fulfilling the saying, 'he shall manage his words with judgement'‖ so that the business entrusted to them is completed, and the matters discussed are fully understood.

As for the sisters' material needs let certain other brothers be responsible for these, chosen after due examination, advanced in years and respectable in conduct and character, so as not to rouse evil suspicions in anyone's conscience, 'For why is my liberty judged by another's conscience?'*

---

* 1 Cor. 10:32.
† 1 Cor. 14:40.
‡ cf. Matt. 18:16.
§ [and let the same good order be preserved not only in the relations of women with men and men with women, but also in those of persons of the same sex.] This passage found here in some manuscripts.
‖ Ps. 112:5.
* 1 Cor. 10:29.

Commentary

Although Basil's reform did end the unregulated mixing described above, this text shows that it did not enforce total separation. The Rules which mention sisters fall into two categories: the first dealing with the *eutaxia* of the ascetic community as a whole, including relations between the male and female parts of the community, and the second with the duties of Superiors. Beyond these texts other Rules can be used to infer details of the life of the sisters. Stramara has made the important point that the usual word for the community, *adelphotês*, which is normally translated 'brotherhood', is in fact gender neutral and can refer to a double community.[13] In Basil's mind there were, therefore, probably many more than thirteen Rules referring directly to female ascetics.[14]

Meeting the other sex

In our Rule Basil begins, through his use of 1 Corinthians 7, by setting the relations between the brothers and the sisters in the context of celibacy. We have seen how Paul's concern for community made this letter a popular text for him. Celibacy is connected with the typically Basilian concern for the avoidance of distraction, and it is also related to a standard ancient theme of the cares of marriage. As Basil is dealing with the way of life pleasing to God, he is thus concerned that one does not aim to please human beings. If one should not act to please a man, how much less should a celibate man act to please a woman – this text is obviously addressed to male ascetics. Meetings are thus only to be allowed in case of necessity and according to the commandment of love of neighbour. This is defined as 'what is pleasing to God both regarding bodily needs and the care of souls'. The ascetic thus serves both aspects of the human person. These two reasons are also found in other texts: Shorter Rules 108 and 110 show brothers giving spiritual help to the sisters and Shorter Rule 154[15] together with the last part of this Rule show material help being given. The former would include spiritual guidance and possibly liturgical celebrations, whereas the latter may have included heavy work and the exercise of certain crafts. The mention of 'the sister entrusted with the wool' in Shorter Rule 153 suggests that female ascetics were involved in traditional woman's work with textiles, which may have been of use to the brothers.

The main concern of our Rule is with the regulation of the meetings to which such contact gave rise. David Amand was shocked by these restrictions and spoke of Basil imposing 'extraordinary and unheard of precautions' to regulate all relations between monks and sisters.[16] Gribomont takes a more realistic and balanced view in commenting on Shorter Rule 154, entitled 'If it should happen that the brothers, being few in number and serving a larger number of sisters, are compelled to separate from one another, is such a situation free from danger?' He points out that Basil in his answer refuses to exaggerate the danger of men working in a predominantly female community. He does however prescribe strict precautions both in our Rule and in Shorter Rule 220. One remembers the quotation from Letter 55 given above. These safeguards are to preserve good order and he uses 1 Corinthians 14:40 in the same context in Shorter Rule 108. They are also to avoid 'every shadow of evil suspicion', and to preserve the values of seriousness and modesty Basil does warn against the tyranny of suspicion in Shorter Rule 109. Special senior brothers and sisters are to be chosen for such meetings and Basil is particularly concerned that more than one person of each sex be present. In a characteristic comment he states that he does not want more than six to meet, as by this people could avoid work. Both here and in Shorter Rule 220, Basil desires to justify this caution from Scripture, using in the latter answer the quotation 'Woe to the solitary man, if he falls there is none to raise him up' (Eccles. 4:10). It is clear that the fall here is into unchastity. This is not the only concern, however, and we also see a desire for prudence and efficiency which is connected with the zeal for work.

Basil and homosexuality

The passage from our Rule which is found in a footnote on page 214 (§) shows a similar concern with precautions and good order but this time 'not only in the relations of women with men and men with *women, but also in persons of the same sex*.' It is not present in all manuscripts and has been shown by Gribomont to be an addition.[17] He notes that a freedom from concern about homosexuality is a way of distinguishing genuine Basilian sources from later works attached to his name.[18] An example of the latter is the sermon in the Great Asceticon entitled 'On the Renunciation of the World' which contains the passage:

> If you are young in either body or mind, shun the company of other young men and avoid them as you would avoid a flame. For through them the enemy has kindled the desires of many and then handed them over to eternal fire, hurling them into the vile pit of the five cities[19] under the pretence of spiritual love.[20]

This theme is also absent from the first generation of Egyptian ascetic literature but is found in later writings such as this Saying of Abba Isaac of the Cells: 'Do not bring young boys here. Four Churches in Scetis are deserted because of boys.'[21]

Connected with this theme is that of particular or exclusive friendships among the ascetics. This is another area where most of the evidence used by modern commentators comes from works that are spurious or of dubious authenticity, in this case primarily the first *Ascetic Discourse*.[22] Here the word *prospatheia* does refer to particular friendships among the brothers which 'injure the common harmony'. The author's ideal is for an equal love to be shown to all. The same word occurs three times in Longer Rule 34, but there it refers to favouritism by 'those who distribute the necessities of life'. This is a different problem, similar to its use in the context of favouritism in admission to ordination in Letter 54. All other occurrences of the word in the genuine works refer to a vain attachment to worldly things.[23] One can therefore conclude that, despite his emphasis on good order in community and interest in love of neighbour, Basil was not unduly concerned about particular friendships. This concern, like the fear of homosexuality, may have emerged in the Basilian communities at a later stage reflected in the *Ascetic Discourse*.

The autonomy of the female community

Many aspects of the female ascetic community can be reconstructed from texts that concern the brothers or are not gender specific. It is clear from references to the two Superiors, however, that Basil was dealing with double, or perhaps twin, communities rather than mixed ones. The autonomy of the two communities, or two parts of the community, is shown by Shorter Rule 111, where he sharply rejects male interference in the female community. The same is found in Shorter Rule 108 where the male Superior is told not to give spiritual direction to a sister in the absence of the female Superior. Basil is thus concerned to protect the autonomy of the female community. In the case of double monasteries it is clear that each half had its own Superior, but there was almost certainly one major Superior over the whole community. Stramara suggests that this could have been a woman, although the evidence is not conclusive.[24] It is not certain that Macrina's double monastery, of which she seems to have been major Superior, is a fair guide to Basil's later practice.

The female Superior is called *Presbytera* in Shorter Rules 110 and 111 and *Proestota* in Shorter Rule 108. Our text uses the plural *presbyterai* which may indicate a class of senior sisters. Shorter Rule 82 deals with the sins of *presbyterai*. These are not necessarily female Superiors as the word could mean older women in general, but if they are it would suggest that male Superiors were able to take action against the sins of female Superiors. Perhaps in this case the men concerned were major Superiors in double monasteries?

Basil on the division of the sexes: equal but different

In reading the texts dealing with relations between the brothers and sisters, one remembers Basil's early ascetic life in Pontus with his mother and sister on the other bank of the River. As these Rules mainly concern prudent relations between the two communities Clarke says, 'the safeguards mentioned in the Rules may perhaps be regarded as a substitute for the River Iris'.[25] Basil accepted equality on the formal, organisational and theoretical level, but this did not extend to issues of economics and spiritual direction.[26] It would thus seem clear that Basil, while accepting the equality of the sexes at the level of capability for virtue, rejected the ideal of identity.

In Shorter Rule 210 he answers the question 'What is the manner of dress prescribed by the Apostle?' by saying that it is one that is appropriate to the person's *skopos*: 'for reason prescribes different covering in winter and summer, nor will the workman and the man of leisure have the same clothes ... or *a man and a woman.*' Unlike other contemporary ascetic teachers Basil believed in preserving the distinction between the sexes.[27] We have already noted that his female ascetics depended on men for spiritual and material assistance, and the former contrasts with the spiritual leadership of women that was practised in the groups deemed heretical. There is however a certain ambiguity here as Gregory of Nyssa reveals that Basil himself had been given spiritual guidance by a woman, Macrina – though he himself never mentions this. Perhaps women, despite having no official teaching role in Basilian communities, nevertheless gave spiritual guidance in a more informal way. The female Superior must have exercised some teaching role in her own community.

From all this it would appear that Basil's underlying theory on the division of the sexes is close to that which is found in modern Roman Catholic teaching: that they are equal but at the same time have different divinely-ordered roles. That he presumes this distinction in ascetic life, which he organised on very different principles than the prevailing society of Late Antiquity, would imply that he believed that the division of the sexes was of more importance in God's plan than the enthusiasts or his brother would allow. There is no evidence that he believed in an originally sexless first creation of humanity.

In relations between the sexes, as elsewhere, the Apostle's precept quoted in Shorter Rule 108, 'Let all things be done decently and in order', is the organisational principle of the life of the ascetics, both male and female.

Double monasteries in later history

Elm calls Basil 'the first great reformer of communal ascetic life'.[28]
She argues that one of his most important innovations was to replace
the mixing of the sexes in the Homoiousian communities with a new
model. This allowed men and women to live together, no doubt both
for practical and scriptural reasons, but separated them into two
distinct units within the one community. There was unity in spirit
but strict and prudent boundaries at the bodily level. Silvas rejects
Elm's thesis and suggests that it was Eustathius, under the influence
of Macrina, who first reformed mixed communities into double ones.
She states that the Small Asceticon reveals Basil following his master
in this.[29] There is insufficient evidence for a firm conclusion, but it
is certain that the Eustathius of Gangra was associated with the
mixing of the sexes and that Basil, from the start, followed the double
model which later became prevalent.

This was not to last, however, and in the twentieth Canon of the
second Council of Nicaea we see a further retreat from the symbiosis
of male and female as practised in Basil's twin communities. At the
same time this authoritative text still sees his model as normative for
existing communities:

> We decree that from now on no more double monasteries are
> to be started, because this becomes a cause of scandal and a
> stumbling block for ordinary folk. If there are persons who wish
> to renounce the world and follow the monastic life along with
> their relatives, the men should go off to a male monastery
> and their wives enter a female monastery; for God is surely
> pleased with this. The double monasteries that have existed up
> to now should continue to exist according to the Rule of our
> holy father Basil, and their constitutions should follow his ordi-
> nances.[30]

History has seen a periodic return to the idea of double communities.
One thinks of the Anglo-Saxon monasteries such as Whitby with
monks and nuns ruled by a powerful Abbess. There are also the
mediaeval examples of the Gilbertines and the early Premonstraten-

sians. The eventual banning of double communities by the latter and
the very strict precautions of the former show that such a life has
dangers and that Church authorities rarely look on it with favour.
In England, recent times have seen an Anglican mixed monastery
established at Burford and the foundation of an Orthodox double
community at Tolleshunt Knights in Essex. Modern Roman Catholic
legislation does not allow mixed or double monasteries, but the
Basilian spirit is still alive in twin monastic communities which share
a church such as the Benedictines at Turvey in England and Petersham
in the USA.

NOTES

1. Elm, *Virgins of God*. 'Double Monasticism in the Greek East, Fourth through Eighth Centuries', Daniel F. Stramara Jr.
2. Stramara, op. cit. pp. 271–3. He notes that the terms are useful as a methodological distinction although they are, except perhaps 'mixed', anachronistic for the fourth century.
3. Novellae 123:36.
4. Basil, Letter 55; Gregory of Nyssa, 'On Virginity' 23:4:5–13; Gregory Nazianzen, *Epigrams* 10–20. (These are not in the *Palatine Anthology*, but are found in PG 38:86–93).
5. Also Matt. 22:30 and Mark 12:25.
6. PG 30:772. Quoted in Elm, *Virgins of God*, p. 120, the full text is found in PG 30:670–810. Silvas, 'Tracking the influence of Eustathius', pp. 70–1, claims that Sozomen HE 3:14 shows Eustathius condemning celibate cohabitation. The text seems rather to present him opposing *sexual relations* under this pretext.
7. cf. *On Human Creation* 17.
8. *Ambigua 41* 1309A. Tr. in Louth, *Maximus the Confessor* (1996).
9. Letter 2:5.
10. *Homilia in martyrem Iulittam*, PG 31:240.
11. It is, however, found in *Moralia* 20:2, 'What is the inner meaning or the power of Baptism?'
12. Stramara, op. cit. pp. 287–8.
13. Stramara, op. cit. pp. 280–2, and his article 'Adelphotês – Two Frequently Overlooked Meanings'. In the former he notes that in LR 15 both male and female children, when they grow up, may make profession to the same *adelphotês*.
14. Gribomont, *Histoire du texte* p. 54, notes that in some manuscripts many of Basil's responses are addressed to 'sisters'.
15. See Clarke (1925), p. 285, which shows that this Rule refers to material help.
16. *L'Ascèse Monastique de Saint Basile*, p. 244.

17. See n62 in Migne, *PG* 31, p. 999. Gribomont, *É&É* 2:379, states that this is 'une interpolation sans autorité'.
18. In a comment to Derwas Chitty, *The Desert a City*, p. 66. David Amand, in a section entitled 'la lutte contre l'amour homosexuel' (*L'Ascèse*, pp. 246–8) states that Basil was very concerned about homosexuality, but this judgement is based on non-Basilian texts and a misinterpretation of SR 265. The use of non- and dubiously Basilian texts to deduce Basil's attitude to homosexuality is common: White, *Christian Friendship*, pp. 82–3; McGuire, *Friendship and Community*, pp. 6–7, 30–31; Boswell, *Christianity, Social Tolerance and Homosexuality*, pp. 159–60.
19. The cities of the plain among which were Sodom and Gomorrah (cf. Gen. 14:2, 19:25 etc.).
20. *CPG* 2889, Clarke, *Ascetic Works* (1925), pp. 60–71.
21. *The Sayings of the Desert Fathers*, tr. Ward, Isaac, Priest of the Cells 5. Cf. Chitty, *The Desert a City*, p. 66.
22. *CPG* 2891. Cf. White, *Christian Friendship*, pp. 82–3, McGuire, *Friendship and Community*, pp. 29–32.
23. *Moralia* 7:29, LRs 5, 8 (3 times) SRs 17, 234.
24. Stramara, 'Double Monasteries', pp. 298–301.
25. Clarke, *Ascetic Works*, p. 38.
26. Elm, *Virgins of God*, p. 77.
27. cf. Anson, J., 'The Female Transvestite in Early Monasticism: The Origin and Development of a Motif'.
28. Elm, *Virgins of God*, p. 211.
29. Silvas, 'Tracking the influence of Eustathius', pp. 67–72.
30. Translation from Tanner, *Decrees of the Ecumenical Councils* vol. I (1990), pp. 153–4.

Chapter Sixteen

Daily Life: Work and Prayer

Work occupies an important place in Basil's ascetic teaching.[1] The two texts here come from a section of the Longer Rules on the subject[2] and there is a corresponding section in the Shorter Rules.[3] Basil's teaching here has been very influential in monastic history especially concerning the purposes of work and its relation to prayer, the development of the Divine Office (common prayer at fixed times during the day), and the choice of work undertaken. He is also concerned with the inner attitude and disposition of the one working. The context of his teaching was the rejection of work by certain currents of ascetic thought. In these texts we find Basil responding to this problem as well as to other questions raised by the daily life of the brotherhoods. His own teaching seems to have remained remarkably consistent over the years and is rooted in his early lifestyle at Annisa. It is also closely connected with the more inner and spiritual aspects of his ascetic doctrine. Our first text takes us straight into the controversy.

LONGER RULE 37

Whether we must neglect work for the sake of the prayers and psalmody, and what times are suitable for prayer, and first of all whether we should work at all.

Since our Lord Jesus Christ says, 'Worthy of his food is' – not just any or every one but, 'the labourer'* and the Apostle commands us to labour and do honest work with our own hands so that we might be able to share with those in need,† it is clear that one should work diligently (*spoudaiôs*). For we

---

* Matt. 10:10.
† Eph. 4:28.

must not treat the ideal of piety (*skopos tês eusebeias*) as an excuse for idleness or as an escape from hard work, but rather as an opportunity for spiritual combat (*athlêsis*), for more abundant labours and for patience in tribulations, so that we may be able to say, 'in toil and hardship, through many a sleepless night, in hunger and thirst'.*

For such a way of life is useful to us, not only because it involves the mortification of the body,† but also because of love of our neighbour, so that through us God may bring sufficiency (*autarkeia*) to the weak among the brothers, according to the example given to us in Acts by the Apostle when he says, 'By every means I have shown you that we must exert ourselves in this way to support the weak.'‡ And again, 'So that you may have something to share with those in need'§ – that we may be counted worthy to hear the words, 'Come you whom my father has blessed, inherit the kingdom prepared for you since the foundation of the world. For I was hungry and you gave me food, I was thirsty and you gave me drink.'‖

What need is there to say how great an evil is idleness, since the Apostle plainly commands that the one who does not work shall not eat?¶ Just as daily food is necessary for every person, then, so also is work necessary according to one's strength. For not in vain did Solomon write by way of praise, 'she did not eat the bread of idleness'.** And again the Apostle says of himself, 'We did not eat anyone's bread without paying, but with toil and labour we worked night and day',†† although he had authority, since he was proclaiming the Gospel, to live by the Gospel. Moreover the Lord linked laziness with wickedness, saying, 'You wicked and lazy servant'.‡‡ And also the wise Solomon not only praises the worker in the words just recorded but also rebukes the lazy person by comparing him with the smallest creature, saying, 'Go to the ant, you lazy thing'.§§ Thus we should fear lest this be

---

* 2 Cor. 11:27.
† 1 Cor. 9:27.
‡ Acts 20:35.
§ Eph. 4:28.
‖ Matt. 25:34.
¶ cf. 2 Thess, 3:10.
** Prov. 31:27.
†† 2 Thess. 3:8.
‡‡ Matt. 25:26.
§§ Prov. 6:6.

brought up against us on the Day of Judgement when he who gave us the ability to work demands from us work proportionate to that ability. For he says, 'when someone is entrusted with a great deal, of that person even more will be expected.'*

Now since some avoid work with the excuse of prayer and psalmody, one should know that for each separate task there is a special time, as Ecclesiastes says, 'There is a time for everything'.† But for prayer and psalmody, as for many other things, every time is suitable; so that while we move our hands in work we praise God, as it is written, with psalms and hymns and spiritual songs‡ with the tongue if it is possible – and this is useful for strengthening faith – but if not, in the heart. And so while working we accomplish our prayer, giving thanks to him who gave both strength of hand to work and wisdom of mind to acquire skill, and also granted the means by which to work, both in the tools we use and the arts we practise, whatever the work may be. We pray moreover that the work of our hands may be directed towards the end (*skopos*) of pleasing God.

We therefore secure an undistracted (*ameteôriston*) soul when we ask success from God in the performance of each task, and give thanks to him who gave the ability to work, and preserve the aim (*skopos*) of being pleasing to God as we said before. For, unless these are our methods, how is it possible to hold together what was said by the Apostle; 'Pray without ceasing'§ and 'Working night and day'?‖ However we should not imagine that because giving thanks at every season has been commanded by the Law and has been shown to be necessary to our life by nature and reason, the prescribed times of prayer should be neglected in the brotherhood. These we have chosen because each has its own special remembrance of good things received from God:

To begin with, Dawn, so that the first movements of the soul and mind may be dedicated (*anathêmata*) to God, and nothing else taken into consideration before we are made joyful by thoughts of God, as it is written, 'I remembered God and was made joyful.'¶ So that we do not stir up the body

---

* Luke 12:48.
† Eccles. 3:1.
‡ Col. 3:16.
§ 1 Thess. 5:17.
‖ 2 Thess. 2:8.
¶ Ps. 76:4 LXX.

to work before doing what is said, 'To you I will pray, O Lord, in the morning you will hear my voice; in the morning I shall stand before you and I shall see you.'*

Again at the Third Hour we should rise to prayer and gather together the brotherhood, should they be scattered about their various occupations. Remembering the gift of the Spirit given to the Apostles at the third hour, we must worship all together (*homothumadon*) so that we too may be worthy to receive sanctification, asking from him guidance and teaching about what is good, just as it was said: 'Create a pure heart in me, O God, and renew a right spirit within me. Do not thrust me away from your presence and do not take away from me your Holy Spirit. Restore to me the joy of your salvation and strengthen me by your ruling Spirit't and elsewhere, 'Your good Spirit will lead me into open country.'‡ Then after prayer we begin our work again.

If some should find themselves at a distance, owing to the nature of the work or the locality, they must of necessity perform where they are all that is prescribed for common observance without any hesitation, 'for', says the Lord, 'where two or three are gathered in my name, I am there among them.'§

At the Sixth Hour we judge that prayer is necessary according to the example of the saints who said, 'Evening and morning and midday I will tell and declare and he shall hear my voice',|| and, that we may be delivered from accident and the noonday demon, at the same time the ninetieth psalm is also said.

The Ninth Hour is handed down to us as necessary for prayer by the Apostles themselves in Acts; 'Peter and John were going up to the Temple at the hour of prayer, the ninth hour.'¶

When the day is finished, let us give thanks for what has been given us during the day and for what we have done rightly, and let us make confession of what we have left undone, whether intentionally or not, or even perhaps of a secret sin that has been committed, in words or deeds or in the heart itself;

---

* Ps. 5:2–3.
† Ps. 50:12–13.
‡ Ps. 142:10.
§ Matt. 18:20.
|| Ps. 55:17.
¶ Acts 3:1.

appeasing God for all these through our prayers. For the examination of past deeds is a great help in avoiding doing the same again, for which reason it is said, 'What you say in your hearts, feel compunction for on your beds.'*

Again, at the beginning of the night, we ask that our rest be blameless and free from fantasies, and we necessarily say again at this hour the ninetieth psalm.

Paul and Silas have handed down to us Midnight as a necessary time for prayer, as the story of Acts shows, 'But about midnight Paul and Silas were singing hymns to God.'† The psalmist too says, 'At midnight I rose to praise you because of your righteous judgements.'‡

Again we must rise before the Dawn to pray so that we are not caught by the day asleep in bed, according to him who said, 'My eyes anticipate the dawn, that I may meditate on your words.'§

None of these hours must be neglected by those who have chosen to live watchfully to the glory of God and his Christ. But I think it is beneficial to have diversity and variety in the prayers and psalms of the fixed hours, because where there is monotony, the soul often becomes bored (*akêdaô*) and distracted (*apometeôrizô*); but by changing and varying the psalmody and the meaning (*logos*) of each hour, the desire (*epithumia*) of the soul is reinvigorated and sober vigilance restored.

Commentary

Before addressing the question of the relation between prayer and work, Basil assembles an array of scriptural texts to show that one must work. The first two quotations are from the Gospel and the Apostle. While the words of Christ relate work to our daily food, Paul here provokes a wider consideration of the motives for work.

Why work?

Sharing with those in need is a way of obeying the second commandment of love. It also fits well with Basil's other two reasons for

---

* Ps. 4:4.
† Acts 15:25.
‡ Ps. 118:62.
§ Ps. 118:148.

community life: the social nature of man and the solidarity of the Body of Christ. Recommended by Paul in Acts 20:35, it was given as a motive for monastic work by many writers of the patristic period.[4] Basil goes on to situate this in the eschatological context of the sheep and the goats in Matthew 25.[5] It is interesting that *autarkeia*, which is condemned in Longer Rule 7, is here given a positive meaning in relation to one's neighbour. Another motive for work, developed from texts of St Paul, is that it gives an opportunity for *athlêsis* (a word which is used of the ascetic's spiritual combat in the *Life of Antony*[6]). Basil is fond of athletic imagery as in Longer Rule 7 where he speaks of the community as an 'arena for athletics'. In Letter 23, speaking of a newcomer to the ascetic life, he asks for an 'anointer . . . one who would train him well and make of him an approved wrestler to wound and overthrow the universal Lord of the darkness of this world.'[7]

Hard work is thus an occasion for spiritual combat and it is also, in another Pauline theme, mortification.[8] David Amand suggests that Basil's emphasis on mortification springs not from Christianity but from a platonist dualism which regards the body as bad, a 'fleshly prison', and the soul as good and in need of liberation from the flesh.[9] The concern with work, however, with clothing and food, with an austere appearance, with posture and tone of voice all show a concern for the body which is far from hatred. In Letter 2 he makes the structure of the body an occasion for glorifying God and we shall see in Longer Rule 19 that he shows a definite concern for the right treatment of the body. Mortification and hard work thus aim to get the body into a naturally healthy state, not enslaved to pleasure or the passions, so that it will serve the life of piety. Finally, and connected with this, work is necessary to avoid the evil of idleness.[10] Basil uses Paul, Wisdom literature and a Gospel parable to stress this point and again ends by evoking the Day of Judgement. Such a developed argument must mean that the rejection of work was a real danger among his ascetics.

Another reason is given by St Benedict, who begins his chapter on 'The Daily Manual Labour' by quoting from St Basil the words 'idleness is the enemy of the soul'.[11] He makes the purpose of work to provide subsistence for the monks, an ascetical discipline and a surplus to give to the poor.[12] The aim of providing for the community is also found in Pachomian texts but at first it is said of Pachomius and Palamon that 'they toiled not for themselves but remembered the poor'.[13] The absence in the Asceticon of emphasis on working for the community, although the workman is worthy of his food and despite the example of St Paul,[14] leads us into the historical context in which Basil was writing.

'We pray without ceasing': an objection to work

In the *Sayings of the Desert Fathers* we find Abba Lucius being visited by some monks called Euchites (the Greek form of the word Messalian). They say, 'We do not touch manual work but as the Apostle says, we pray without ceasing.' In another saying John the Dwarf says, 'I should like to be free from all care, like the angels who do not work but ceaselessly offer worship to God.'[15] In both cases this antipathy to labour is rejected: in the second example John is returned to orthodoxy by the very practical means of giving him no food until he resumes work.

These examples show a perennial temptation among ascetics which was very prevalent in Basil's time.[16] The commands to pray always and not to be anxious about food and drink[17] provide an objection to the practice of work and it is to this which Basil responds here. The latter command is quoted in Shorter Rule 207 (R 127), where he contrasts it with the command to work in order to give to the poor which is found in Ephesians 4:28 and Acts 20:35. These are the same two texts used here. The reproach of being anxious about food is behind Basil's reluctance to give support for the community as a motive for work. This is developed in Longer Rule 42 where Basil explains away Paul's command that one must work in quietness and earn one's own living (2 Thess. 3:12) as only addressed to the unruly for whom it is a better practice than idleness. The mention in this Rule of the brother in charge of one's needs shows a way out of this problem, although Basil specifically rejects it. With a fully established community, one works for the community and the poor, and then receives one's needs from the community and thus from the Lord.

In our text Basil does not say that some times are for prayer and some for work, but rather that all times are suitable for prayer. Thus one can pray while working, silently if praying out loud is inappropriate. The work itself can give the occasion for prayer and thanksgiving. We have seen how Macrina practised manual labour in her ascetic life and that it was a feature of Basil's from the beginning. His more poetic friend Gregory, when he complains of muck-spreading and other unpleasant tasks in the retreat at Pontus, reveals, if slightly tongue in cheek, that this is true.[18] The clever juxtaposition in our Rule of the texts 'pray without ceasing' and 'working night and day' shows Basil's answer to the Euchites and lead on to his provision that there should be 'prescribed times of prayer' as well as times for work. Basil thus gives structure to the ascetic's day and he also stands at the origin of the Monastic Office.

Times of prayer during day and night: the origins of the Divine Office

It is significant that Basil deals with unceasing prayer before speaking of special times of prayer. For him and for the whole of Christian antiquity there was no distinction between private and public, or liturgical, prayer. There was only the one prayer done sometimes in common and sometimes on one's own.[19]

The fundamental command was to pray unceasingly[20] and this gave rise to various responses. Origen said, 'He prays without ceasing who combines his prayer with necessary works . . . the whole life of the saint is one mighty integrated prayer.'[21] The Egyptian Desert Fathers practised simple manual work such as basket-weaving while praying, and had two periods of formal prayer in the morning and evening, either alone or, on Saturdays and Sundays, in common. We have already noted the response of the Euchites. Later there grew up monasteries of *akoimetai* (sleepless ones) who kept up constant prayer in Church on a rota of shifts.[22] The practice of having a number of times of prayer during the day, as in Palestine and Cappadocia, was not a relaxation of the ideal of unceasing prayer but rather, as our text shows us, a particular way of expressing it.

Special times of prayer during the day and night are mentioned in the first centuries of Christianity. The *Didache* recommends saying the Our Father three times a day and the First Letter of Clement of Rome speaks of fixed times of prayer.[23] Clement of Alexandria mentions prayer at the third, sixth and ninth Hours, the beginning and end of the day and during the night.[24] Origen speaks of morning, noon, evening and night.[25] In North Africa Tertullian and Cyprian witness similar times.[26] There is no generally accepted interpretation of this data, or agreement on whether it is a development of Jewish customs, nor indeed do liturgists agree about the post-Constantinian development of fixed times of prayer in cathedrals and monasteries. It is clear, however, that our text is of primary significance for the development of the Monastic Office.

In the fourth century both cathedrals and Egyptian monasticism, hermits and cenobites alike, had morning and evening services. The cathedrals also had occasional all-night vigils, a Cappadocian example of which is described in Basil's Letter 207. In what Taft calls the 'urban monasticism' of Palestine, Mesopotamia, Syria and Cappadocia a mixed Office emerged incorporating various elements and adding services at the traditional times of private prayer, the third, sixth and ninth Hours. A prayer at bed-time which becomes Compline, various types of Vigil and, in Palestine, a second morning Office were also added.[27] This brings us to our text and to Basil's own organisation of the fixed daily times of prayer.

The Hours of prayer in Basil's scheme

Longer Rule 37 speaks of a morning Office which is mentioned twice. Both references mention dawn (*orthros*), which is the name still used by Greek Christians today for this service. Then comes prayer at the third, sixth and ninth Hours, an evening prayer at which one reviews the day and confesses sin, and a prayer before going to bed which duplicates the evening Office. There is also an Office at midnight, contrasting with the Egyptian custom of an office at cockcrow (about

3 a.m.). Basil's Letter 2 only mentions prayer at daybreak and midnight and so he must have gradually developed the formal structure of our Rule. Although Basil uses the traditional times of prayer here, his words 'these we have chosen (*eklegomai*)' show that his arrangement was not a simple repetition of current practice.

Studying the content and times of the Hours, Taft makes the interesting point that whereas the monks of Palestine and Antioch have a Monastic Office with cathedral elements, Basil seems to have a 'cathedral' structure morning and evening with monastic elements added to it. This would fit well with Basil's identification of his ascetics as Christians, especially if they only gradually evolved out of the normal congregation into separate communities. Urban ascetics, such as the Homoiousians and those of Jerusalem, would have attended the daily cathedral services.

The comments Basil makes on each Hour are also significant. Dawn is connected with the memory of God and the same quotation of Psalm 5 is also used by Origen and Cyprian. Concerning the Little Hours Basil does not use the usual text from Daniel 6:10, 'he got down upon his knees three times a day and prayed.' He connects the third Hour with Pentecost saying that we must worship together (*homothumadon*), an adverb often used in Acts of the Apostolic Community. The sixth Hour uses texts from the psalms and not the more usual account of Peter's vision in Acts 10:9, but the ninth Hour has the standard story of Peter and John going up to the Temple in Acts 3:1. Unlike the third-century document, the *Apostolic Constitutions*, Basil does not connect these three hours with the times of Christ's passion as given in the Gospel of Mark. For prayer at midnight Basil uses the same texts from Psalm 118 and Acts as Origen. The problem mentioned here of brothers who are too far away to come to the Office is also discussed by Pachomius and Benedict and, although there is no direct dependence, they give the same solution as Basil.[28]

The first *Ascetic Discourse*,[29] which is possibly by Basil, speaks of all life being a time of prayer but says that there are 'the Hours of prayer enjoined by the Saints'. These are midnight, mentioning Paul and Silas and Psalm 118:62, morning, noon and evening, Psalm

54:17, the third Hour, mentioning Pentecost, and the ninth Hour, the Passion. This leaves out bed-time prayers and so to fulfil the seven times of prayer mentioned in Psalm 118:64 midday prayer is divided, part before and part after the meal, just like the prayers before and after meals in Letter 2. If this is genuine it could represent Basil's practice after Letter 2 and before he adopted the prayer on going to bed, although one would then wonder why in our text he dropped the connection of the ninth Hour to the crucifixion.

To live watchfully and without distraction

The last paragraph touches on some interesting themes. The description of the ascetic as one who lives 'watchfully to the glory of God' recalls the common idea of monks as the 'watchful ones'. This is often associated with the ever-vigilant angels and, together with the practice of virginity, contributes to the description of monastic life as the angelic life. This concept is not used by Basil but it is found in non-Basilian works associated with the Rules.[30]

The Christian should be *monotropos* but that is no excuse for monotony in worship. The changes mentioned here recall Letter 207 where Basil replies to the charge of changing the psalmody in church and describes the variety of ways of praying during a night-Vigil. Here also this variety is associated with avoiding distraction. The verb for distraction in our text recalls *ameteôriston* and may be another word coined by Basil. The word for boredom recalls the characteristic monastic vice of *akêdia* called the noonday demon, one of Evagrius' eight deadly thoughts.[31] The Rule ends with a characteristically Basilian mention of the importance of desire.

Basil and the Eucharist

One notable absence from this important text dealing with times of prayer in the ascetics' day is the Eucharist. This chief sacrament is similarly almost entirely absent from most other early monastic texts including the Pachomian literature and the *Rule of St Benedict*.[32] It certainly had its place in the life of Basil's followers as we can see from the questions concerning it[33] and the Rules reveal that a few of the brothers, like Basil himself, were priests.[34] Priesthood and the Eucharist however primarily belonged to the Church and only incidentally impinged on the issues of monastic interest, such as the Daily Office, which are discussed in the Rules. Basil would have agreed with Pachomius' words on the Eucharist and priesthood: 'It is better to be subject modestly to the Church of God.'[35]

The Canons of Gangra condemn a eucharistic practice among the ascetics which is at variance with that of the Church. In a parallel case to that covered in Canon 6 of Gangra, we find Basil in Shorter Rule 310 rejecting the celebration of the Lord's Supper in an ordinary house except in an emergency. His ascetics thus attended the Liturgy in the local church unless, as was probably the case with the Basileiados and at Annisa, the community had use of its own Oratory.[36] That other cenobitic founder, Pachomius, first took his brothers to a church he had built in the village and then had one built in the monastery, but even then he went to the village church on Saturdays.[37]

As to the frequency of Communion, Basil says in his famous Letter 93 to the Patrician Caesaria that daily Communion is 'good and beneficial' but that the usual custom is to receive on Sunday, Wednesday, Friday and Saturday and at the commemoration of a Saint. In the same Letter he makes the interesting comment, 'all who live the monastic life in remote places (*hoi kata tas erêmous monazontes*), where there is no priest, keep the Communion at home and partake of it from their own hands' as do all, even the laity (*tôn en laô telountôn*) at Alexandria and in Egypt. This may well have been the custom in some of the more remote of his communities and it shows the Eucharist playing a greater part in ascetic life than that revealed by the Rules.

This Rule shows us that prayer and work are essential elements in the ascetic's day. While Basil is a very important figure in the development of the Monastic Office, the formal times of prayer he demands are subordinate to the command to pray always. The next Rule follows on from this and its title is self-explanatory.

LONGER RULE 38

Having been adequately shown both that prayer should never be omitted and that work is necessary, it follows that we should be taught what crafts are appropriate for our profession (epangelma).

It is no easy matter to define suitable crafts specifically, since different groups pursue different crafts according to the special characteristics of their localities and the suitability of business openings in each district. But generally speaking, one may recommend the choice of those crafts that preserve the peaceful and untroubled nature of our life, needing neither much trouble to get the requisite material, nor much anxiety to sell what has been made, and which do not involve us in undesirable or harmful meetings with men and women. But in everything we must consider that simplicity and cheapness are set before us as our proper aim (skopos), and we must avoid serving the foolish and harmful desires of men by working to satisfy their requirements.

In weaving we should make what is appropriate to our way of life, not what is devised by the unchaste to trap and ensnare the young. Similarly in shoe-making, let us serve by our craft those who are looking for basic necessities. Building and carpentry and metalwork and agriculture, however, are in them-selves necessary for life and give many benefits, and are not to be rejected in themselves. Yet when they cause us disturbance, or break the unity of the life of the brethren, then let us necessarily avoid them; preferring those crafts which preserve for us an undistracted life of devotion to the Lord,* one which drags away those who devote themselves to the ascesis of piety (eusebeia) neither from the time of psalmody, nor from prayer, nor from the rest of the well ordered (eutaxia) life. But since there is nothing in these crafts which harms the special purpose of our life, they are preferable to many. Agriculture is the best of them since by it we get the necessities of life, and it preserves its workers from much wandering or running to and fro. But only if, as we have said before, it brings upon us no troubles and disturbances from neighbours or fellow inhabitants.

---

* 1 Cor. 7:35.

Commentary

Basil here applies his principles to the choice of a type of work for the brothers. This must avoid disturbance and undesirable contact with the world, produce simple necessities and not luxuries,[38] maintain unity and not keep the brother or sister from prayer or psalmody. In mentioning avoidance of distraction he quotes 1 Corinthians 7 which deals with Christian celibacy.

The choice of work in monastic tradition

Basil notes that it is hard to prescribe specific crafts as the situation of different communities vary. This concern with context and reluctance to make absolute decisions was later to be a characteristic of Benedict's Rule.[39] As to the precise crafts, Basil mentions a number: weaving, shoe-making, building, carpentry, metalwork and agriculture. This points to diverse economic activities which would, despite Basil's reluctance, serve the needs of the community as well as producing goods for sale. Another type of work not mentioned here is helping in the hospital which Basil discusses in Shorter Rule 155. The Pachomians also came to practise various trades and became a major economic force in Egypt. We have little information about the later history of Basil's communities but their small size should have enabled them to avoid the disadvantages of riches.

It is interesting that Basil prefers agriculture as 'by it we get the necessities of life', for he had been reluctant to name the provision of necessities for the community as a motive for work in the previous Rule. Cassian notes that agriculture is a cause of distraction as monk-gardeners are 'working outdoors every day . . . running about in the airy void not only in the flesh but even in the mind, scattering their thoughts everywhere in the open with their bodily activity'.[40] Rejection of agriculture for similar reasons is also taught by the *Rule of the Master*,[41] although Benedict allows it in cases of necessity and implies that work in the garden is a normal monastic activity amongst the various crafts.[42] Gardening also figures in a list of monastic crafts given by St Jerome, together with basket-making, beekeeping, making fishing nets and copying books.[43] The *Lausiac History* lists the workmen at the Pachomian monastery of Panopolis as including tailors, metalworkers, carpenters, camel-drivers, fullers, gardeners, shoemakers, swineherds, bakers, basketmakers and scribes.[44]

The presence of writing as an activity in these lists – it counted as manual work – raises the question of whether this typically monastic activity was practised in Basil's fraternities. Although Basil and Gregory compiled the *Philocalia* in their retreat at Pontus, there is no evidence of copying in the Rules, only the spiritual practices of reading and learning the Scriptures and the teaching of the young.[45] Basil's Answers themselves were presumably written down in the communities where they were given and manuscripts were certainly preserved in the Basileiados and a community in Pontus. In Letter 223, mentioning the composition of his work *Against Eunomius* on the way to Lampsacus, he speaks of Eustathius' shorthand writers (*tachygraphoi*). In Letter 135, however, Basil bemoans the lack of a fast copyist 'for to such a state of poverty has the once envied condition of the Cappadocians come!'

Interface with the world

An unavoidable distraction, but one to be minimised, is caused by interaction with the world as a result of selling the products of labour and obtaining necessities. Longer Rule 39 teaches that it is better to sell at a lower price if this can avoid long journeys. If this is impossible then a group must go together to market 'each bearing the products of his own work' and reciting psalms and prayers. These must lodge together at night to celebrate the Hours of prayer and to help keep watch on each other.[46] Longer Rule 40 tells the ascetics to avoid buying and selling at the assemblies (*synodoi*) at Martyr's tombs, which connects with Canon 20 of Gangra. It is interesting that Basil expects that they will meet 'grasping and extortionate men' and his main concern is the avoidance of harm. All this is an exception to his principle that 'it is more fitting to remain in one place'.

Work thus leads to a certain interaction with those outside the community, as also does love of neighbour. We have already noted that when the brethren work in the hospital, piety is the guiding principle. It is the same with alms for the poor. Good order demands that only those entrusted with the task should give alms.[47] For anyone else to do so is self-will and contrary to poverty. Concerning the official Almoner, Basil notes that the command to 'give to everyone that asks' refers only to situations when one is forced to, whereas usually one should only give to the poor.[48] This restrictive policy is explained in Letters 91 and 150. In the former it is noted that Basil said that one needed experience to discern between genuine and false beggars, the latter deserving 'no pity on grounds of want'. In the latter it is mentioned that:

> ... he (Basil) said that experience was necessary for distinguishing between the man who is truly in need and the man who begs through avarice. And while he who gives to the afflicted has given to the Lord, and will receive his reward from him, yet he who gives to every wanderer casts it to a dog that is troublesome on account of his shamelessness, but not pitiable because of his need.

Work and inner attitude

As one would expect, other Rules discuss the disposition of the ascetic who is working. One of Basil's particular concerns here is the perennial danger of self-will. This is a pleasing of self and is particularly condemned in Longer Rules 41 and 42 which end the section on work. To refuse the work assigned or to do something other than this, even if it is over and above what is commanded, is condemned as self-will and contrary to the virtue of obedience.[49] There is, however, the possibility of discussing onerous tasks with the Superiors, as we have already seen. Shorter Rule 125 says that self-will is displeasing to God and breaks the bond of peace. As a remedy he offers a favoured quotation, 1 Corinthians 7:24, 'let each one remain in the state in which he was called'.[50]

Proprietary rights over one's will are related to the private ownership of property. Basil was very hostile to private ownership[51] and in Longer Rule 41, concerning tools, he contrasts the Greek legal terms *despoteia,* which indicates absolute ownership, and *chrêsis* which indicates merely the use of something. The tools are the common property of all and are only to be used with the permission of the Superior. Thus the values of community, poverty and obedience, together with stability and order, are shown in this most practical area to be of central importance in Basil's monastic teaching.

This section has shown how Basil is concerned with very practical issues. The great themes of his spiritual teaching cannot be understood unless they are seen in action within the daily round, just as he himself cannot be fully understood unless one takes into account Gregory's picture of Basil pushing a cart and spreading muck.

NOTES

1. For a thorough study of the monastic attitude to work see *Towards a Benedictine Theology of Manual Labour* (Illinois 1951) D. Rembert Sorg OSB.
2. LRs 37 to 42.
3. SRs 141 to 156.
4. For example: *Didache* 4:5–9; Jerome, *Letter 52;* John Chrysostom, *Homilies on Matthew* 8:5; *Historia Monachorum in Aegypto* 18; John Cassian, *Institutes* 10:21.
5. He does the same in Longer Rule 42, entitled 'The aim *(skopos)* and intention *(diathesis)* with which the workers should work'.
6. Life of Antony 10, cf. Heb. 10:32.
7. cf. Eph. 6:12.
8. 1 Cor. 9:27. See in addition the use of Col. 3:5 in LR 41 which also connects mortification with hard work.
9. *L'Ascèse Monastique de Saint Basile,* pp. 191–19.
10. cf. SR 61 on the idle brother who will neither work nor learn psalms.
11. *Rule of St Benedict* 48, quoting R 192.
12. *RB 80,* p. 96.
13. *First Greek Life of Pachomius* 6.
14. 2 Thess 3:7, cf. also 1 Thess. 2:9, 2 Cor. 11:9, 12:4.
15. *Apophthegmata Patrum* Lucius 1, John the Dwarf 1, cf. also Silvanus 5.
16. On the same subject see: Augustine, *On the Work of Monks;* Cassian, *Conferences* 24:10, 11, quoting St Antony; Athanasius, *Life of Antony* 3.
17. 1 Thess. 5:7 and Matt. 6:25–33.
18. Gregory Nazianzen, *Letter 5.*
19. For this and the rest of this section I am much indebted to Robert Taft's *The Liturgy of the Hours in East and West.*
20. 1 Thess. 5:16–18, Eph. 6:18, Col. 4:2, Luke 18:1, Luke 21:36.
21. Origen, *On Prayer* 12.
22. See Desprez, *Le Monachisme Primitif,* pp. 337–8.

23. 1 Clement 40:1–4.
24. *Stromata* 7.7.40, 7.7.49. *Pedagogue* 2:9–10.
25. Origen, *On Prayer* 12.
26. Tertullian, *On Prayer* 25. Cyprian, *On the Lord's Prayer* 34–6.
27. Cassian describes the Egyptian customs in Book 2 of the *Institutes* and the Palestinian and Mesopotamian Office in Book 3. On the interpretation of this see Taft, pp. 58–70, 76–80.
28. *Precepts of Pachomius* 142, *Rule of St Benedict* 50.
29. *CPG* 2891.
30. *On the Renunciation of the World* 204A, *Ascetic Discourse* 320B, *Monastic Constitutions* 561D. In the *Homily on Thanksgiving* PG 31:227A the angelic life is associated with joy.
31. *Praktikos* 12.
32. The only references in the three-volume *Pachomian Koinonia* are *Bohairic Life* 25, 208, *First Greek Life* 27, 29 (repeating Bo. 25), *Precepts* 75 and *Regulations of Horsiesius* 14. De Vogüé speaks of a 'half-dozen furtive mentions' in the *Rule of St Benedict* and shows that it is similarly rarely mentioned in the other Western Rules, *Doctrinal and Spiritual Commentary*, p. 159.
33. SRs 292, 309, 310. A similar concern with the disposition with which one receives Communion is shown in the *Regulations of Horsiesius* 14.
34. SRs 64, 231(?), 264(?).
35. *First Greek Life* 27, *Bohairic Life* 25. Even in the Church as a whole, there was a certain reticence about discussing the Eucharist, cf pp. 97–8.
36. *Life of Macrina* 16, 22; Basil, Letter 176, if *mnêmê* is in fact a memorial chapel. See the note in *St Basil: the Letters*, tr. Deferrari, pp. 460–1 n2, and the reservations expressed by Rousseau in *Basil of Caesarea*, p. 141.
37. *Bohairic Life* 25, cf. *First Greek Life* 29.
38. A concern for honest and useful crafts is expressed by Augustine in *On the Work of Monks* 14.
39. cf. *Rule of St Benedict* ch. 40 on drink and ch. 55 on clothing.
40. *Conferences* 24:4, cf. 24:12:4.
41. *Rule of the Master* 86.
42. *Rule of St Benedict* 48:7–9, see also 7:63, 46:1, 66:6.
43. Jerome, *Letter* 125.
44. *Lausiac History* 32.
45. LR 15, SRs 96, 235, 236.
46. On journeys see also SR 120 and LR 44. The latter has the same stress on not travelling alone and on watchfulness, with the added precaution that one must give an account of all one's expenses to the Superior on one's return.
47. SRs 87, 91.
48. SR 91.
49. SRs 119, 121, 125 and also 142 on receiving work without permission.
50. Also used in similar contexts in SRs 100, 136, 141, 147.
51. cf. SR 85: 'Is it lawful to have any private property in the Brotherhood? . . . Whoever says that anything is his private property has made himself an alien to the Church of God and to the love of the Lord . . .'

Chapter Seventeen

Self-Control: Food and Laughter

Enkrateia is a fundamental theme in the Rules. It means self-control, temperance or continence. In Latin it is often translated by *continentia*. The first two texts we shall examine here are taken from the section in the Longer Rules devoted to this subject.[1] The first looks at the important issue of the ascetics' food. The second deals with laughter, and then goes on to sing the praises of *enkrateia* and deal with a typical Basilian concern: the outward appearance and demeanour of the ascetic. This connects with our last text which, although it is from the section on renunciation, deals with silence and speech in the context of *enkrateia*.

LONGER RULE 19 (R 9)

What should be the degree of self-control (enkrateia)?

As regards the passions of the soul, there is one degree of self-control: complete abstinence from all that tends to harmful pleasure. But regarding food, as different people have different needs which vary according to age and occupation and proportionately to the state of the body, so also there are different amounts of food required and different customs regarding its use. It is thus impossible that all who are being trained in piety (*gymnasia tês eusebeias*) should be included under the same rule. But having defined the measure to be observed by those of the ascetics who are in health, we allow those responsible for administration to make wise deviations from it to meet individual circumstances.

For it is not possible to deal with every single case in these instructions, but only with the broad outlines of generally applicable teaching. Whether it is the sick who need food to increase their strength, or someone exhausted after strenuous work, or one who needs food to prepare for a journey or other hard task, the Superiors will always arrange things according to the need, as in the saying, 'distribution was made to each as any had need'.* It is impossible, therefore, to fix the same hour for taking food or the same manner or measure; but let the satisfying of the need be the aim (*skopos*) in each case.

For to have the stomach full to excess, and weighed down with food, is worthy of a curse, since the Lord said, 'Woe to you that are full now'.† It also makes the body itself useless for activities, inclined to slumber, and exposed to injuries. Nor indeed should we make pleasure the end of eating, but rather necessity in order to preserve life, avoiding the immoderation of pleasure. To be enslaved to pleasures is nothing else than to make one's belly one's god. For since our body, which is always being emptied and diminished, needs to be filled – and because of this our appetites for food are natural – the right concept (*logos*) of the use of food demands the filling up of what has been emptied in order to support the animal nature (*zôon*), whether the need be for dry or liquid nourishment.

Whatever then is going to free us from our need with the least trouble should be used. The Lord himself shows this by the way in which he entertained the weary multitude in the desert, 'lest they collapse on the road'.‡ For although he had the power to extend the miracle in the desert by concocting an extravagant feast, he prepared a meal for them so frugal and simple as to consist of barley loaves and a little fish besides the bread.§ Drink is not even mentioned, since they could get water, which is available to all from nature, and is sufficient for our needs; unless indeed such a drink is harmful to someone on account of their infirmities and therefore to be avoided in accordance with Paul's advice to Timothy.‖ In fact all things which are manifestly harmful are to be avoided. For it is absurd to take food in order to sustain the body, and then by means of this very food to wage war with the body and hinder it in observing the commandments. The same principle teaches us to accustom our soul to avoid what is harmful, however pleasurable it may be.

We must however by all means prefer what is easily obtained, so that we

---

* Acts 4:35.
† Luke 6:25.
‡ Matt 15:22.
§ cf. John 6:9.
‖ 1 Tim. 5:23.

do not on the pretext of self-control take pains to get expensive foods, seasoning our dishes with costly sauces. But in each district we must choose what is easily obtained and cheap and ready for the use of the local people. We should only use imported foods that are essential for life, such as oil and the like, and whatever is necessary for the diet of the sick; but even these only if they can be got without fuss, disturbance and distraction.

Commentary

This Rule shows that *enkrateia* is of central importance in Basil's ascetic teaching, but in his Canonical Letters he condemns a group called the Encratites.[2] There is an ambiguity about this word which is not revealed by Basil's positive use of it in the Rules.

The Christian encratite tradition

Although *enkrateia* is not common in the New Testament,[3] there is a great stream of Christian encratite tradition through the early centuries of the Church. It was especially strong in Syria where it is associated with the convert philosopher Tatian, and it influenced many of the apocryphal Acts and Gospels. At first it was more a collection of ideas than a sect, and as such it caused a major crisis in the Church during the second century.[4] Encratism was ascetic and focused on sexual renunciation, thus contrasting with Basil, and it can be divided into two broad sections. One rejected marriage, had a strong dualist flavour and was opposed by writers in the Christian mainstream such as Irenaeus and Clement of Alexandria. The other, consisting of writers such as Clement and Origen, formulated a more moderate orthodox encratism, just as Clement had also defined an orthodox gnosticism. In the fourth century, while the extremist current continued, as shown by Basil's Canons and Epiphanius's collection of heresies in his *Panarion*,[5] this orthodox encratism came into its own with the increased importance of asceticism and virginity and the growth of monasticism in the Church. Ambrose, Jerome, Athanasius, the Cappadocians, John Chrysostom and many others praised self-control in its various forms, especially virginity.

Basil is firmly in this tradition but is keen to distance himself from deviant Encratites. In Longer Rule 18, entitled 'That it is necessary to eat all that is set before us', Basil says, while advocating self-control, that we must 'avoid falling into the same error as the enemies of God', who 'abstain from food which God created to be received by the faithful with thanksgiving... – everything created by God is good.' The appetite for food is thus natural and it aims to sustain the 'animal nature'. The restrictions demanded by *enkrateia* in food, as in sexuality, are not designed to protect one from what is evil but rather to purify one's disposition, mortify the passions and free the spirit from servitude to the flesh. This was well put by Basil's brother Gregory when he said: 'This is the most perfect goal of self-control (*ho teleôtatos tês enkrateias skopos*): not to concentrate on the sufferings of the body, but on the efficient working of the instruments of the soul.'[6] Such explicit rejection of Manichean dualism is common in the Fathers[7] and serves to distinguish them from at least the more extreme currents of heretical Encratism.

Food, sex and pleasure

There is very little about sexual self-control in the Rules, although it is their presumed context. Basil's main interest in the section on *enkrateia* is with food. For Evagrius, followed by Cassian, gluttony is the primary sin, and they put it before lust at the head of the vices.[8] It would seem that the same was true for Basil. It was certainly so for the author of the pseudo-Basilian treatise 'On Renunciation of the World', for whom it was the sin by which Adam fell, that evil-eating we have noted above in Basil's Homily quoted in Chapter Ten. The power of gluttony is 'in desire and little tastings' and he has never seen 'one who ate on the sly or who was gluttonous' restored to spiritual health.

In our Rule Basil starts by distinguishing *enkrateia* in eating, which needs to be done and so must be moderated, from *enkrateia* concerning the passions of the soul which tend to harmful pleasure, primarily lust, which should be totally cut off. Right at the start he has the main enemy in his sights, pleasure (*hêdonê*). This word has a broad range of meanings and was much discussed in ancient philosophy.[9] While Plato and Aristotle can speak of pleasure in the virtuous life as something good, the general use is of bodily pleasures which make us act badly. It is in this latter sense that Basil uses it here. In our text he contrasts pleasure with necessity as the basic principle for eating. In Longer Rule 16 he has already said that 'in speaking of self-control we do not mean complete abstinence from food. . . but abstinence from pleasures', and in Longer Rule 17 we are told, 'pleasure is the great bait used by evil, by it we humans most readily fall into sin'. *Hêdonê* is thus not the spiritual joy that Basil contrasts with hilarity in Longer Rule 17, but a pleasure which lures to excess and sin and is associated with the passions. These are the ideas conjured up by the word hedonism.

For Basil, pleasure increases the danger. Gregory of Nyssa, in his treatise 'On Virginity', speaks of the necessity of estrangement from all bodily pleasure, especially 'the pleasure of taste, because somehow this seems to be the most persistent, being practically the mother of all that is forbidden'. When pleasure is mixed with need, however, it is not necessary to avoid satisfying this need.[10] In Shorter Rule 126, 'How can one avoid taking pleasure in eating?', Basil says that one should take appropriateness as a guide whether the food is pleasant or unpleasant. Shorter Rule 140 is interesting as it asks if the brothers should look after – probably in the hospital – one who does not practice self-control in eating. Basil's answer is that this is reasonable but only if his soul can be cured of its vice. If not he should be left until his pain cures him of lack of self-control.

Basilian moderation: what and when should we eat?

Satisfying need is the *skopos* of eating and in the first paragraph Basil recognises that different people have different needs. The key text here is Acts 4:35, which is also used of the one who gives out food in six other Rules.[11] This apostolic order is clarified in Shorter Rules 131 and 135 where it is made clear that the giver and not the recipient of the food decides what is necessary. In the first of these it is said that to seek special food, possibly on the pretext of ill-health, is wrong. One general principle is that 'those responsible for administration' – the Superior is not mentioned in this early text – should modify the usual diet for those with special needs. This is an attractive example of Basilian moderation and an attitude also characteristic of Cassian and Benedict.[12]

The usual arrangements for food, which are not clear from the Rules, would however strike a modern person as austere rather than moderate. In Letter 2 Basil says:

> For someone in good health bread will suffice, and water will quench thirst; such dishes of vegetables and fruits may be added as help strengthen the body for its necessary tasks... Not even at table should one let the mind forget to think of God, but one should make the very nature of the food and the structure of the body that takes it an occasion for his glorification... Let there be one fixed hour for taking food, always the same in a regular course, that of all the twenty-four hours of the day and night barely this one may be spent upon the body. The rest the ascetic should spent in spiritual exercises.[13]

Here Basil only allows one meal a day, the custom of the Egyptian anchorites.[14] The Pachomians usually had two meals a day,[15] and this practice is suggested by the title of Longer Rule 21 which mentions *ariston* (lunch) and *deipnon* (supper). This title is however not original, it is not in the corresponding answer in the Small Asceticon (R 10), and the text only speaks of *ariston*. This connects with Shorter Rule 136 where one who deliberately misses lunch must 'remain without food until the fixed time on the following day'. The first *Ascetic Discourse*,[16] possibly by Basil, speaks of one meal at the sixth Hour which may have been his normal custom, although there is much latitude for exceptions. Shorter Rule 180 shows that at least some communities had reading during meals and Cassian says that this custom originated in Cappadocia 'to prevent arguments among themselves'.[17] Basil also deals with the ascetics' meals in Longer Rule 20 when he discusses food given to the guests,[18] where the same principles as in our Rule are normative. In Longer Rule 21 he says that, to avoid all fighting for the lowest seat, the one to whom it is entrusted should determine place at table.

As to what is eaten, Basil avoids being too prescriptive but he does lay down certain principles. Necessity is the main criterion, which Basil describes in a very basic way as 'the filling up of what has been emptied'. Simplicity is another rule, for which Basil uses the food with which Jesus fed the five thousand as an example. Using Paul's advocacy of a little wine he orders harmful things to be avoided and thus reveals that the true encratite is not hostile to the body. What can be easily obtained in the locality is a final criterion. All these criteria are really just aspects of necessity. There is also special attention to the sick and a typically Basilian emphasis on avoidance of distraction. Two Shorter Rules, 71 and 72, provide little vignettes of ascetics who do not follow the rule of necessity, seeking delicacies, eating too much (*koros*), or behaving indecorously. These provoke Basil to respond that one must endeavour to cure them compassionately and he uses two favourite quotations from that Letter which so often guides his thoughts on community: 1 Corinthians 14:40, which we have already met, and 10:31 'whether you eat or drink. . . do all to the glory of God'.[19]

Fasting and self-will

Ascetic texts often pay attention to food, and this is frequently in the context of fasting. Two of Basil's extant homilies are devoted to this subject. The section of the Shorter Rules on food is mainly concerned with fasting, which is obviously an aspect of *enkrateia*. The danger with which Basil is most concerned is self-will, for '*enkrateia* does not consist in refraining from material foods. . . but in the complete giving up (*anachôrêsis*) of one's own will.'[20] When asked which we should give up when fasting makes us too feeble for work, he answers that we should do both according to piety and the commandments and quotes 1 Corinthians 10:31.[21] There is thus no place in Basil's teaching for the competitive asceticism one sometimes meets in Egyptian and Syrian sources. There is an austerity which would seem extreme to us moderns, even monks,[22] but it is firmly subordinated to the community and the commandments of Scripture. Our next text begins by looking at self-control in a different area.

LONGER RULE 17 (R 8)

That it is also necessary to control laughter (gelôtos enkratôs echein).

This, neglected by most people, calls for appropriate watchfulness on the part of ascetics. For to be overcome by unrestrained and immoderate laughter is a sign of intemperance, of a lack of control over one's emotions and of failure to suppress the soul's frivolity by a strict rule (*akribês logos*).

It is not improper, however, to reveal a joyful soul by a cheerful smile, though only as far as Scripture allows when it says, 'a joyful heart makes a cheerful face';* but raucous laughter and an uncontrollable shaking of the body is not fitting for one who has his soul under control, is of proven virtue, or has mastered himself.† The author of Ecclesiastes condemns this sort of laughter as being especially subversive of stability of the soul in the words, 'I said of laughter, it is error', and, 'as the crackling of thorns burning under a pot, so is the laughter of fools'.‡ Moreover the Lord seems to have experienced the necessary passions (*pathê*) of the flesh, as well as those that witness to virtue, such as weariness on the one hand and compassion for the oppressed on the other; but he appears never to have laughed, as far as we can tell from the gospel story. On the contrary he declared those prone to laughter to be unhappy.§

Let us not be deceived by the ambiguity of the word laughter (*gelôs*). Scripture often calls the joy of the soul and the cheerful disposition (*diathesis*) caused by good fortune, laughter. So Sarah says, 'God made laughter for me;'‖ and, 'blessed are you who weep now, for you will laugh';¶ and the passage in Job, 'he will fill a true mouth with laughter'.** For in all these places the word is used for exultation of soul (*kata psychên agalliasis*) not hilarity (*hilarotês*). Thus he who rises superior to all passions, and experiences no stimulation because of pleasure, or at least does not show it, but remains firm and in

---

* Prov. 15:13.
† Some Mss. add here Sirach 21:20 LXX.
‡ Eccles 2:2, 7:6.
§ Luke 6:25.
‖ Gen. 21:6.
¶ Luke 6:21.
** Job 8:21.

control of himself: he is perfectly self-controlled (*enkratês*). Such a one is obviously free from all sin. But sometimes one must even refrain from things that are allowed and necessary for life, when the abstinence is for the benefit of our brethren. As the Apostle says, 'if food is a cause of my brother's falling, I will never eat meat.'* And even though he had a right to earn his livelihood from preaching the Gospel, he made no use of this right, lest he put an obstacle in the way of the Gospel of Christ.†

Self-control (*enkrateia*) therefore takes away sin, detaches from passions (*pathê*), mortifies the body with its natural passions (*pathêmata*) and desires (*epithumia*); it is the beginning of spiritual life, the introducer of eternal blessings, and it destroys the sting of pleasure (*hêdonê*). For pleasure is the great bait used by evil, by it we humans most readily fall into sin; by it every soul is dragged to death as if by a hook. So whoever is not emasculated or broken down by it has attained complete avoidance of sins. Nevertheless if such a person has escaped most incitements to sin, but is mastered by one, he is not self-controlled (*enkratês*); just as he is not healthy who is troubled by one bodily illness, and he is not free who is under the authority of anyone, whoever it might be.

Other virtues, being practised in secret, are seldom apparent to other people; but self-control makes its possessor stand out the moment one meets him. For as firm flesh and a healthy colour characterise the athlete, so the Christian is marked out by emaciation of body and paleness, which is the bloom of self-control, showing that he is truly an athlete of Christ's commandments. For he overcomes his enemy by the weakness of his body, and displays his strength in the contests of religion (*eusebeia*), as it is written, 'when I am weak, then I am strong'.‡ How rewarding it is just to see the self-controlled person (*enkratês*), reluctantly and sparingly using the necessities of life, ministering to nature as a burdensome duty and begrudging the time spent in it, and quickly springing away from table in his zeal (*spoudê*) for work. For I think that no sermon would teach the soul of the undisciplined glutton, or move him to conversion, so much as merely meeting the self-controlled person (*encratês*). This, I think, is the meaning of eating and drinking to the glory

---

* 1 Cor. 8:13.
† cf. 1 Cor. 9:12.
‡ 2 Cor. 12:10.

of God;* so that even at table our good works may shine to give glory to our father who is in heaven.†

Commentary

In the Small Asceticon this is the second half of Answer 8 and follows directly on from what became Longer Rule 16. Thus although we have seen the importance of self-control in food, Basil immediately follows his general exposition of *enkrateia* with a discussion of self-control in the area of laughter. It would have been good to have commented on Longer Rule 16, but with limited space it seemed better to examine *enkrateia* in two specific areas and deduce general principles from these.

A holy sorrow: *penthos* and the avoidance of laughter

The primacy given to restraint of laughter seems very strange to the modern mind which invariably sees laughter as a sign of happiness and thus to be valued and encouraged. In the patristic tradition, however, and especially in Eastern monastic texts, laughter is almost unanimously condemned. Iréné Hausherr has shown that this is closely connected to the disposition called *penthos*: compunction, a godly sorrow or mourning, which was so highly valued by the Fathers.[23] Speaking of his female ascetics in Letter 207 Basil evokes 'a sorrow which is deemed blessed'. St John Chrysostom said:

> Even as it is difficult, or rather impossible, to mix fire and water, so it seems to me that pleasure and compunction are incompatible. One brings forth tears and sobriety, the other laughter and foolishness.[24]

Our Rule is cited by Hausherr as a classic statement of the patristic view although, as we will see, it is somewhat nuanced. Other Fathers who condemn laughter include Clement of Alexandria, Origen, Gregory Nazianzen, Ephrem the Syrian, Dorotheus of Gaza, Theo-

---

* 1 Cor. 10:31.
† cf. Matt. 5:16.

doret of Cyrrhus and Theodore the Studite. This remained a common theme in the monastic tradition. Abstaining from laughter was taught to laymen and so Basil's text here is in no way a specifically monastic document. In one thirteenth-century Egyptian source laughter is listed among the vices renounced at baptism.[25] If we ask why it is condemned, we see in the text from Chrysostom that it is seen as a product and sign of pleasure. Basil also, as we have seen, rejects pleasure and here associates both it and the passions with laughter, which is thus linked to sin. It is the lack of control and stability which is particularly offensive. In this passage his controlled austerity makes one think of the ideal of the stoic sage, but it would be a mistake to think that Basil and the Fathers are just adopting a pagan Greek model.

Compunction is profoundly biblical: 'Blessed are those who mourn' (Matt. 5:4). The Fathers based their case against laughter firmly on the Bible, however much they were influenced by philosophical ideas. Basil's austere statement that Jesus 'appears never to have laughed' seems absurd today but is hard to refute. The Scriptures do, however, modify the prevailing gloom.

A cheerful smile: joy in the midst of mourning

In Shorter Rule 31 (R 53) Basil invokes *penthos* in giving an uncompromising negative to the question '*Must we not laugh at all?*' He answers:

> Since the Lord condemns those who laugh it is obvious that there is never a time of laughter for the believer, especially when there is so great a multitude of those who by transgression of the law dishonour God and are dead in sins, for whom one should mourn and grieve.

Our Rule does, however, allow one 'to reveal a joyful soul by a cheerful smile', but Hausherr suggests that it is earlier than the text just quoted and that Basil's thought developed in a more rigorous direction. This tolerance of smiling does, though, occur in other writers influenced by Basil such as Gregory Nazianzen, Dorotheus of Gaza and Theodore the Studite.[26] Joy and a cheerful disposition are valued in the Bible. Hausherr notes that Basil mainly uses Old Testament quotations to justify his smile and the text from Chrysostom quoted above goes on to suggest that the New Testament was more severe on the subject. One obvious text is Sirach 21:20, 'The fool lifts up his voice in laughter, but a wise man will scarcely smile quietly', and this is found in our Rule in some manuscripts. Although this is probably a gloss and not by Basil, the text, with its allowance of the smile balancing hostility to laughter, may be the source of his unusual teaching here. The Jewish writer Philo, despite being influenced by the prevailing philosophy, comments on Sarah and the birth of Isaac in a most un-Basilian way saying that laughter is 'that most exquisite joy of all pleasures'.[27]

Basil uses a rather forced distinction between laughter meaning *agalliasis*, which is good, and laughter meaning *hilarotês*, which is not. It is true that laughter is ambiguous in the New Testament. *Gelôs* is only used once, in James 4:9, 'let your laughter be turned into mourning (*penthos*)', and the verb *gelaô* three times in the Blessings and Curses in Luke 6:20–26. Here it is said 'Blessed are you that weep now, for you shall laugh. . . Woe to you who laugh now, for you shall mourn and weep' which suggests an eschatological motive for not laughing that may be behind Basil's teaching. *Agalliasis* (extreme joy) and its related verb are used 16 times in the New Testament. This is always with a positive meaning, but the same is true of *hilarotês* (cheerfulness – Rom. 12:8) and *hilaros* (2 Cor. 9:7 – 'God loves a cheerful giver'). Basil was also familiar with the evening hymn *Phôs Hilaron* (O Joyful Light) which he quotes in *On the Holy Spirit* 29 (73). Thus his justification of a smile and response to the positive use of laughter in Scripture seems to show him caught between a tradition of seriousness to which he is deeply committed and the evidence of the Word of God. Perhaps also his innate sociability influenced his views. The obscure passage on refraining from things that are allowed may reflect this tension. Centuries later Thomas Aquinas in the Latin West was to use Aristotle's positive evaluation of *eutrapelia*, a playful wit and jollity, to counter this patristic seriousness.[28] Basil's defence of the smile may have played a similar but much smaller role in the Greek East.

The example of the pale encratite

The last paragraph of this Rule, which is an addition to the text of the Small Asceticon, is a praise of the virtue of *enkrateia* and especially of the one who possesses it. He is called an *Enkratês*, an Encratite,[29] which means that one can call Basil's teaching orthodox encratism. The teaching that one is not an encratite if one is mastered by just one incitement to sin recalls the words of the Preface to the Longer Rules that in breaking one commandment we break all. At the end of Longer Rule 16 Basil says of *enkrateia*, 'do you see how round this one commandment all the commandments are grouped as in a chorus.' This interrelationship of virtues and vices is a commonplace idea of the period and is particularly prominent in Evagrius.

Basil says that *enkrateia* is a public virtue and the picture he draws of the Christian encratite reveals a typically Basilian concern with the outward manifestation of inner realities. We have already noticed this concerning clothing, and it is related to Basil's interest in both inner disposition and the mechanics of community life. We have here a very vivid picture: 'emaciation of body and paleness', ministering to the body 'as a burdensome duty' and 'quickly springing up from table in zeal for work'. This is closely related to Basil's ideal in Letter 2 where barely one hour out of the twenty-four should be expended on the body and, 'the humble and abject spirit is attended by a gloomy and downcast eye, neglected appearance, unkempt hair and dirty clothes.'[30] The 'athlete of Christ's commandments' is contrasted to the secular athlete. We have already noted Basil's use of athletic imagery in Longer Rule 35 where in the context of uniting brotherhoods he speaks of a *sunathlêsis*, with his typical stress on community and unity.

The distinctive outward appearance is seen as an example to the undisciplined glutton, just as the frugality of 'the table of Christians' in Longer Rule 20 enables the worldly person to 'learn from works what words did not teach him'. There Basil uses the same text, 1 Corinthians 10:31, and the reason for his concern with external matters is succinctly put in the words 'the life of the Christian is consistent and has one aim – the glory of God.' In the next Rule we see another part of this aspect of Basil's teaching.

LONGER RULE 13

That the practice (gymnasion) *of silence is valuable for novices* (eisagomenoi).

The practice of silence (*siôpê*) is indeed good for novices. For in gaining control of the tongue they will both give sufficient proof of self-control (*enkrateia*) and will also learn in quietness (*hêsychia*), eagerly and attentively, from those who are skilled in instruction, how they should ask questions and give answers in particular cases. For there is a tone of voice, a moderation in speech, an appropriateness to the occasion, and a special vocabulary which are proper to religious people (*tois eusebesin*) and can only be learned by one who has unlearned his former habits. Silence both leads to forgetfulness (*lêthê*) of the past through lack of practice and provides leisure for what is good. Consequently silence should be kept, except of course for the singing of psalms, unless there is a special reason to talk concerning the cares of one's own soul or an emergency in the work in hand or a similar question that requires an answer.

Commentary

This Rule is from the section on renunciation which deals with entrance to the community, but it makes clear at the start that in treating of silence it is concerned with an aspect of *enkrateia*. It is not in the Small Asceticon and thus probably a late text. It is distinguished by having no scriptural quotations, which is strange as there are many texts on this theme as shown in Shorter Rule 208 (R 136) which answers the question '*Generally speaking is it good to ractice silence?*' It also recalls certain aspects of the texts we examined in the second part: the *eisagomenoi* of Longer Rule 4 and the theme of memory of God and forgetfulness of the past.

Why be silent?

The main subject of this text, however, is silence. This is highly valued by Basil in his theological writings as a 'therapy' against the tendency, which he saw in his opponent Eunomius, to subject sacred tradition to analysis and criticism.[31] In the ascetic life, the renunciation of speech has been from the first a characteristic of monasticism.[32] Early writers teach silence as a sign of or way to humility, a means to avoid sin or as a response to unjust accusations. Here Basil relates it to formation in asceticism. It is a practice of self-control enabling one to forget one's old way of life and learn the modes of speech and behaviour proper to religious. He uses the word *hesychia* here to mean that tranquil atmosphere which is the best context for learning, just as in Letter 2 it is the context for prayer. This word does not have in Basil the technical meaning it was later to acquire as describing the life of the hesychast monk, devoted to prayer and solitude.[33]

Words out of silence

Our Rule teaches that silence is practised so that one may learn how to speak. Shorter Rule 208 says that 'whether silence is good or not depends on the time and person', but some need complete silence to learn how to speak. Letter 2 also refers to the start of the dedicated life when it says 'the very beginning of the soul's purgation is *hesychia*, in which the tongue is not given to discussing the affairs of men, nor the eyes to contemplating rosy cheeks or comely bodies.' In this early letter silence leads to the mind ascending to the contemplation of God, whereas in our later texts it is a means of learning how to speak. There was thus a development in Basil's thought. With the emergence of a group in the Community of those 'who have been entrusted after trial with the dispensation of the word' we find another group, in Letter 22 called 'the workers', whose normal state is silence. It is clear that silence was an important but relative value in Basil's communities and the way in which it was practised varied as they developed. Basilian balance is shown at the end of this Rule where it is made clear that even for the novices silence is not absolute. There was no need for them to develop sign-language like the medieval Cistercians.

As spiritual dialogue was a defining characteristic of Basil's communities, so he frequently shows a concern with appropriate ways of speech and behaviour. He pronounces judgement on idle words in Shorter Rule 23 but his main concern seems to be with the right regulation of speech.[34] Even Letter 2 from his Pontic solitude devotes a long section to the proper way of speaking in different circumstances. At the same time there does seem to be a gradual acceptance of two groups in the community, with the charism of speech providing the dividing line between them.

Eating and speaking, as well as one's clothes and behaviour, are thus all determined by the values of community and self-control. The Christian should be conspicuous in all these areas, thus giving an outward manifestation to the inner values which are so important in Basil's teaching. The inner and the outer should be in harmony.

NOTES

1. LRs 16–23.
2. Letter 188 Canon 1, Letter 199 Canon 47.
3. Acts 24:25, Gal. 5:23, 2 Pet. 1:6; with the related verb *enkrateuomai* in 1 Cor. 7:9, 9:25, and *enkratês* at Titus 1:8.
4. See: the article 'Encratisme' in *DSp* 4A:628–42; Brown, *The Body and Society*, pp. 90–102; Giulia Sfameni Gasparro, 'Asceticism and Anthropology: Enkrateia and "Double Creation" in Early Christianity', in *Asceticism* (1995), ed. Wimbush and Valentasis, pp. 127–46.
5. *Panarion* 47 says that there were many Encratites in Phrygia and Pisidia, but one must be careful in interpreting the writings of heresiologists.
6. 'On Virginity' 22:2. A chapter entitled 'That one should not practice *enkrateia* more than is necessary'.
7. e.g. Augustine, *de moribus ecclesiae catholicae et de moribus manichaeorum* 1:65–73; Gregory of Nyssa, 'On Virginity' 7, 'That marriage is not to be despised'; Jerome, *Against Jovinian* 2:6, 16; *Lausiac History* Prol.:9–14; Cassian, *Institutes* 5:22.
8. Evagrius, *Praktikos* 6, 7; Cassian, *Institutes* 5–6, *Conferences* 5:4.
9. See for example Guthrie's *History of Greek Philosophy*, vol. 5, pp. 199–200 on Plato's Philebus, and vol. 6, pp. 376–84 on Aristotle.
10. Gregory of Nyssa, 'On Virginity' 21.
11. LR 34, SRs 93, 131, 135, 148, 252.
12. cf. Cassian, *Institutes* 5:5, *Rule of St Benedict* 40.
13. Letter 2, tr. Jackson (modified).
14. cf. *Apophthegmata*, Poemen 168.
15. Rousseau, *Pachomius*, p. 84.
16. *CPG* 2891.
17. *Institutes* 4:17. One may suspect the reason Cassian gives, which he contrasts with the strict silence of his heroes the Egyptians.

18. SR 124 forbids eating with heretics and pagans.
19. This latter text is also used in a variety of contexts: LRs 5, 22, 55 where it ends the Longer Rules; SRs 139, 196, 220, 276, 299.
20. SR 128, cf. also SRs 129, 137 and 138.
21. SR 139, see also SR 196 which asks the meaning of 1 Cor. 10:31.
22. This is the theme of de Vogüé's little book, *To Love Fasting*. It compares the almost total lack of this practice in modern monasticism with the more healthy example of the Fathers, which the author himself follows with joy.
23. Hausherr, *Penthos*, pp. 94–105.
24. *De Compunctione ad Stelechium* 2:3, quoted in Hausherr, *Penthos*, p. 97.
25. Ibn Saba, *The Precious Pearl* 31, cited in *Penthos*, p. 104 and Špidlik, *The Spirituality of the Christian East*, p. 216.
26. Gregory, *Oration 12*; Dorotheus, *Doctrina* 24 (dubia); and Theodore, *Great Catechesis* 54. All cited in *Penthos* 100–101 where Hausherr notes that the last reference is the only passage in Theodore's works that he has found where 'he allows such a free rein to permissiveness'. It may well be that Basil is at the root of this lightening of patristic gravity.
27. Philo, *On the Change of Names* 131, see in general sections 130–76.
28. Eph. 5:4 uses *eutrapelia* in a bad sense as buffoonery and vulgar talk, and this would appear to have been the common use among the Greek Fathers. For an overview of the history of this word in Christian spirituality see Hugo Rahner's article, 'Eutrapélie', in *DSp* 4B:1726–9 where the pseudo-Basilian *Monastic Constitutions* are cited among the Greek writings which follow Ephesians in hostility to the term.
29. Found only once in the New Testament in Titus 1:8 in a list of the virtues expected of a bishop.
30. A similar description is found in the non-Basilian Letter 45 (*CPG* 2900) which revels in a grotesque description of the effects of fasting on the ascetic's body.
31. See Rousseau, *Basil of Caesarea*, pp. 120–21.
32. For example: *Apophthegmata* Arsenius 2, where the Lord tells him 'flee, be silent, pray always'; Isidore of Pelusia 1, 'To live without speaking is better than to speak without living'; Poemen 37, 47; Sisoes 42. Pachomius *Precepts* 31, 33, 34, 59, 60, 68, 88, 94, 116, 122; *Institutes* 18. Augustine, *Ordo Monasterii* 7, 9. Jerome, *Letter* 22:35. Cassian, *Institutes* 2:10:1–2. *Rule of St Benedict* 6.
33. cf. Miquel, *Lexique du Désert*, 'Hèsychia', pp. 144–80.
34. See SRs 208, 266.

Epilogue

The spiritual teaching we have been studying was given by St Basil to men and women who were attempting to conform their lives to the commandments of Christ. Their burning desire to attain the aim of a life pleasing to God is the context of the Asceticon. The Rules are thus not primarily a source for the historian of Late Antiquity, but rather a practical document for the serious Christian. As such they have been read throughout the ages and as such, with allowance for changing circumstances, they still retain their value today.

With this in mind, the last word may be left to Gregory of Nazianzus, in an epigram written after the death of his friend:

> There is one God who rules on high,
> and our age saw but one worthy high-priest,
> you, Basil, the deep-voiced messenger of truth,
> the Christian's bright eye,
> shining with the beauty of the soul,
> the great glory of Pontus and Cappadocia.
> Continue even now, I implore you,
> to stand offering up your gifts for the world.

Appendix: The Canons of the Council of Gangra

Titles

Canon 1	On those who condemn legitimate marriage.
Canon 2	On those who condemn the use of meat.
Canon 3	On slaves who rebel against their masters, on the pretext of the Christian life.
Canon 4	On those who form a conscientious objection against communicating at the eucharist of married priests.
Canon 5	On those who do not value any of the assemblies in Church.
Canon 6	On those who celebrate liturgies outside the Churches.
Canon 7	On the offering of ecclesiastical dues against the decision of the bishop.
Canon 8	On the offerings for the poor made apart from the bishop.
Canon 9	On those who practice virginity out of abhorrence of marriage.
Canon 10	On those who are lifted up in regard to virginity.
Canon 11	On those who cast ridicule on the charity meals offered to the poor
Canon 12	On those who use the cloak and scorn those who wear the *beros*.
Canon 13	On women who dress in men's clothes.
Canon 14	On women who desert their husband.
Canon 15	On those who, on the pretext of piety, neglect their children.
Canon 16	On those who, on the pretext of piety, neglect their parents.

Canon 17	On women who, on the pretext of piety, have their head shaved.
Canon 18	On those who fast on Sunday.
Canon 19	On those who do not observe the ecclesiastical fasts.
Canon 20	On those who detest the Synaxes of the Martyrs.

These are taken from Gribomont, *Évangile et Église*, pp. 21–5. He translated them from the classical Byzantine canonical text as given in Joannou, *Les Canons des Synodes particuliers* (1962).

Bibliography

Primary Sources

ST BASIL

Complete Works in Greek and Latin: *PG* 29–32

(Small Asceticon) *Basili Regula a Rufino Latine Versa*, ed. Klaus Zelzer, *CSEL* 86 (Vienna 1986)

(Great Asceticon and other ascetic works) *PG*:620–1428

BASILEIOS HO MEGAS, (MEROS 3) (Athens 1976); Greek text from *PG*. That of the *Moralia* and Longer Rules improved by Gribomont

The Ascetic Works of St Basil, tr. W. K. L. Clarke (London 1925); includes *Moralia*, Longer Rules, Shorter Rules and 7 short ascetic treatises

Basil of Caesarea, Ascetical Works, tr. M. Monica Wagner, *FC* 9 (Washington D. C. 1950); includes *Moralia*, Longer Rules, 7 short ascetic treatises, On Baptism, and 6 ascetic homilies

Les Règles monastiques, tr. Léon Lèbe (Maredsous 1969)

Les Règles morales et portrait du chrétien, tr. Léon Lèbe (Maredsous 1969)

Die Mönchsregeln, tr. K. S. Frank (St Ottilien 1981)

Opere Ascetiche, tr. Umberto Neri and Maria Benedetta Artioli (Turin 1980)

Ad Adulescentes: To Young Men, on how they might Derive Profit From Pagan Literature, in Deferrari, *Letters* 4:379–435

Basil of Caesarea, Exegetic Homilies, tr. Agnes Clare Way, *FC* 46 (Washington D. C. 1963)

Basile de Césarée, Sur le baptême, ed. U. Neri, tr. J. Ducatillon, *SC* 357 (Paris 1989)

Gateway to Paradise: St Basil the Great, tr. T. Witherow (London 1991); a selection from various works

St Basil, Letters, 2 vols., tr. Agnes Clare Way, *FC* 13, 28 (Washington D. C. 1951)

– *St Basil, The Letters*, 4 vols., tr. Roy J. Deferrari, Loeb Classical Library (1950–53); includes Greek text

– *Letters and Select Works*, NPNF2:8, tr. Blomfield Jackson; Letters, Homilies on the Hexameron and On the Holy Spirit

St Basil the Great on the Holy Spirit, tr. B. Jackson, rev. D. Anderson (New York 1980)

(with Gregory Nazianzen) *The Philocalia of Origen*, tr. George Lewis (Edinburgh 1911)

Pseudo-Basil *Dans la tradition basilienne. Les Constitutions ascétiques, l'Admonition à un fils spirituel et autres écrits*, SO 58 (Bellefontaine 1994)

ST GREGORY NAZIANZEN

Epigrams in *The Greek Anthology*, Books VII–VIII, W. R. Paton, Loeb Classical Library (1917)

Funeral Orations by St Gregory Nazianzen and St Ambrose, L. P. McCauley, Fathers of the Church 22 (New York 1953)

Gregory of Nazianzus: Autobiographical Poems, ed. & tr. Carolinne White, Cambridge 1996

Saint Grégoire de Nazianze: Lettres, 2 vols., ed. & tr. Paul Gallay (Paris 1964)

St Gregory of Nazianzus: Three Poems, tr. D. M. Mehan, FC 75 (Washington D. C. 1987)

Select Orations and Letters, NPNF2:7, tr. C. G. Browne and J. E. Swallow

ST GREGORY OF NYSSA

Ascetical Works, tr. Virginia Woods Callahan, FC 58 (Washington D. C. 1967)

Encomium of St Gregory Bishop of Nyssa on His Brother St Basil Archbishop of Caesarea, ed. & tr. J. A. Stein, CUA Patristic Studies 17 (Washington D. C. 1928)

Grégoire de Nysse, Lettres, ed. & tr. Pierre Maraval, SC 363 (Paris 1990)

Gregorii Nysseni Opera Ascetica, ed. W. Jaeger, J. Cavarnos, V. W. Callahan (Leiden 1952)

On the Soul and the Resurrection by St Gregory of Nyssa, tr. Catharine P. Roth (New York 1993)

Select Writings and Letters, NPNF2:5, tr. W. Moore and H. A. Wilson

Traité de la Virginité, ed. & tr. Michel Aubineau, SC 119 (Paris 1966)

Vie de Sainte Macrine, ed. & tr. Pierre Maraval, SC 178 (Paris 1971)

OTHER PRIMARY TEXTS

Athanasius of Alexandria, *Vie d'Antoine*, ed. & tr. G. J. M. Bartelink, SC 400 (Paris 1994)

Athanasius: The Life of Antony and the Letter to Marcellinus, tr. Robert C. Gregg, Classics of Western Spirituality (New York 1980)

Augustine of Hippo and his Monastic Rule, George Lawless (Oxford 1987)

Barsanuphe et Jean de Gaza: Correspondance, tr. monks of Solesmes (Solesmes 1993)

Barsanuphius and John: Questions and Answers 1–124, ed. & tr. Derwas Chitty, *Patrologia Orientalis* 31:3 (Paris 1966)

Basil of Ancyra, *On Virginity*, PG 30:669–809

Decrees of the Ecumenical Councils, 2 vols., ed. N. P. Tanner (London/Washington 1990)

– *The Seven Ecumenical Councils*, NPNF2:14, tr. H. R. Percival

Eugippii Regula, ed. Villegas, F. and A. de Vogüé, CSEL 87 (Vienna 1976)

Évagre le Pontique: Traité Pratique ou le moine, 2 vols., ed. & tr. A. and C. Guillaumont, SC 170, 171 (Paris 1971)

Evagrius Ponticus: The Praktikos and Chapters on Prayer, tr. J. E. Bamberger, CS 4 (Kalamazoo 1978)

Historia Monachorum in Aegypto, *The Lives of the Desert Fathers*, tr. N. Russell (Oxford 1981)

John Cassian, *Institutions Cénobitiques*, ed. & tr. J.-C Guy, SC 109 (Paris 1965); ET *The Monastic Institutes, St John Cassian*, tr. Jerome Bertram (London 1999)

John Cassian, *Conférences*, 3 vols., ed. & tr. E. Pichery, SC 42, 54, 64 (Paris 1955, 1958, 1959); ET *John Cassian, the Conferences*, tr. Boniface Ramsey, ACW 57 (New York 1997)

John Cassian, *Cassian on Chastity*, tr. Terence Kardong (Richardton 1993)

Justin Martyr, *Writings of St Justin Martyr*, tr. T. B. Falls, FC 6 (Washington 1948)

Maximus Confessor: Selected Writings, tr. George C. Berthold, Classics of Western Spirituality (London 1985)

Origen: Commentary on the Gospel of John, 2 vols., FC 80, 89, Washington 1989, 1993)

Origen: Contra Celsum, tr. Henry Chadwick (Cambridge 1965)

Origen: Homilies on Leviticus 1–16, tr. G. W. Barkley, FC 83 (Washington 1990)

Origen: The Song of Songs, Commentary and Homilies, tr. R. P. Lawson, ACW 26 (1957)

Pachomian Koinonia: The Lives, Rules and other Writings of St Pachomius and his Disciples, 3 vols., tr. Armand Veilleux, CS 45–7 (Kalamazoo 1980–82)

Pachomius, *The Life of Pachomius (Vita Prima Graeca)*, tr. Apostolos Athanassakis, Scholars Press 1975 (Contains Greek text)

Palladius: The Lausiac History, tr. Robert T. Meyer, ACW 34 (Westminster/London 1965)

Philo, *The Works of Philo*, tr. C. D. Yonge, updated (Peabody 1993)

Photius, the Bibliotheca, tr. N. G. Wilson (London 1994)

Rufinus, *The Church History of Rufinus of Aquileia*, tr. Philip R. Amidon (Oxford 1997)

RB 80: The Rule of St Benedict, ed. Timothy Fry and others (Collegeville 1981)

The Rule of the Master, tr. Luke Eberle, CS 6 (Kalamazoo 1977)

The Sayings of the Desert Fathers, tr. B. Ward (Oxford 1975)
– *Les sentences des pères du désert. Collection alphabétique*, tr. L. Regnault
  (Solesmes 1981)
– *The Wisdom of the Desert Fathers*, tr. B. Ward (Oxford 1981)
– *Les sentences des pères du désert. Séries des anonymes*, tr. L. Regnault, *SO* 43
  (Solesmes/Bellefontaine 1985)
– *Les chemins de Dieu au désert. Collection systématique des apophtegmes*, tr. L.
  Regnault (Solesmes 1992)
– *Les sentences des pères du désert. Nouveau receuil*, tr. L. Regnault (Solesmes
  1970)
– *Les sentences des pères du désert. Troisième receuil et tables*, tr. L. Regnault
  (Solesmes 1976)
Socrates and Sozomen, *Ecclesiastical Histories*, PG 67
Theoderet of Cyrrhus, *A History of the Monks of Syria* (Religious History), tr. R.
  M. Price, *CS* 88 (Kalamazoo 1985)

Secondary Works

ST BASIL

Amand de Mendieta, E. (D), *L'ascèse monastique de saint Basile: Essai historique*
  (Maredsous 1949)
Bamberger, J. D., 'MNEME-DIATHESIS: The Psychic Dynamisms in the Ascetical
  Theology of St Basil', *Orientalia Christiana Periodica* XXXIV:2 (1968) 233–51
Clarke, W. K. L., *St Basil the Great: A Study in Monasticism* (Cambridge 1913)
de Vogüé, A., 'The Greater Rules of St Basil – A Survey', in *Word and Spirit* 1
  (1979) 49–85
Elm, S., *Virgins of God: The Making of Asceticism in Late Antiquity* (Oxford 1994)
Fedwick, P. J., (ed.), *Basil of Caesarea: Christian, Humanist, Ascetic, A Sixteenth
  Hundredth Anniversary Symposium*, 2 vols. (Toronto 1981)
Fedwick, P. J., *Bibliotheca Basiliana Universalis 3, Ascetica . . .* (Turnhout 1997)
Fedwick, P. J., 'A Chronology of the Life and Works of Basil of Caesarea', *CHA*
  1:3–20
Fenwick, John, *The Anaphoras of St Basil and St James, An Investigation into their
  Common Origin*, Orientalia Christiana Analecta 240 (Rome 1992)
Fitzgerald, Wilma, 'Notes on the Iconography of Saint Basil the Great', *CHA*
  2:533–64
Gribomont, J., *Histoire du texte des Ascétiques de s. Basile*, Bibliothèque du
  Muséon 32 (Louvain 1953)
Gribomont, J., *Saint Basile, Évangile et Église: Mélanges*, 2 vols., Spiritualité
  Orientale 36, 37 (Bellefontaine 1984) includes:

'Commandments du Seigneur et Libération évangélique', 2:295–322

'L'exhortation au renoncement attribué à saint Basile', 2:365–90

'Eustathe de Sébaste', 1:95–106

'Eustathe le Philosophe et les voyages de jeune Basile de Césarée', 1:107–16

'Le monachisme au IVeme siècle en Asie Mineure: du Gangres au messalianisme', 1:26–42

'Le monachisme au sein de l'Église en Syrie et en Cappadoce', 1:3–20

'Obéissance et évangile selon saint Basile le Grand', 2:270–9; ET in *Hallel*, Summer 1984

'La prière selon saint Basile', 2:426–42

'Les Règles Épistolaires de saint Basile, Lettres 173/22', 1:157–91

'Le Renoncement au monde dans l'idéal ascétique de saint Basile', 2:322–63

'Saint Basile et le monachisme enthousiaste', 1:43–64

'La tradition johannique chez saint Basile', 1:209–28

Lèbe, Léon, 'S. Basile et ses Règles Morales', *Revue Bénédictine* 75 (1965), 193–200

Meredith, A., 'Asceticism – Christian and Greek', in *Journal of Theological Studies*, NS vol. XXVII (1976), 313–32

Meredith, A., *The Cappadocians* (London 1995)

Meyendorff, J., 'St Basil, Messalianism and Byzantine Christianity', in *St Vladimir's Theological Quarterly* 24 (1980) 219–34

Morrison, E. F., *St Basil and his Rule* (Oxford 1912)

Murphy, M. G., *St Basil and Monasticism*, CUA Patristic Studies 25 (Washington 1930)

Patrucco, Marcella Forlin, 'Social Patronage and Political Mediation in the activity of Basil of Caesarea', *Studia Patristica* XVII, 1102–7

Pelikan, J., *Christianity and Classical Culture* (New Haven/London 1993)

Pouchet, Jean-Robert, 'Basile et la tradition monastique', *Collectanea Cisterciensia* 60:2 (1998) 126–48

Pouchet, Robert, *Basile le Grand et son univers d'amis d'après sa correspondance: un stratégie de communion* (Rome 1992)

Rousseau, Philip, *Basil of Caesarea* (Berkeley 1994)

Silvas, Anna Margaret, 'Tracking the influence of Eustathius on Macrina the Younger and her family', *Tjurunga: An Australasian Benedictine Review*, 57 (1999) 59–72

Špidlik, T., 'L'ideal du monachisme basilien', in *CHA* 1:361–74

Stramara, Daniel F., '*Adelphotês* – Two Frequently Overlooked Meanings', *Vigiliae Christianae* 51 (1997) 316–20

Stramara, Daniel F., 'Double Monasticism in the Greek East, Fourth through Eighth Centuries', *Journal of Early Christian Studies* 6:2 (1998) 269–312

Tsichlis, S. P., 'Monastic Themes in the Second and Twenty-Second Letters of Basil the Great', in *Cistercian Studies* XIX (1984:4) 289–295.

Voicu, Sever J., 'P. Antin 111: Un testimone ignorato delle *Erotapokriseis* di Basilio', *CHA* 2:565–9

White, C., *Christian Friendship in the Fourth Century* (Cambridge 1992)

St Basil and St Benedict

Butler, C., *Benedictine Monachism* (London 1919)

  Dom Cuthbert Butler said, 'St Benedict owed more of the ground-ideas of his Rule to St Basil than to any other monastic legislator.'

Lienhard, J. T., 'St Basil's Asceticon Parvum and the Regula Benedicti,' in *Studia Monastica* 22 (1980) 231–42

de Vogüé, A., *La Règle de Saint Benoit*, vols. 1–6 (Paris 1971–72)

de Vogüé, A., *Community and Abbot in the Rule of St Benedict*, 2 vols., CS 5/1, 5/2 (Kalamazoo 1979)

de Vogüé, A., *The Rule of St Benedict: A Doctrinal and Spiritual Commentary*, CS 54 (Kalamazoo 1983)

de Vogüé, A., *Reading St Benedict: Reflections on the Rule*, CS 151 (Kalamazoo 1994)

  An idea of Dom Adalbert de Vogüé's views on the influence of Basil on Benedict can be gained by using the indices in the above volumes. He has said, 'We believe that Egyptian influence, communicated in its essentials through Cassian, is much more evident in St Benedict than that of Basil.' The following articles illustrate the controversy on this subject between him and Dom Gribomont.

Gribomont, J., 'Sed et Regula s. Patris nostri Basilii', *É&É* 2:521–34; ET *Benedictina* 27 (1980) 27–40

Gribomont, J., 'Les commentaires d'Adalbert de Vogüé et la grande tradition monastique', in *Commentaria in S. Regulam I*, Studia Anselmiana 84 (Rome 1982) 109–43; ET *ABR* 36:3 (1985) 229–62

de Vogüé, A., 'Twenty-five years of Benedictine Hermeneutics – an Examination of Conscience', *ABR* 36:4 (1985) 402–52

Other Secondary Works

Anson, J., 'The Female Transvestite in Early Monasticism: The Origin and Development of a Motif', *Viator* 5 (1974) 1–32

Binns, J., *Ascetics and Ambassadors of Christ: The Monasteries of Palestine, 314–631* (Oxford 1994)

Blowers, M., *Exegesis and Spiritual Pedagogy in Maximus the Confessor* (Notre Dame 1991)

Bonner, Gerald, *St Augustine of Hippo: Life and Controversies* (Norwich 1986)

Boswell, John, *Christianity, Social Tolerance and Homosexuality* (Chicago 1980)

Bouyer, Louis, *Eucharist: Theology and Spirituality of the Eucharistic Prayer* (Notre Dame 1968)

Bouyer, Louis, *The Spirituality of the New Testament and the Fathers*, History of Christian Spirituality 1 (London 1960)

Brown, P., *The Body and Society: Men, Women and Sexual Renunciation in Early Christianity* (New York 1988)

Burton-Christie, Douglas, *The Word in the Desert* (Oxford 1993)

Chitty, D. J., *The Desert a City: An Introduction to the Study of Egyptian and Palestinian Monasticism under the Christian Empire* (Oxford 1966)

Chryssavgis, John, 'Aspects of Spiritual Direction: The Palestinian Tradition', *The Sixth Century, End or Beginning?* (Brisbane 1996) 126–30

Clark, Elizabeth, *The Origenist Controversy: the Cultural Construction of an Early Christian Debate* (Princeton 1992)

Clark, Elizabeth, *Reading Renunciation* (Princeton 1999)

Crouzel, H., *Origen*, ET (Edinburgh 1989)

de Vogüé, A., *Histoire littéraire du mouvement monastique dans l'antiquité 3* (Paris 1996)

Desprez, Vincent, *Le Monachisme Primitif, Des origines jusqu'au concile d'Éphèse*, SO 72 (Bellefontaine 1998)

Gould, *The Desert Fathers on Monastic Community* (Oxford 1993)

Guillaumont, A., *Aux origines du monachisme chrétien*, SO 30 (Bellefontaine 1979)

Hausherr, Irénée, *Penthos*, ET CS 53 (Kalamazoo 1982)

Hill, Edmund, *Being Human* (London 1984)

Kelly, J. N. D., *Golden Mouth: The Story of John Chrysostom, Ascetic, Preacher, Bishop* (London 1995)

Larchet, Jean-Claude, 'Ancestral Guilt According to St Maximus the Confessor: a Bridge between Eastern and Western Conceptions', *Sobornost* 20:1 (1998) 26–48

Louth, Andrew, *Maximus the Confessor* (London/New York 1996)

McGuire, Brian Patrick, *Friendship and Community, the Monastic Experience 350–1250* (Kalamazoo 1988)

Meyendorff, John, *Byzantine Theology* (Oxford 1975)

Miquel, Pierre, *Lexique du Désert*, SO 44 (Bellefontaine 1986)

Osbourne, Catherine, *Eros Unveiled, Plato and the God of Love* (Oxford 1994)

Patrich, J., *Sabas, Leader of Palestinian Monasticism* (Washington 1995)

Rousseau, Philip, *Pachomius: The Making of a Community in Fourth Century Egypt* (Berkeley 1985)

Rubenson, Samuel, *The Letters of St Antony: Monastic Tradition and the Making of a Saint* (Minneapolis 1990)

Sorg, Rembert, *Towards a Benedictine Theology of Manual Labour* (Illinois 1951)

Špidlik, T., *The Spirituality of the Christian East*, CS 79 (Kalamazoo 1980)

Stewart, Columba, *Cassian the Monk* (Oxford 1999)

Stewart, Columba, '*Working the Earth of the Heart*': The Messalian Controversy in History, Texts and Language to AD 431 (Oxford 1991)

Taft, Robert, *The Liturgy of the Hours in East and West* (Collegeville 1986)

Ware, Kallistos, *How Are We Saved: The Understanding of Salvation in the Orthodox Tradition* (Minneapolis 1996)

Wimbush, V. L. and Valantasis, R. (eds), *Asceticism* (Oxford 1995)

Zona, James W., ' "Set love in order in me". Eros-Knowing in Origen and Desiderium-Knowing in St Bernard', *Cistercian Studies Quarterly* 34:2 (1999)

Index of Scriptural Quotations

Index of Greek Terms

General Index

admission to the community (*see also* profession) 183, 186, 193–201, 254

Aerius 30, 40

Akoimetai 230

Alexandria 13, 17, 31, 122, 206, 234

almsgiving 238

Amand de Mendieta, David xvii, xviii, 216, 228

Ancyra, Synod of (358) 36

angels 80, 83, 84, 123, 146, 178, 198, 233

Annisa 6, 7, 9, 10 n11, 14, 15, 16, 17, 19–21, 26, 31, 35, 36, 37, 111, 158, 223, 230, 234

Anomoeans 29–30, 36, 37

anthropology 90–3, 117, 132–6, 148, 153, 169

Antioch 28, 39, 40, 49, 169, 195, 232

Antony of Egypt 17, 26, 84, 95, 111, 143–4, 147, 228

Apostolic Community in Acts 93, 142, 144, 148, 150–2, 156, 245

Aquinas, Thomas 252

Arian controversies 29–30, 35, 38

Aristotle 91, 245, 252

Armenia xix, 28, 48

asceticism in the early Church (*see also* household asceticism) 24–7

Athanasius 27, 36, 71, 72, 95, 243

Athens 3, 5, 8, 9, 13–15, 17, 30–1, 41, 64, 156

athlete 107, 116, 142, 224, 228, 253

Athos, Mount xx, 49

Augustine 27, 65, 71, 133, 144–6, 152, 156

Bamberger, John Eudes 115–16, 119, 122

Baptism 86, 97–8

Barsanuphius and John 51

Basil and Sophronius 41

Basil of Ancyra 30, 36

On Virginity 30, 211

Basil the Elder 5, 6, 29, 199

Basil the Great

    Basilian maximalism 74–5, 197

    Basilian moderation 30, 95, 197, 242, 245, 246, 255

    liturgical cult 13, 21 n1, 23 n33

    Asceticon xv–xxi, 15, 17, 19, 24, 26, 34–5, 37–9, 42, 46–55, 60 *passim*.

    recensions of the Asceticon 47–9; origins and genre 49–52, 62, 177

    Small Asceticon xxi, 37, 47–8, 77, 82, 91, 113, 131, 144, 206, 220; (R 2) 70, (R 7) 103, (R 8) 248–54, (R 9) 206, 241–7, (R 10) 99, 246, (R 11) 201–8, (R 12) 104, 172, (R 13) 170–2, (R 14) 118, (R 15) 104, 172, (R 55) 125 n37, (R 57) 123, (R 65) 189, (R 69) 189, (R 89) 162 n32, (R 116) 104, (R 117) 103, (R 123) 103, (R 138) 103, (R 171) 205

    Longer Rules 52, 59, 63, 70; (Preface) 100, 117, 130, 155, 253, (1) 52, 62–7, 152, (2) 65, 68–88, 117, 118, 120, (3) 65, 73, 89–96, 147, 148, (4) 96–106, 196, 254, (5) 53, 102–3, 107–26, 129, 131, (6) 65, 94, 110, 124 n5, 125 n36, 127–38, 146, 147, 148, 155, 159, (7) 65, 93, 94, 110, 112, 128, 129, 139–63, 228, (8) 73, 94, 116, 136, 195, (9) 195, (10) 53, 103, 193–201, (11) 195, (12) 195, (13) 122, 124 n5, 195, 196, 254–6, (14) 195, 200, (15) 117, 178, 195, 199,

Macrina the Elder 5
Macrina the Younger 3, 5, 6, 7, 8, 9, 11
n24, 34, 52, 117, 200, 204, 210, 212,
218, 219, 220, 230
Manichaeans 39, 244
Marathonius of Nicomedia 29
Mark the Monk 51, 135
marriage 28, 42, 113, 195, 211, 213, 215
martyr 189, 199
Maximus the Confessor 51, 63–4, 117,
212
medicine 115, 182, 184–6
memory of God 78–9, 84, 102, 107–11,
116, 118–24, 128, 132, 135, 225, 246,
254
Meredith, Anthony xvi, 74, 91
Messalians 40–1, 99, 210, 211, 229, 230
mixed monasticism 209–13, 220–1
Modestus, Prefect 38, 169
monasticism 54, 93–4, 146, 152, 200,
204, 231, 234, 255
monasticism, origins 26–7
Mount of Olives, monastery on 47
Murphy, Margaret Gertrude xvii,
171–2

nature 68, 74–5, 78, 82, 85, 91, 93, 110,
127, 132, 133, 136, 153, 159, 225, 242,
244
nature and grace 60, 74–5, 82, 85, 86,
149
Naucratius 3, 5, 7, 8, 11 nn18 & 19, 14,
35, 157
Nazarites of Caesarea 36, 37, 158
Neocaesarea 4, 5, 6
Neocaesarea, Synod of (c.339) 8, 28
Newman, John Henry 12
Nicaea, First Council of (325) xx, 29
Nicaea, Second Council of (787) xx,
210, 220

obedience 80, 154, 170–2, 174, 182–92,
238, 239
Oeconomus 178, (229)
Origen 5, 7, 13, 17, 25, 30, 71–3, 76,

84–7, 98, 122, 186, 230, 231, 232, 243,
250
original sin 60, 132–8, 205, 212, 244
Overseer of Work 178

Pachomius 26, 93, 122, 144–6, 160, 172,
177, 196, 197–8, 206, 232, 233, 234,
236, 237, 246
Palestine xix–xx, 31, 159–60, 230, 231,
232
passions 64, 117, 131, 140, 228, 241, 244,
245, 248, 251
Paul 90, 94, 95, 96, 187, 205, 206, 227,
228, 229, 242
perfection 34, 97, 102, 194, 196
Peter of Sebaste 7, 200, 210
Philo of Alexandria 25, 116, 122, 252
philosophy 14, 15, 20, 21, 64, 197, 199,
205, 252
Plato 52, 74, 76, 77, 118, 120, 136, 228,
245
pleasing God 53, 84, 108, 111, 113, 119,
130, 139, 153, 155, 207, 215, 225, 259
pleasing men 53, 110, 213, 215, 237
pleasing self 140, 142, 153, 154, 237
pleasure 6, 124, 200, 228, 241, 242, 245,
248, 249, 252
Plotinus 71, 74, 76, 77
Pneumatomachoi 41
Pontus 3, 4, 5, 6, 7, 8, 10, 16, 18, 24,
36, 37, 48, 52, 195
poverty 7, 9, 43, 195, 201, 202, 204, 206,
229, 237, 239
prayer 64, 68, 120, 121, 123, 127, 130,
132, 136, 223, 225–36, 255
priesthood 19–21, 28, 35–6, 234, 259
profession and vows 98, 193, 195, 197,
198, 199–201, 202, 235
psychology 63, 114–16, 118–19, 122
Pythagoras 149

relatives 95, 108, 129
renunciation 110, 116, 128, 195, 254, 255
repentance 62, 197